D1560590

The Adaptive School

Revised Printing

The Adaptive School

A Sourcebook for
Developing
Collaborative
Groups

Second Edition

Revised Printing

Robert J. Garmston and Bruce M. Wellman

ROWMAN & LITTLEFIELD PUBLISHERS, INC.
Lanham • Boulder • New York • Toronto • Plymouth, UK

Every effort has been made to contact copyright holders for permission to reproduce borrowed material where necessary. We apologize for any oversights and would be happy to rectify them in future printings.

"The Polarity/Paradox Map"® is based on the work of Barry Johnson and Polarity Management Associates and is used with permission. Polarity Management Associates, 1496 Manitou Lane, Middleville, Michigan 49333. 269-205-4263.

Published by Rowman & Littlefield Publishers, Inc.
A wholly owned subsidiary of The Rowman & Littlefield Publishing Group, Inc.
4501 Forbes Boulevard, Suite 200, Lanham, Maryland 20706
www.rowman.com

10 Thornbury Road, Plymouth PL6 7PP, United Kingdom

Copyright © 2013 by Robert J. Garmston and Bruce M. Wellman
Second Christopher-Gordon Publishers, Inc., edition published 2009
New material for revised printing copyright © 2013 by Robert J. Garmston and Bruce M. Wellman
Rowman & Littlefield revised printing published 2013

All rights reserved. No part of this book may be reproduced in any form or by any electronic or mechanical means, including information storage and retrieval systems, without written permission from the publisher, except by a reviewer who may quote passages in a review.

ISBN 978-1-4422-2399-8 (cloth : alk. paper) — ISBN 978-1-4422-2400-1 (electronic)

∞™ The paper used in this publication meets the minimum requirements of American National Standard for Information Sciences—Permanence of Paper for Printed Library Materials, ANSI/NISO Z39.48-1992.

Printed in the United States of America

Contents

Foreword

Jay McTighe

Today's educators face unprecedented and unrelenting accountability pressures in the forms of high-stakes testing, adequate yearly progress (AYP) reviews, rigorous professional standards, and stringent accreditation requirements. Concurrently, education experts offer a plethora of proposed remedies to improve educational practices or reform the entire enterprise. Some recommendations address substantive facets of schooling (e.g., power standards, curriculum mapping, interim assessments, differentiated instruction), whereas others are structural in nature (e.g., block schedules, professional learning communities, charter schools, multigrade looping). Although each of these suggestions might have merit for raising student achievement, educators are cautioned against rushing to embrace a particular reform or improvement initiative without thoughtfully considering the need as well as the school's history, culture, and context.

It is in the contextual realm that this book makes a vital contribution. *The Adaptive School* addresses the essential *process* aspects of schooling (e.g., culture, community, communications) that are too often overlooked in the frenzy to address the programmatic or structural aspects of educational improvement. The authors offer a conceptually rich construct for helping readers to better understand the dynamics of school culture, adult learning and collaboration, and the process of facilitating educational change. Beyond just stating the theoretical, they provide an extraordinarily detailed and practical menu of tools, strategies, and protocols for enacting necessary school improvements.

In addition to providing substantive content, this book fuses a refreshing mix of research, stories, and analogies with practical strategies and tips. The writing style weaves together the scholarship of academicians, the practical wisdom of veteran educators, and the lyrical flow of accomplished storytellers.

The book includes an appendix of facilitation protocols, a treasure trove of practical and proven methods that in itself would justify the cost of the book. However, don't be tempted to bypass the dinner for the dessert. Enjoy the succulent, full-course meal that this valuable book offers.

Introduction

This edition of *The Adaptive School* represents much of our learning about school systems and groups in the past 15 years as we have worked with educators in settings that span the globe. Although each school is unique, there are social patterns that are easily recognizable when people gather in groups to work together. Drawing on these experiences and looking at group work through the theoretical filters of biology, ecology, quantum physics, complexity science, systems thinking, and cognitive and social psychology, we offer a practical set of principles and tools for developing and facilitating collaborative groups.

The Adaptive School is about developing strong schools in which collaborative faculties are capable of meeting the certain challenges of today and the uncertain challenges of tomorrow. Some schools are flourishing. Others are making remarkable gains in improving student achievement, increasing attendance, attaining higher postschool accomplishments, and developing satisfying relationships with their communities. Some schools produce only fair results; others languish. We believe that all can be better.

As realists, we recognize that difficult and different challenges beset schools and communities in their quest to serve students. Issues differ from school to school. Urbanism and ruralism bring their own special problems. Defeatism, extremism, apathy, or politics infect some schools. Schools can become obsessed with ensuring predictable results, or they can struggle to overcome the effects of extreme poverty, neglected children, or the burdens of ponderous bureaucracy. Money can bring its own problems. Some affluent communities lobby for traditional definitions of success at the expense of other needs. In some districts, the teachers and the students struggle daily with inadequate and outdated materials and facilities. Regardless of the nature of the issues, our premise is that the means for improvement exist within the school community. The practical ideas and tools in this book show how to activate these resources if they are dormant and focus them if they are scattered.

We believe that leadership is important and that the most effective leadership is informed, deeply developed, and widely distributed. To be adaptive and meet the demands of omnipresent change requires more than linear thought, old problem-solving formulas, and recycled strategic plans. In the work of school improvement, human energy matters as much as the elements of good management do—maybe more.

How to Use This Book

This book is informed by the central notion of adaptivity, five principles of dynamic systems, and focusing questions that bring attention to fundamental issues for capacity building in schools (see sidebar). These ideas are initially mentioned in chapter 1 and elaborated in the following 10 chapters. They form the conceptual backbone of the chapters and provide a rationale for the tools and approaches that we present.

The book is designed as a sourcebook to support you in developing and facilitating collaborative groups to improve student learning. You can use it as a basic text for yourself or with a study group and as a reference book for diagnosis and problem solving. We encourage you to choose the approaches that best serve your interests and needs.

Read from the beginning to the end. The chapter content is designed sequentially, with each chapter building on the preceding ones.

Check the table of contents for an issue of specific interest and read that chapter. It will provide references to other chapters.

Refer to the problem-based user's guide (Table I-1) to search the text for information about specific problems.

A major section of this book is the toolkit of strategies, which makes up Appendix A.

Adaptive: Changing form, clarifying identity

Dynamic principles:

More data do not lead to better predictions.

Everything influences everything else.

Tiny events produce major disturbances.

You don't have to touch everyone to make a difference.

Both things and energy matter.

Focusing questions:

Who are we?

Why are we doing this?

Why are we doing this this way?

Table I-1. Problem-Based User's Guide

1. What to do about group members who:

(a) don't listen	PAG/PAU	Appendix A
	Attention First	Appendix A
	Show, Don't Say	Appendix A
	Round-Robin Reflection	Appendix A
	Norms Inventories	Appendixes B–E
	Grounding	Appendix A
	Trios PPPI	Appendix A
(b) are uncomfortable speaking up	Paraphrasing	p. 33
	Gatekeeping	Appendix A
	Grounding	Appendix A
	Learning Partners	Appendix A
	Round-Robin Reflection	Appendix A
	Norms Inventories	Appendixes B–E
(c) dominate	Presuming Positive Intentions	p. 38
	Caping	Appendix A
	Stop and Redirect	Appendix A
	Balance Participation	p. 67
	Learning Partners	Appendix A
	Satisfy, Satisfy, Delay	Appendix A
	Round-Robin Reflection	Appendix A
	Airplane Stacking	Appendix A
(d) are unaware of the effects of their behaviors on others	Meeting Inventory	Appendix L
	Challenge Relevance	Appendix A
	Set & Test Working Agreements	p. 70
	Round-Robin Reflection	Appendix A
	Group-Member Capabilities	p. 27
	Norms Inventories	Appendixes B–E
	Structuring Conversations about Data	Appendixes I & J

2. What to do about groups that:

(a) are resisting	Focusing Questions	p. 10
	Reenergize	Appendix A
	Group Groan	Appendix A
	Ask for Sabotage Ideas	Appendix A
	Six-Position Straw Pile	Appendix A
	Change Formula	p. 154
	Transitions	p. 154
(b) don't stay on task or don't process	PAG/PAU	Appendix A
	TAG/TAU	Appendix A
	Posted Outcomes	p. 83
	Meeting Inventory	Appendix L
(c) lack clear standards for collective performance and products	Meeting Inventory	Appendix L
	Naive questions	Appendix A
	Develop Standards	p. 65
	Anticipate Transitions	p. 106
	Done/Yet-to-Do Questions	Appendix A
	Responsibility Charting	Appendix A
	Assessing the Six Domains of Group Development	p. 116
	Contracting for Facilitation Services	Appendixes G & H
	Structuring Conversations About Data	Appendixes I & J

(d) have difficulty with decision making	Decide Who Decides	p. 58
	Force-Field Analysis	Appendix A
	Rule of One- Third	Appendix A
	Combine Opposites	Appendix A
	Ranking	Appendix A
	Forced-Choice Stickers	Appendix A
	Eliminate the Negative	Appendix A
	Six-Position Straw Poll	Appendix A
	Steps in Decision Making	Table 5-1
	Slip Method	Appendix A
	Close the Discussion	Appendix A
	Sufficient Consensus	Appendix A
	1-2-6	Appendix A
	Existing State–Desired State Map	Appendix A
	Focusing Four	Appendix A
	Freeing Stuck Groups	Appendix A
	Is/Is Not	Appendix A
	Not A or B but C	Appendix A
	Spend a Buck	Appendix A
	Thumbs Up	Appendix A
	100% Consensus	Appendix A
(e) have unproductive meetings	Decide Who Decides	p. 58
	Define the Sandbox	p. 59
	Design the Surround	p. 62
	PAG/PAU	Appendix A
	1-2-6	Appendix A
	Agenda Design	p. 80
	Final Planning Tips	p. 83
	Round-Robin Reflection	Appendix A
	Meeting Inventory	Appendix L

(f) need help with prob-lem finding and problem solving	Futures Wheel	Appendix A
	Spot Analysis	Appendix A
	Fishbone Diagram	Appendix A
	Is/Is Not	Appendix A
	Sensing Interviews	Appendix A
	Issues Agenda	Appendix A
	Causal Loop Diagram	Appendix A
	Fix What Shows, Not What Is Broken	p. 145
	Brainstorm Questions	Appendix A
	Elephant Walk	Appendix A
	Outcome Mapping	Appendix A
	Facilitator's Contracting Conversation	Appendixes G & H
	Polarity Mapping	Appendix M
	Define Fairness	p.136 & Appendix M
	Denominalize	p. 143
	Histomap	Appendix A

3. What to do about increasing your effectiveness in:

(a) influencing the thinking of others	Paraphrasing	p. 33
	Probing for Specificity	p. 36
	Placing Ideas on the Table	p. 38
	Balancing Advocacy and Inquiry	Table 3-2
	Balcony View	p. 50
	Choose Voice	Appendix A
	Putting Inquiry at the Center	p. 34
	Assumptions Wall	Appendix A
	Listening Set-Asides	p. 28
(b) managing your fear during conflict	Presuming Positive Intentions	p. 38
	Pausing	p. 32
	Paraphrasing	p. 33
	Balcony View	p. 50
	Managing Emotions	p. 147
	Depersonalize the Conflict	p. 147

(c) fighting gracefully	Paying Attention to Self and Others	p. 38
	Balancing Advocacy and Inquiry	Table 3-2
	Balcony View	p. 50
	Define Fairness	p. 136
	Elicit and Label Social Norms	p. 137
	Managing Emotions	p. 147
	Depersonalize the Conflict	p. 9
	Polarity Mapping	Appendix M
	Disagreement Grid	Appendix A
	Grounding	Appendix A
	Clearing	Appendix A
	100% Consensus	Appendix A
	Decontaminate Problem Space	Appendix A
	Third Point	Appendix A
(d) exercising your meta-cognitive skills as a group member	Group-Member Capabilities	p. 27
	Pausing	p. 32
	Monitoring Dialogue	p. 48
	Monitoring Discussion	p. 50
	Round-Robin Reflection	Appendix A
(e) maintaining your individuality while being a productive member of a group	Group-Member Capabilities	p. 27
	Round-Robin Reflection	Appendix A
	Pay Attention to Self and Others	p. 38
	Polarity Mapping	Appendix M

Chapter 1   What Is an Adaptive School?

When pioneering navigators first sailed away from the coasts of Asia, Africa, and Europe, they were guided by their dreams, the stars, and primitive compasses—sailing into territories marked on their fanciful charts as unknown lands and seas of mystery. Undoubtedly, many in the ship's crews cast apprehensive glances at the receding shores of the familiar, trusting in the soundness of their vessel and the courage and skills of their leaders. The results of these voyages were both heroic and tragic, opening new vistas yet dramatically altering the lives and cultures of the people these early explorers encountered.

In current times, we too are leaving the shores of the familiar as the forces of change roil the educational seas. Demographic shifts in student and staff populations, social and political upheavals, advances in learning theory, the revolution in cognitive psychology, and the pulse of technological innovation all shape the environment around and within schools and school systems.

Our personal and organizational maps for this new world are in many ways incomplete. There are no preprogrammed global positioning technologies to plot future voyages and alert us to the turns ahead. What we most need to develop are the mental, emotional, and social tools for finding our way in these shifting landscapes. We also need new lenses to see the world not as a reflection of ourselves but as images of the many possibilities within the human landscape.

New tools help us to see new sights, think new thoughts, and do new things. For productive school improvement efforts, many of these new tools are both cognitive and cultural. How we think influences the ways that we work together. How we work together influences the ways that we think about that work.

Evolutionary forces shaped human brains and response systems to meet the demands of much earlier times. If a saber-toothed tiger were to bound through the door, these systems would immediately trigger a host of chemical, physical, and emotional reactions. Modern humans still possess automatic routines for Pleistocene-era problems.

The fast reflexes that supported our hunting and gathering ancestors will not help educators to develop the forms of schools and schooling that we need in this new era. These demands require new minds and models that are better suited for the challenges of today. Most of all, educators need new sensitivities that can discern what is not readily apparent to the senses and help to craft new ways of improving schools for the journey ahead.

As educators, authors, and consultants, we are actively exploring new possibilities and developing ways of thinking about adult interactions in schools. Our own thinking is influenced by the emerging sciences of quantum mechanics, complexity theory, fractal geometry, evolutionary biology, and systems thinking as they apply to social organizations. We are also influenced by constructivist psychology, as it relates to learning and leadership; our personal histories in a variety of roles in education—teacher, curriculum consultant, staff developer, principal, superintendent, and professor; and our current work as consultants with schools throughout North America and in Africa, Asia, Australia, Europe, and the Middle East.

Learning From the New Sciences

As we struggle to understand ways to improve schools, the new sciences reveal a world in which chaos and order are parts of the same system. We live not in a world of either-or but in the dawning world of both-and. We learn that schools are complex dynamical systems that are continually influenced by many variables, just as a weather system is influenced by wind, temperature, and moisture. Weather systems and the course of school improvement are both unpredictable in their details but not in their patterns (Lorenz, 1993).

Teams, too, are dynamical systems affected by the ratio of positive to negative communication within their interactions and the ratio of inquiry into the ideas of others to advocacy for personal positions (Danner, Snowdon, & Friesen, 2001). Even mild and fleeting positive affect creates large benefits in the long run, underscoring the realization that outcomes are not always proportional to inputs, and, as with weather systems, seemingly trivial inputs produce major changes.

Nonlinear relationships govern dynamical systems. Dynamical systems differ from linear systems like automobiles, in which direct cause-and-effect reasoning supports problem solving and the ability to isolate and repair discrete malfunctioning parts. John Briggs (1992)

describes this new world as follows:

> It appears that in dynamical systems chaos and order are different masks the system wears: in some circumstances the system shows one face; in different circumstances it shows another. These systems can appear to be complex; their simplicity and complexity lurk inside each other. (p. 20)

The second law of thermodynamics—entropy—tells us that all physical systems run down as energy dissipates. Ultimately the system decays into a state of disorganization known as thermodynamic equilibrium. For instance, if you leave a bicycle out in the yard for long enough, it will eventually become a mound of rust.

Living systems counter the law of entropy by creating order out of disorder. Living systems do not nullify the second law of thermodynamics; they merely keep the forces of dissipation at bay by maintaining a state of active positive energy potential. These complex interactions produce a state called negative entropy. Molecular biologists who study these processes at life's fundamental levels note that organisms engage in a highly efficient intake, storage, and output of energy and material. In this way they sustain an ongoing relationship with their environment (Ho, 1998).

Social organizations, including schools and school districts, are living systems, and like all living systems they are capable of self-organization, creating order out of chaos. Biological systems self-organize through their genetic codes. Social systems self-organize through cultural codes; they do so by both default and design (Gharajedaghi, 2006).

When beliefs, values, and assumption lie below the surface and are not illuminated by the light of inquiry, the system defaults to established patterns and predictable outcomes. By applying principles and practices of purposeful design, systems thinkers expose, consider, and reshape the counterproductive deeper structures of the organization. These revitalized values and norms then shape behaviors as the energies of cooperation, collaboration, and caring flow through the system.

Our premise is that information and metaphors from the new sciences can reframe and clarify challenges for educational leaders. These new challenges are not about working harder—there is hardly a profession in which people pour out as much energy and work—but about working in new ways within the principles suggested by the new sciences. In adopting these lenses, however, we are not refuting what has been learned in the past 80 years of research on school improvement.

The History of School Change

School improvement research parallels and intertwines with organizational development research and practice. As far back as the 1930s, education, government, and business thinkers developed lenses and tools for improving organizational focus and productivity.

Important findings endure from each decade. Efforts from the 1930s through the 1950s focused on innovation and diffusion of ideas. During the 1960s, parallel to the work in organizational development, school research emphasized organizational health and stages in the change process. The 1970s saw increased attention to activities related to the whole organization: building mutual trust, removing barriers to communication, establishing positive climates, and encouraging participation in decision making.

During the 1970s researchers increased their understanding of the processes of change in schools and the means of technical assistance for promoting it. The Concerns-Based Adoption model, widely disseminated and applied, is a product of this era (Hall & Hord, 1987). These findings are still being employed successfully in school improvement efforts.

The RAND change-agent study in the late 1970s brought to light fundamental principles of school change. These include (a) the importance of staff efficacy, (b) the value of participation in decision-making, and (c) the necessity for both bottom-up and top-down change efforts. These factors are now taken for granted in improvement efforts.

The 1980s and 1990s brought wide exposure to the effective-schools research. The efforts to apply this were largely rationalistic and behavioral, resulting in lists, inventories, and attempts to install various desirable characteristics in school life. The meta-analysis of school improvement designs by such authors as Michael Fullan, Larry Cuban, Mathew Miles, Richard Elmore, and Seymour Sarason informed further change efforts as they drew on the larger knowledge bases developing in the field of organizational development.

In the current century, serious efforts focus on eliminating the achievement gaps related to race and poverty. The standards-based accountability-driven models are developing increasingly reliable data points that frame and energize the conversations about school and instructional improvements to serve all students' needs.

An important perspective on school change is that the sole issue is not innovation. Deep patterns of inquiry must be embedded as essential organizational patterns—a form of adaptive DNA to guide and shape responses to any innovation and to the changing environment. Although change might start with innovation, it must also include the basic more linear management skills of implementation, fidelity, impact, institutionalization, maintenance, and replication (Louis, Toole, & Hargreaves, 1999).

This growing knowledge base points strongly to the influence of organizational culture on employee behavior. As Richard Elmore (2002) has clearly pointed out, American schools know how to change; "they do it promiscuously and at the drop of a hat." He notes that what schools have trouble doing is engaging and sustaining continuous progress toward meaningful goals over longer periods.

Lasting improvement efforts require clearly articulated theories of learning for both the students and the adults who serve them. Such efforts also require a cohesive theory of the system called school to organize and guide these learning efforts.

As systems thinking has evolved in recent decades, important governing ideas keep appearing in different types of social organizations. System results emerge from four interacting factors: design, participation, iteration, and second-order learning (Gharajedaghi, 2006).

Design. At a basic level for schools, design includes physical space, calendars, schedules, contracts, and rewards and punishments. These elements are fundamentally influenced by the beliefs, assumptions, and goals that guide the organization. Schools that talk about collaboration but don't provide or protect quality time or space for adult interactions display their deeper, more entrenched values when they construct the yearly calendar and negotiate teachers' contracts.

Participation. Who talks and what is talked about says much about life in classrooms, staff rooms, and meeting rooms. Information is one of the most important energy flows within the system. It requires both the dispositions and the skills for collaborating with others; this is true for both adults and students. Classrooms without tables to meet around, for instance, send the message that learning is a personal rather than a collective effort.

Iteration. From the study of fractals we learn that this new geometry is the mathematical modeling of patterns across scale. A head of broccoli is an example of a fractal pattern. Each floret is a miniature version of the whole. In an organization, values and beliefs form patterns across the layers of the organization. Cooperation and trust are patterns, stretching from parents to board members to administrators to teachers to students. Power and control is another, and potentially more debilitating, pattern that iterates throughout the system. Pattern is the ultimate teacher, the ultimate cumulative effect. By searching for and breaking dysfunctional patterns, systems designers establish the groundwork for making new and more productive patterns within and across the organization.

Second-order learning. First-order learning is the development of new knowledge and skills; this is classically the purpose of most staff development efforts. In many ways these are quantitative changes that result in measurable improvements in student performance. In first-order change efforts, the variables that guide these performances are analyzed, assessed, modified, and remeasured after some intervention. Second-order learning is the adaptive learning that leads to more qualitative changes and requires challenging the core assumptions that are shaping behaviors. Teachers who work in isolation often assume that they are free agents, able to choose idiosyncratic methodologies and materials based on personal values or knowledge transmitted from their own mentors. By investigating the cumulative effects on student learning of these choices and examining long-term data sets, practitioners begin to see the downside of hyperautonomous cultures.

From all these decades of effort and research, three fundamental questions remain for school improvement efforts: (a) Are teachers and students doing things differently in classrooms? (b) Are these differences improving student learning? (c) Are schools learning from experience so they can be increasingly effective in response to ever-changing needs? This book attempts to make a modest contribution in answering the third question.

"Thing" and "Energy" Models of the World

Marshalling, focusing and developing energy, information and relationships becomes the role of leaders.

— Margaret Wheatley (1992)

Improving schools requires two ways of looking at the world. One view focuses on "things," the basic stuff of good management. "Thing" ways of seeing and working get the details handled, the bills paid, and the buses running on time and making the right stops in the right neighborhoods. "Thing" thinking is the historical foundation of all management systems in modern organizations.

Another leadership perspective focuses on energy. Margaret Wheatley (1992) observes that the quality of human relationships creates the energy source that produces all organizational work. This is the energy with which organizational members commit, persevere, and relate. With the special lenses explored in this book, such energy can be discerned, modified, and focused.

The celebrated revolution in physics called quantum mechanics clarifies the essential distinctions between matter and energy and simultaneously blurs the line between them. The very term *quantum mechanics* means bundles of energy (quantum) in motion (mechanics) (Capra, 1991). This book describes ways to shape this energy through collaborative norms, well-structured meetings, new frames for conflict, and communication practices that make a difference for student learning.

As Richard Elmore (1995) reminds us, the real work of changing schools lies in changing norms, knowledge, and skills (energy) at the individual and organizational levels before we attempt to change the structure of schools (things). In fact, without new norms, knowledge, and skills, structural changes such as block scheduling, site-based decision making, multiage classrooms, and inclusive classrooms will have little or no effect on student learning.

In adaptive schools, leaders pay attention to both things and energy and to the flow and interchange of energy. Energy becomes an avenue to attainment. We will expand on this idea in chapter 2 with descriptions of four leadership roles and in chapter 7 with an elaboration on one of the roles (facilitator).

Adaptive, Not Adapted

Evolutionary biology is the source for a central notion in our work: adaptivity. To be *adaptive* means to change form in concert with clarifying identity. This is quite different from being *adapted*, which means to have evolved through specialization to fit specific conditions within tightly defined boundaries.

Monarch butterflies are a good example of an adapted species. Across North America, the summer fields sparkle with their flight. Monarchs, as most schoolchildren learn, lay their eggs only on milkweed plants. When the larvae hatch, they feed on the milkweed leaves, growing and developing until it is time to spin a chrysalis that is attached to the milkweed plant. The larvae metamorphose into adult butterflies, and the cycle repeats. Without milkweed there would be no monarchs. The monarch's nutritional and habitat needs are firmly adapted to this one type of plant.

An example of adaptivity within a species can be found on another continent. As primatologists study the social lives of chimpanzee

5

groups, they discover a remarkable range of behaviors within individuals and within populations that are isolated from one another. They are now using the term *culture* to describe variations in food-gathering techniques that include prepositioning hammer stones for cracking nuts in anticipation of ripening, using grass stalks as tools to fish termites from holes, and sharpening sticks to use as thrusting spears when hunting small monkeys. These cultural variations spread through local populations and to the next generation but remain unique to a given region.

Organizations, like species, also need to contend with being adapted to existing environments and becoming adaptive to changing conditions. This usually means letting go of existing *forms* and continually clarifying the core *identity* of the enterprise. As we write this volume, Verizon Communications is actively selling off its landline telephone business in New England. Note that Verizon itself is an outgrowth of the old American Telephone & Telegraph Company, which long had a monopoly on that form of communication. Verizon is actively focusing its business on developing wireless and high-speed fiber optic networks to transmit the exploding forms of digital information across the ether and through spun glass strands. As video, data, and text messages become the dominant conduits of information, the profit potential in voice transmission is diminishing every day. Copper wires strung from poles will someday be as anachronistic as the "clickity-clack" of telegraph keys or the hand-cranked phone on a kitchen wall.

Form and identity confusions are rampant in schools. One of the most significant changes in recent years has been the transformation of the role of the school librarian. This was first brought to our attention several years ago at a seminar we were conducting, when a participant stopped by at a break to share her struggles with this issue. As the head librarian for a medium-size school district, she described all the professional changes she had experienced since completing her master's degree in library science in the early 1970s. As a supervisor, she supported several librarians who were also struggling with similar changes. She noted that as librarians they were taught to be quality filters and to stock the shelves with reliable and authoritative reference materials. When students and teachers asked for resources, the librarians were able to supply the best sources available and took professional pride in knowing and having these materials on hand.

As students and teachers became increasingly computer savvy, the librarians were feeling devalued. The budget for reference materials switched to online resources, and the librarians become concerned about the quality of the information that students and teachers access through Google® and Wikipedia®. Being a quality filter was a form that gave the librarians pride in their work. They have found that they now have to be *teachers* of quality filtering. The deep transition is therefore a change not in the knowledge base of the librarians but in the ways that they applied their knowledge within their new identities.

All around us we see examples like this. As Internet-based courses for students become common, what it means to be a teacher and to have a class will dramatically shift. The very concept of the schoolhouse will increasingly be seen as a historical artifact rather than a current reality. With many museums "wired" to provide virtual field trips, the springtime ritual of the class trip with the bus ride, snacks, and souvenirs might also become another historical artifact from "the good old days." Rising fuel costs could even accelerate this possibility.

Voice-recognition software, along with high bandwidth, cheap digital storage, and artificial intelligence, will most likely dramatically change the teaching of foreign languages. It is not hard to imagine digital environments in which students or their avatars interact with native speakers of the language they are learning. The scenes will come complete with full cultural settings, appropriate body language and nonverbal messages, and an oscilloscope-like readout displaying the voice inflections of the native speaker compared to the voice inflections of the novice learner. Conversations can be repeated with this patient tutor until they are fully mastered. In such an environment the form of specialty teacher of one language is replaced by the identity of master of second-language learning. This identity is accompanied by the elements of designer, motivator, manager, and clinician. The number of languages to be taught is limited not by personnel but by the availability of software and hardware

Table 1-1 sums up the relationship between form and identity in the examples we have discussed.

The traditional North American high school serves as a striking example of an adapted, rather than an adaptive, system. Designed in another time for the purposes of that time, the typical high school often shows a remarkable lack of flexibility, with staff members clinging to tightly defined niches within increasingly fragile specialties. Richard Elmore (2002) claims that U.S. high schools are either third or tied for second as "the most pathological social institutions in our society after public health hospitals and prisons."

The essential design of the "modern" high school dates to 1892, when an august body called the Committee of Ten met to develop uniform entrance requirements for colleges. Their goal was to create a smoother transition from high school to college for the elite students of the day. In 1890, only 360,000 students ages 14–17 (i.e., approximately 6.7%) attended high school in the United States. A much smaller percentage was college-bound (DeBoer, 1991).

The basic course structures that the Committee of Ten recommended are still in place today. In an ever-changing world, we cling to the comfort of tradition and do not effectively question the roots of our institutions and norms. The students we serve and our expectations for them are substantially different from the forms that contain them.

Nevertheless, when alternative schools emerge to engage students whose needs are not being met by existing school structures, very few people question the schooling and teaching practices that are not meeting these needs in the first place. The very label *alternative school* means that this is an alternative to the "real" school down the hall or down the road, into which these problematic students can't seem to fit.

Table 1-1. Form vs. Identity

Example	Form	Identity
Verizon	Telephone company	Information transmission company
Reference Librarian	Quality filter	Teacher of quality filtering
Foreign Language Teacher	Specialist in one language	Specialist in second-language learning

Demographic, technological, economic, social, and political pressures drive our rapidly changing world from many different directions. For many educators and parents, the surety of the past is a greater solace than the vagueness of the future. Their response to change is to embrace tradition. This could well turn out to be the equivalent of training Linotypists to work with hot lead in an era of digital design and production.

The great challenge for schools is to let go of the comforts of adapted behaviors and to develop the patterns and practices of adaptivity. This is especially true in climates in which the metaphorical milkweed might not live forever. Adaptivity consists of flexible responses interacting with changing environmental conditions. This is true for individuals, species, and organizations. It requires a clear identity and a lack of attachment to form.

Schools Are Nonlinear Dynamical Systems

Schools change through different mechanisms than researchers have often supposed. Schools are nonlinear dynamical systems in which cause and effect are not tightly linked. In nonlinear systems, the parts do not add up to the same sum each time they are combined. Fresh combinations result in different outcomes. For teachers, the curriculum combines with instructional and assessment practices to support student learning. Yet every school year turns out differently as the pedagogical mix blends with a new crop of students.

A blend of regularity and irregularity shapes nonlinear systems, producing patterns of stability and instability. Critical choice points present new possibilities and new forms of order. Instability permits creative life in school systems. The self-organizing interactions between people develop feedback loops that recur and amplify across the scale of the organization.

Management thinker Ralph Stacey (1992) observes the following:

> Top managers cannot control this, but through their interventions they powerfully influence it. It is their prime responsibility to understand the qualitative patterns of behavior that their interventions may produce. Order through installations by designing minds is replaced by order emerging from instability through a process of self-organization. (p. 13)

Self-organization develops through meaningful adult interactions about students, student work, and the purposes and processes of schooling. To be productive, such interactions must be infused with and guided by shared values and norms of collaboration. The environment must encourage reflection, inquiry, challenge, and deprivatization of practice for both teachers and administrators. This in turn requires skills in dialogue, discussion, planning, and problem solving. At times the work is messy and nonrational. Habitual, linear ways of thinking will work for some issues but not for the increasingly complex and ill-structured problems that beset many schools today.

The modern history of the shipping industry offers a striking example of the ways in which system change occurs. For centuries, ships were loaded and unloaded by gangs of workers who, manually and with the aid of cranes, lugged, rolled, and stored cargoes in the bowels of ships. Cargo handling at either end of the voyage produced as much as 50% of the costs of moving goods. The actual voyage itself accounted for less than 12% of the costs (Levinson, 2006).

In the early 1950s a trucking magnate named Malcom McLean and his colleagues began the process that produced the shipping-container industry that we know today. McLean was not limited by the identity of being a trucker. He realized that he was in the moving-goods business and that trucks, trains, and ships could work in harmony to move material if that material was placed in uniform-size containers and a supporting infrastructure facilitated the rapid deployment of these containers across the globe.

This revolution rapidly reduced the costs of moving goods and negated the need to have sources of production and storage close to ports. The waterfronts of the world swiftly shed manufacturing industries, and warehouses were transformed into high-status housing and recreation areas in many locales. In 1964 the five boroughs of New York City were home to manufacturing concerns that employed nearly 900,000 workers. By the mid-1970s more than one-third of those jobs were gone. Cheap transportation motivated the search for cheaper labor and lower manufacturing costs. Distance was no longer an obstacle to commerce. This example illuminates five underlying principles, described below, that guide dynamical systems such as the shipping industry, weather systems, and schools.

1. *More data do not lead to better predictions.* Malcom McLean did not need to know all the economic data points about the industries that were his customers. He merely needed sufficient data about his own business and the appropriate metrics to guide his business plans. Meteorologists have more data than at any time in history, yet their radars and computer models lose meaning beyond a four-day window. Many schools we work with are data-rich and information-poor. They collect endless surveys and pour over spreadsheets but don't take the time to dialogue and make meaning from their experiences and the knowledge they have within them.

2. *Everything influences everything else.* The rise of the shipping container made the economic boom possible both in Asia and for Wal-Mart and other big-box discount stores. These forces have fueled growing prosperity as well as environmental damage across the globe. In weather systems, temperature changes affect wind patterns, which affect precipitation patterns, which in turn influence climate changes, including droughts and floods. In schools, the affective climate of the building and classrooms influence what adults feel about their work as well as the academic results for students.

3. *Tiny events create major disturbances.* Putting a stack of boxes in and on ships is in many ways a tiny event. Yet this simple revolution has changed economies throughout the world, changed labor relations by making loading ships highly technical skilled work, and changed the balance of power as emerging countries flex their new financial and political muscles. As tropical storms develop off the coast of the African continent and swing across the Atlantic Ocean and into the Caribbean Sea, encountering water that is as little as one-fourth degree warmer tips the storm into a raging hurricane. In collaborative groups, a participant who is skilled in paraphrasing and inquiry opens up the thinking of others and deepens the meaning that these conversations produce.

4. *You don't have to touch everyone in the system to make a difference.* Malcom McLean didn't have to run around the globe and get all the policy makers and decision makers in place and on board before starting his venture. He designed some sturdy boxes, converted some old tanker ships, and built some special cranes at the sending and receiving ports. The rest of the system responded over time to these innovations. Weather systems affect behaviors by their mere presence. Whether these systems are hot or cold, wet or dry, environments and organisms respond to these influences without the right to vote. In the same way, a school culture shapes the behavior of its members. That is why school cultures are so tenacious in the face of personnel changes. The real work of school improvement, then, is the work of "recultur-

ing" by shaping the norms, beliefs, and values of those cultures.

5. *Both things and energy matter.* Ships, boxes, cranes, trucks, and trains are all things. They have to work together in a timely fashion to move the goods that move the economy. They also represent the energy of commerce— the innovating, buying, selling, and improving of products that engage human minds and imaginations. Wind, sun, and rain are all tangible phenomena, but it is the energy they contain and transmit that moves windmills, sprouts plants, and produces waterfalls. Schools require books and bells, halls and balls, but again it is the energy of caring and commitment that moves minds and produces learning.

How Schools Become Adaptive

So far we have discussed the importance of adaptivity and the need to clarify identity, both as individuals and as organizations, without clinging to outmoded forms. We've suggested a rationale for why this is important by framing schools as nonlinear dynamical systems in which cause-and-effect linkages are not so easily drawn. We will now briefly describe how schools can achieve this. The chapters that follow will expand, elaborate on, and share many of the concrete tools we have learned to use from our work with successful schools.

We encourage departments, committees, councils, and faculties to reflect frequently on three focusing questions: (a) Who are we? (b) Why are we doing this? and (c) Why are we doing this this way? The by-product of this reflection is action for improving student learning.

Who Are We?

Principal Kathy Dunton of Vine Hills Elementary School in California told us that these three questions transformed her school. She encourages teachers and parents to ask them

frequently and to explore them in depth. The question "Who are we?" leads directly to the issue of identity. This issue forces the related questions of "About what do we care?" and "How much do we dare?" The form taken by a school, team, department, or teacher's assignment is less important than identity. Identity represents the story that a group tells itself to organize its values and beliefs. A group's beliefs determine its behavior. Collectively, its behavior affects student learning (Dilts, 1994).

Identity cannot be found in a mission statement. It displays itself in hallways, faculty lounges, meeting minutes, and student academic results. Identity reveals itself in periods of stress: What a group strives to preserve or fights to protect describes its identity. The very definitions of success, the awards and rewards for both students and staff members, symbolize driving values and beliefs.

Why Are We Doing This?

Folk wisdom, tradition, and unexamined habit rule much of what schools do. The agricultural calendar, factory schedules, and athletic practices continue to frame yearly and daily time use. Bus schedules and teacher contracts exert powerful and often unexamined influences on student learning. Yet these and other features of school life go unquestioned. "It's just the way we do things around here," one is told when bold enough to inquire.

A classic story captures the essence of this issue. A little girl, watching her mother prepare a ham for the oven, wanted to know why her mommy was cutting the end off before placing it in the roasting pan. "I don't really know," her mother replied. "That's the way my mommy did it."

So the little girl went to see her grandmother and asked her why she cut the end of the ham off before putting it in the roasting pan. "I don't really know," her grandmother replied. "That's the way my mommy did it."

So the little girl went to see her great-grandmother and asked her why she cut the end of the ham off before putting it in the roasting pan. "Well," the old woman explained, stretching her arms wide, "I grew up on the prairie in a little sod house, and our hams were this big." Bringing her hands closer together, she concluded, "And our oven was this big. We had to cut the end off the ham to fit it in the oven."

In many settings, educators continue to "cut the end off the ham" long after the original rationale has passed. The deep structure of schooling is set on foundations of "hams and end scraps" from earlier eras. Unquestioned assumptions form the "ovens" in which they "cook." Many current practices are rooted in beliefs about the need for power and control over others and over resources (Sarason, 1990). Such beliefs were at the heart of the management literature during most of the 1800s and 1900s. They are the source of conflicts over curriculum and at the center of most tensions around any form of shared decision making. The question "Why are we doing this?" brings attention and choice to practices that have become unquestioned habits.

Why Are We Doing This This Way?

The "this" that we are doing could be grouping students for instruction, developing learning experiences, or deciding time allotments for activities. This last question, valued so highly by California principal Kathy Dunton, brings focus not to the *what* and *why* of the activity but to the *how*. Walk through any school with a notebook in hand, because this question will have you scribbling rapidly.

The daily schedule is a good starting point. Anyone who has observed the sleeping and waking patterns of adolescents knows that 8 a.m. is

not peak time for anything not conducted in a prone position, yet district schedules organized by transportation patterns typically have high schools starting around that hour. On the other hand, many 5- and 6-year-olds are up and bustling, ready to get on with the new day. Schools might, in fact, have the daily time schedule for the various levels of schooling in reverse order from what would be a better fit with physical development patterns.

The question "Why are we doing this this way?" could be restated as "Who benefits from the current system?" Exploring this form of the question provides insight into the forces that keep current practices in place. As Kathy Dunton found, these three focusing questions open up new ways of seeing school practices. Once revealed, they can be acted on and modified. Left unexamined, they keep the institutional drivers on autopilot and the "map" stuffed in the "glove compartment."

This Book Teaches New Songs

All cultures have creation stories to explain the coming of the world and their own place in it. The Aboriginal people of Australia believe that their land is covered with a web of invisible pathways. These "dreaming-tracks" or "songlines" first appeared during the Tjukurpa (djook-oor-pah) or "Dreamtime," when ancestral beings wandered over the featureless landscape, singing the world into existence. These totemic ancestors sang out the name of everything that crossed their path. They sang out the names of plants, animals, rocks, rivers, salt pans, and waterholes, coding and wrapping the world in a web of song (Chatwin, 1987).

When an Aboriginal mother is pregnant and feels the baby kick for the first time, she calls the shaman to identify that child's totemic spirit guide. Physical features at the site of the kick are then interpreted, and the spirit of the child—the child's "dreaming"—is thus identified. This dreaming can be one of any number of mammals, insects, birds, or reptiles. As the child grows, he or she learns the song of this spirit guide. Coded into the song are the features of the local landscape—where to find food, water, shelter, and safe travel routes. Song is the oldest mnemonic device, far easier for a nomad to carry than any road atlas.

An Aborigine who goes "walkabout" on a journey of discovery or on a hunting foray calls on this song to guide him or her. Along one's "songline," one has safe passage, meeting others who share the dreaming along the way. Memory carries the traveler to the limits of the song. At the boundaries Aborigines meet and, through ritual, swap songs. This sharing relationship extends the territory of each and binds one to another through song.

To find new territory and new routes, we all need to learn new songs. This earth and its workings are not as we were once taught. At the limits of our songs, we need one another so that we can be adaptive in a world made of bundles of energy in motion.

Chapter 2   The Importance of Professional Community

The term *professional community* is striking when it is applied to the working cultures of schools. The word *professional* has its roots in *profess*, meaning to declare, to own, and to claim some body of knowledge; it therefore implies a level of expertise with a strong technical core that can be clearly articulated by practitioners. The word *community* has its roots in the word *common*, and its relationship to the word *communicate* implies that the body of expertise is shared. The practitioners in a professional community talk regularly about their collective practice and work together to extend and effectively apply this knowledge base.

The characteristics of developing shared expertise and working with common purpose are vividly present in the schools that are beating the odds and making a difference for student learning (Bryk & Schneider, 2002; Dufour, Eaker, & Baker, 1998; Louis, Marks & Kruse, 1996; McLaughlin & Talbert, 2006).

Unfortunately, the notion of shared practice within a school or a district is not as universal as we would like. Richard Elmore (2000) points out that schools and schooling are governed by the principle of "loose coupling" (p. 6), with many decisions about what and how to teach residing in individual classrooms and not in the surrounding organization. Loose coupling tied to a weak technical core is a recipe for disaster. As the value-added research of Sanders and Rivers (1996) so clearly demonstrates, the effects of both effective and ineffective teachers are felt for years. The issue, then, is how to enhance and spread good practice throughout the school to produce cumulative and lasting effects for all learners, not just those who are fortunate enough to learn the material the way it is presently taught.

It is the current system and ways of running schools that produce the current results. The deep structure of North American schools and the ways of organizing and operating them has remained fairly stable throughout this century and up to the present day. Students, parents, educators, and the greater public all seem to know what a "real school" is. This cultural template provides stability and legitimacy to the school as an institution in society and support for many of the practices that occur within the institution (Tyack & Cuban, 1995).

One of the most stable factors in schools over the years has been the relative isolation of teachers from one another throughout their workday and work year. What sociologist Dan Lortie (1975) described in his groundbreaking study is still true in many schools today. In what he calls "egg-crate" schools, he observed a work life in which autonomous teachers were organized by a culture of presentism, individualism, and conservatism. In these schools teachers lived from moment to moment in their classrooms and sought routines that were efficient and energy conserving. They were careful not to tread on the territory of others and were proactively conservative about changes in curriculum and instruction. Such behaviors and attitudes are still deeply embedded in many schools today and do not contribute to building the kinds of practices that will be flexible and adaptive for meeting the challenges of changing demographics and of increased academic demands to serve the learning needs of a society in rapid transition.

The Elements of Professional Community

In our work, we have not discovered a magic elixir that will improve schools once and for all. Our intent in this book is to share what we are learning about ways in which staffs can better interact to improve results for all students. We offer ways to build professional communities in schools so that difficult things can be talked about, hard questions about teaching and learning can be asked, and adults can actively learn from one another.

The fundamental definition of adaptivity, with the accompanying dynamical principles and focusing questions that we introduced in chapter 1, directly applies to the work of developing true professional communities in schools. These factors interact to produce adaptivity and work together to energize the emergence of a professional community. The combined effects of these relationships (Figure 2-1) produce increased student learning.

The emerging research base supports the importance of the essential elements of profes-

Figure 2-1. Adaptive Schools and Professional Community

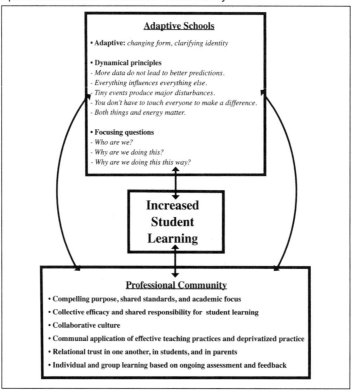

sional community. We are drawing here from three arenas: (a) research on the effects of the adult culture on student learning, (b) research on the impacts of teacher collective efficacy on student learning, and (c) research on the effects of teachers' academic optimism on student learning.

Six essential factors work in concert to produce a sense of shared responsibility for student success. They are a prime example of the principle that everything influences everything else. Each principle on its own is important but not sufficient for the task of energizing instructional improvements. The six factors are as follows:

1. Compelling purpose, shared standards, and academic focus

2. Collective efficacy and shared responsibility for student learning

3. Collaborative culture

4. Communal application of effective teaching practices and deprivatized practice

5. Relational trust in one another, in students, and in parents

6. Individual and group learning based on ongoing assessment and feedback

These shared efforts produce schoolwide gains in student achievement. When teachers take collective responsibility for students, they conceive their work to be a joint enterprise (Little, 1990). They have a greater sense of personal and collective efficacy and assume that learning is a result of school rather than nonschool factors (Lee & Smith, 1996). In high schools where this sense of collective responsibility was strong, the students made larger gains in mathematics, reading, history, and science than in schools where the collective sense was weaker. These outcomes were especially true for minority students and students from low socioeconomic backgrounds.

Compelling Purpose, Shared Standards, and Academic Focus

Communities come into existence and thrive because of a common purpose for working together. A group's compelling purpose establishes reciprocal expectations for its members. Louis and colleagues (1996) assert that teachers' professional communities operate with a sense of moral authority and moral responsibility for making a difference in the lives of students. Such purpose must be grounded in clearly articulated standards for both student and teacher performance. Defining and refining the meaning of doing good work is the task of a professional learning community. Understandable performance and product standards are an important catalyst for conversations among colleagues and for focusing conversations with students and parents.

The work on academic optimism by Hoy, Tarter, & Woolfolk-Hoy (2006) emphasizes the significance of establishing and maintaining a strong academic focus in the school and is at the center of the work of any professional community. Without such a focus, groups spend their time talking about and around peripheral issues instead of working on the work of learning and teaching.

Collective Efficacy and Shared Responsibility for Student Learning

The personal efficacy of individual teachers is a well-studied phenomenon (Tschannen-Moran, Woolfolk-Hoy, & Hoy, 1998). Highly efficacious teachers believe that their teaching knowledge and skills can overcome external factors to make an important difference for their students. Teachers with stronger personal efficacy beliefs consistently outperform teachers in the same settings with weaker beliefs.

These applications in education are based on the concepts of self-efficacy that Albert

Bandura (1977) introduced more than a quarter century ago. Self-efficacy is the belief in our capacity to organize and carry out a plan of action to produce some goal.

More recent work (Goddard, Hoy, & Woolfolk-Hoy, 2004) extends these concepts into the collective realm of teaching. To have a high degree of collective efficacy means that group members believe that they and others, individually and together, are capable of producing increased student success and of overcoming obstacles to that goal. These collective expectations are a powerful element in a school and in a team's working culture, influencing the behaviors and choices of both the individuals and the group as a whole.

Goddard and colleagues (2004) report that being able to influence instructionally relevant school decisions is the most important factor in developing a robust sense of collective efficacy. Participating in decision making contributes strongly to teachers' beliefs in the capabilities of their peers, fosters commitment to school goals, and promotes gains in student achievement.

Collaborative Culture

Who teachers are to one another is as important as who they are to their students. In high-performing and improving schools, studies show that collaboration is the norm (Little, 1982; Newman & Associates, 1997). We are not talking here about project-based collaboration or the "contrived collegiality" described by Hargreaves and Dawe (1990) in which administrators create tasks and agendas to occupy teachers' collective energies. Rather, we are referring to sharing expertise and perspectives on teaching and learning processes, examining data on students, and developing a sense of mutual support and shared responsibility for effective instruction.

Collaboration and collegiality in this way is part of one's professional identity. It does not happen by chance; it has to be taught, practiced, and learned. Developing collaborative cultures is the work of leaders who realize that a collection of superstar teachers working in isolation cannot produce the same results as interdependent colleagues who share and develop professional practices together. From such interactions come growth and learning for teachers, teams, and schools as adaptive organizations.

Communal Application of Effective Teaching Practices and Deprivatized Practice

The norm of privacy has deep roots in "real schools." Once the classroom door is closed, the teacher is God. In this sphere of autonomy lies both greatness and sorrow. Within the zone of isolation, some teachers still find ways to develop craft knowledge, content knowledge, and compassion for their students. These extraordinary individuals manage to stimulate their teaching and continually renew their passion for daily interactions with young minds. All too often, however, this same isolation buffers mediocrity and hides high performers from those who might learn from their modeling, consultation, and coaching.

When practice is deprivatized, teachers visit one another's classrooms to observe master teaching, to coach each other, to mentor, and to solve problems in the living laboratory of instructional space. Students are the beneficiaries of shared teaching repertoires. Although many schools and districts have spent much time and energy developing coherent curriculum maps, shared instructional maps are equally important. When students proceed to the next grade or next subject in a secondary school, having possession of a predictable learning repertoire (such as an understanding of a palette of graphic organizers) energizes learning and increases success—especially for the least successful learners.

By developing communities of practice, teachers establish a working zone between the macroworld of district initiatives and resources and the microworld of their classrooms (McLaughlin & Talbert, 2006). In this way they develop more coherent instructional approaches that represent shared understandings of their unique setting.

Relational Trust in One Another, in Students, and in Parents

In their work on the effects of academic optimism on student achievement, Hoy and colleagues (2006) point out that collective efficacy is the cognitive side of the equation, academic emphasis is the behavioral side, and faculty trust in one another, in students, and in parents is the affective side. Given the powerful biochemical connections between thinking and feeling in our bodies and our brains, it is difficult to separate these functions in practice.

Trust is the glue that binds community members to one another. This is equally true for teacher communities, classroom communities, and parent communities. When all three parties hold the expectations for their relationships, and these expectations are grounded in shared goals and values, trust is a powerful resource for learning.

Bryk and Schneider (2002), in their seminal work in Chicago schools, name four elements of relational trust: respect, competence, personal regard for others, and integrity. Respect comes in the form of basic civility and a willingness to listen deeply to what each person has to say. Parents, students, and teachers need opportunities to talk with and influence one another and to believe that they can positively affect educational outcomes. Competence is the

sense that each party has the ability to carry out its appropriate roles and produce desired outcomes. This applies to both academic results and teacher-student relationships. When gross incompetence goes unchecked, it erodes trust and undermines shared efforts toward improving learning. Personal regard for others deepens relational trust. We are a social species, wired for relationships and reciprocity. Mutual support and mutual caring fuel these associations. Extending ourselves to and for others is like making a deposit in the trust account; the interest in this account compounds with each deposit. Integrity is the congruence between saying and doing. In trusting relationships, this means we believe that a sense of morality and ethics is operating in others and in the ways we are relating. Following through with agreements and commitments is a key aspect of integrity.

Individual and Group Learning Based on Ongoing Assessment and Feedback

"Learning is a basic, adaptive function of humans. More than any other species, people are designed to be flexible learners and active agents in acquiring knowledge and skills" (Bransford, Brown, & Cocking, 1999, p, xi). Cognitive science tells us that learning is socially constructed and individually integrated; learning therefore requires engaging with other learners and is an active process for all involved. Individual and collective learning is one of the key characteristics of effective professional learning communities (Bolam, McMahon, Stoll, Thomas, & Wallace, 2005).

For adult groups, learning how to learn together requires conscious attention, purposeful structures, and meaningful feedback. One form of feedback arises when teachers look at student work together to explore what is working and what might require modification in their curricular and instructional approaches. Groups apply another form of feedback when they take time to reflect on their own processes and outcomes to consider which practices to continue, which to abandon, and which to modify.

From time to time a group or team will share with us that it has some great number of years of combined teaching experience. Their assumption is that learning is additive, when in fact the group members have merely been involved in side-by-side processes. Engaging in parallel play without feedback and reflection is usually a poor teacher.

Developing Teachers' Professional Communities

Despite the existence of these descriptors of schools that make a difference for students, the question of how we get there remains. Schools require frameworks, role clarity, and self-renewing tool kits for collaborative practice. Based on our understanding of the literature on school change, organizational development, and teaching and learning, as well as our experiences with schools the past several years, we offer the following four frameworks as organizers for this journey:

- Twin goals: developing organizational capacities and developing professional capacities

- Four "hats": facilitating, presenting, coaching, and consulting

- Five energy sources: efficacy, flexibility, craftsmanship, consciousness, and interdependence

- Seven norms of collaboration: pausing, paraphrasing, posing questions, putting ideas on the table, providing data, paying attention to self and others, and presuming positive intentions

Figure 2-2 shows the interaction of the first three frameworks.

Figure 2-2. Adaptive Schools

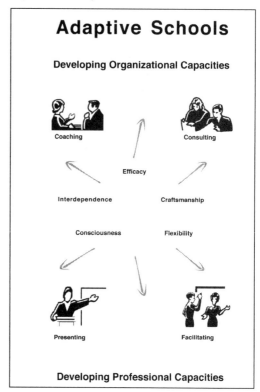

To address problems in languishing schools (see box on next page), districts and schools must continually apply energy and resources to both production and production capacities. Leaders of adaptive schools simultaneously develop two goals related to the organization's ongoing need for self-improvement. The first goal expands six organizational capacities for adaptivity. The second goal strengthens six professional capacities for adaptivity. These 12 capacities for organizational and professional adaptivity are the source of and focus for reflective dialogue in professional communities. Exploration of these 12 areas helps communities to focus their work and strengthen their ties to one another. We offer them here as lenses for examining schools and teaching practice in the hope that they will become focal points for important dialogues and discussions in schools, departments, teams, and governing councils. We will provide brief descriptions here and elaborate on them in chapter 10.

Organizational Capacities for Adaptivity

The six organizational capacities for adaptivity are (a) vision, values, and goal focus, (b) systems thinking, (c) initiating and managing adaptation, (d) interpreting and using data, (e) developing and maintaining collaborative cultures, and (f) gathering and focusing resources.

Vision, Values, and Goal Focus

Clarity of vison, values, and goals is a hallmark of successful schools. The most important goals are the academic goals for the students. These in turn are an expression of the value system that governs the organization. Healthy schools and organizations hold a vision for themselves of how they wish to operate in the world. This is a vision of values and goals in action. Such a vision is informed by real-world

The Languishing High School

At the languishing high school, many students proactively disengage from learning. They slump in their seats on the days that they even bother to come to class. Students ignore homework assignments, and remediation needs outweigh the coverage of new material. External rewards such as grades, honor rolls, and college admissions requirements hold little or no motivational power. Teachers are attempting to deal with this situation by embracing tradition, enforcing standards, and struggling to maintain the integrity of teaching methods and materials. The net result of all these interactions includes departments with abnormally high failure rates, decreased enrollments in advanced courses, falling attendance, and increased dropout rates. Staff morale and teacher efficacy plummet.

This is a classic situation in which the five principles of dynamic systems are at work:

1. More data does not lead to better predictions. Additional surveys and reports about attendance, dropout rates, test scores, and staff attitudes will not improve this school.

2. Everything influences everything else. Tough standards only raise the bar higher for students who lack basic jumping skills. Poor student performance lowers expectations and teachers' professional pride and sense of purpose. Parental concerns and complaints cause defensiveness and withdrawal.

3. Tiny events create major disturbances. Student expulsions, a dropped section of an honors course, and half-full classes create ripple effects throughout life in the school.

4. You don't have to touch everyone in the system to make a difference. A belief that everyone in the school must be ready for change before any action can be taken blocks movement and innovation.

5. Both things and energy matter. Rules, routines, and procedures will count for little unless you also attend to the qualities of human relationships in the school.

measures of student achievement and other goal accomplishments.

At the languishing high school, vision, values, and goals require rethinking and refocusing. English literature might not be the most appropriate course to teach students who have fundamental literacy needs.

Systems Thinking

Systems thinking and vision, values, and goal focus are the major organizers of adaptivity. Helping others to see systems places the work of schools in a larger context. This framework reveals influential interactions and helps to answer the question "What part of the system can we influence to create positive change?"

One major concept in systems work is the idea of feedback loops. These can be either negative or positive. School systems governed by reward and punishment based on test scores operate with negative feedback loops that attempt to keep test scores within acceptable parameters, which are usually calibrated by political pressures.

Positive feedback loops work the other way—the more there is, the more that develops. How people talk to one another is an example of a positive feedback loop that iillustrates the dynamical principle of how a little input can have a major influence. In the next chapter we will discuss the seven norms of collaboration as examples of positive feedback loops within organizations.

Systems thinking, whether explicitly labeled as such or not, is what professional communities do. It is an essential entry point at the low-performing high school. Administrators and teachers would gain much perspective by stepping back and looking at the interactions of the parts of the system in which they are involved.

Initiating and Managing Adaptation

Adaptation is the work of leaders at all levels of the school and professional community. Inquiry is an essential tool of adaptation. The three focusing questions offered in chapter 1 are resources: "Who are we?" "Why are we doing this?" and "Why are we doing this this way?"

Adaptation is not limited to external events. Adaptive schools help all players to learn how to cope with the psychological transition related to change.

The three focusing questions do not seem to be asked at the languishing high school. The questions, if asked persistently by all players, would positively perturb the system and produce enough shared dissatisfaction to create a willingness to consider changing entrenched patterns and practices.

Interpreting and Using Data

Data have no meaning on their own. Meaning is a result of human interaction with data. Many schools are data-rich and meaning-poor. Adaptive groups develop the capacity to discern what data are worth paying attention to and what collaborative practices help people to engage with data in ways that increase ownership and willingness to act on conclusions.

Data can be quantitative or qualitative. Schools are difficult places to motivate and govern with numbers. A 6% rise in student reading scores is often not as compelling as a teacher's tale of the slow reader who makes a breakthrough. Reasoning by anecdote is often more common than reasoning with data. Interpreting and using data is a learned skill that takes time and practice to develop.

The languishing high school usually has enough data about the system but little knowledge. Knowledge, meaning, and commitment result from dialogue and discussion about what story is told by the data. Without organized story making, people in organizations make up their own explanations for events. Part of the reason for this is protection from unwanted truths.

Developing and Maintaining Collaborative Cultures

Collaboration is the essence of teachers' professional community in schools. Collaborative and group development work hand in hand. In chapter 8 we will discuss ways to help groups become more interdependent and cohesive.

Collaboration operates within and between groups. When students work with units of measure as they quantify lab materials, interdependence connects the math teachers to the science teachers. Success in the lab builds on math skills learned in other settings. Laboratory applications further reinforce the practical nature of algorithms learned in math class.

Collaboration fuels group development when individual members envision (a) the potential of the group as a collective force in the school, and (b) the expanding capacity of the group for accomplishing important work that individuals working in isolation would not be able to achieve.

A sense of collaboration is lacking at the low-performing high school. The teachers and the departments feel besieged, hunkering down and fighting their own fights for some sense of accomplishment and dignity. The students and the teachers do not see themselves aligned in a shared task. Each sees the other as an adversary, with small victories and losses accumulating on a daily basis.

Gathering and Focusing Resources

Time, money, and human energy are some of the resources that support goal accomplishment in schools. Overload and fragmentation are the enemies of success. Resources must be focused where they will make the greatest difference. Ultimately this leads to some hard decisions in schools. Resource allocation and goal accomplishment are directly linked. What receives attention gets done.

This last organizational capacity for adaptivity cannot work without clarity in the others. Values and goals point out resource needs. Systems thinking frames where to target resources. To initiate and manage adaptation means to apply and manage resources. Data use and interpretation set up essential feedback loops that reflect whether and how goals are being achieved. Collaboration is the glue that allows groups to both agree upon and work toward the goals.

All this is missing at the languishing high school. Energy, time, and money are thrown at problems to fix the most visible ones. Doing anything is considered good enough. The goal is to protect individuals and the organization from the accusation of not working hard enough. Without a clear focus and without honest feedback systems, however, this only saps resources and increases the magnitude of the problems.

Professional Capacities for Adaptivity

The six professional capacities for adaptivity are (a) collegial interaction, (b) cognitive processes of instruction, (c) knowledge of the structure of the discipline, (d) self-knowledge, values, standards, and beliefs, (e) a repertoire of teaching skills, and (f) knowing about students and how they learn.

Collegial Interaction

In many respects, collaboration needs to be taught. Past practices and workplace culture influence the capacity for collaboration. So does gender and school organization (elementary, middle, or high). Attitudes, knowledge, skills, and practices can be taught; these are the focus of chapters 3–7 and 9. The capacity to be a colleague is different from other capacities of good teaching. It draws upon craft knowledge, self-knowledge, and interpersonal skills to form a web of reciprocal relationships and services.

Norms of privatism are strong at the languishing high school. Each teacher operates as an independent artisan. There is no craft guild with which to share professional knowledge and concerns. Small breakthroughs with students are personal victories to be savored and fleetingly enjoyed in quiet moments.

Cognitive Processes of Instruction

Instructional thinking occurs in four phases: planning, teaching, analyzing and evaluating, and applying what has been learned to future work.

The more cognitively adept a teacher is, the better the results are in classrooms and with colleagues. This capacity includes the abilities to manage multiple goals simultaneously, to align one's work with that of one's colleagues, and to learn from experience in the classroom.

Teachers in the languishing high school feel as if they have no time to reflect. The pace of survival puts action ahead of reflection on most personal and collective agendas. Peer coaching programs sputter out in the press for time. Formal supervision is pro forma and ritualized. Administrators are mostly satisfied with teachers who "keep the lid on" in a classroom and keep kids out of the office.

Knowledge of the Structure of the Discipline

Knowledge of the structure of the discipline moves beyond content knowledge, which is necessary but not sufficient for good teaching. The former involves knowing the organiz-

ing schema of the field, including the significant ideas in the discipline and how they relate to one another. Anticipating major misconceptions and barriers to learning and understanding the significant ideas are also important here. These inform curricular choices and the selection and use of resource materials.

This area is looming as an important entry point for instructional improvement. In chapter 10 we will elaborate on the connections between teacher knowledge of the structure of the discipline and student achievement. Just as there are no teacher-proof curricula, there are no knowledge-free curricula. To interact flexibly with students in the flow of instruction, teachers need to deeply know their content and the organizing principles of that content.

Little attention has been given to matters of curriculum at the low-performing high school beyond periodic textbook adoptions. Teachers' knowledge of their fields is not always up to date. In fact, more than a quarter of the staff might be teaching outside their areas of certification or in areas in which they did not major in college.

Self-Knowledge, Values, Standards, and Beliefs

The knowledge of what one stands for is the most important assest a professional educator has to maintain a steady course through the ups and downs of life in schools. Having clarity about personal standards for good work and good behavior and effectively communicating these standards to students is a basic skill of all good teachers.

Such clarity is not bestowed with teaching credentials; it is the result of trial and error, reflection and experimentation, and dialogue and iteration with colleagues. Values and beliefs about learning, collegiality, and relating to students and parents are all shaped by personal reflection and interaction with other professionals. Reflective dialogue serves the dual purpose of developing shared understanding and helping individuals to clarify personal thinking to ground their actions.

A lack of deep professional interaction does not serve teachers in the languishing high school. Many are unsure of themselves and insecure in the changing world in which they find themselves. Old touchstones, such as grades, course syllabi, and school traditions no longer provide comfort and a sense of purpose in the world. Some cling tightly to known elements even in the face of evidence of their negative effects. The comforts of the past hold memories of the way things are supposed to be.

A Repertoire of Teaching Skills

In chess, the queen is the most powerful piece on the board because she has the most flexibility of movement: She can move forward or backward, left or right, and diagonally, for any number of spaces. Like a chess queen, teachers with an expanded repertoire of teaching skills have the most flexibility of movement and thus the most options.

No one knows it all in the classroom. Craft knowledge is a lifetime in the making. There is always something new to learn as research, technology, and professional practice continually expand both the knowledge base of teaching and the answers to the questions about what works and why. The revolution in brain biology that is driving new understanding of cognitive psychology and pedagogy will continue to push the need for repertoire building for all practicing professional educators throughout their careers.

Teachers at the languishing high school cling to old ways of doing business in the classroom. Lectures, videos, reading from textbooks, note taking, and quizzes prevail. Students play out their part of the ritual, minimally complying with this production. Alternative teaching techniques such as simulations and project-based learning are usually rejected as "not my style."

Knowing About Students and How They Learn

Just as educators can never know enough about the structure of their disciplines, themselves, and their teaching repertoire, they can never know all there is to know about their students and how they learn. This capacity is divided into two parts. The first, knowing about students, means knowing them as people—who they are and where they come from. This is the stuff of genuine relationships that nurture and motivate learning. The second part, knowing how students learn, is informed by knowledge of learning styles, developmental stages of intellectual growth, cultural differences, and gender differences.

Students in the languishing high school are often viewed as problems to overcome. They are the objects of instruction, not the constructors of meaning. All too often, relationships between teachers and students are strained in the battle for power and control. Each side needs the other but does not always know how to cross the gap that divides them.

The Four "Hats" of Shared Leadership

In adaptive schools, all players learn to "wear four hats," or play four roles. By all players we mean administrators, teachers, support staff, students, and, when appropriate, parents. In such schools all the players must have the knowledge and skills to manage themselves and influence and lead others.

Leadership is a shared function in meetings, staff development activities, action research, and classrooms. Recognizing the "hats" and knowing when and how to change them is shared knowledge within the organization. When values, roles, and work relationships are clear, decisions about appropriate behavior are easy. We offer definitions to illustrate the major functions of four leadership roles and the distinctions among the roles.

Facilitating

To facilitate means "to make easier." A facilitator conducts a meeting in which the purpose is dialogue, shared decision making, planning, or problem solving. The facilitator directs the processes used in the meeting, choreographs the energy within the group, and maintains a focus on one content and one process at a time. The facilitator should never be the person with role or knowledge authority (described in chapter 7). The role of facilitator is central to the ideas in this book. Many of the templates, tools, and strategies provided here apply to it. We have therefore elaborated on this role in chapter 7.

Presenting

To present is to teach. A presenter's goals are to extend and enrich knowledge, skills, or attitudes and to enable these to be applied in people's work. A presenter may adopt many stances—expert, colleague, novice, or friend—and use many strategies of presentation—lectures, cooperative learning, study groups, or simulations. Touchstones of effective presentations include clarity of instructional outcomes, of standards for success, and of ways to assess learning (Garmston, 2005; Garmston & Wellman, 1992).

Coaching

To coach is to help a group take action toward its goals while simultaneously helping

it to develop expertise in planning, reflecting, problem solving, and decision making. The coach takes a nonjudgmental stance and uses open-ended questions, pausing, paraphrasing, and probing for specificity. The skillful coach focuses on group members' perceptions, thinking, and decision-making processes to mediate resources for self-directedness.

Consulting

To consult is to have your expertise be used by others. A consultant can be an information specialist or an advocate for content and/or process. As an information specialist, the consultant delivers technical knowledge to the group. As a content advocate, the consultant encourages group members to use a certain instructional strategy, adopt a particular curriculum, or purchase a specific brand of computer. As a process advocate, the consultant influences the group's methodology, such as by recommending an open rather than a closed meeting to increase trust in the system. To effectively consult, one must have trust, commonly defined goals, and the group's desired outcomes clearly in mind (Block, 1981).

Marshaling the Energy for Changing Schools

Carl Glickman (1998) writes that without the will to change for the better, all resources and management schemes will have little effect. "This issue of will—wanting to be better—is critical to understanding how long-term policies, allocation of resources, and work conditions can or cannot work" (p. 3).

Two major problems related to change confront all groups. One is adapting to and surviving in the external environment. The other is developing internally to support daily functioning and increase the capacity to adapt (Shein,

2004). Groups either develop toward greater inclusion and effectiveness or dissolve through fragmentation and disarray. Changing the structure of the group or teaching group members skills does not guarantee growth toward increased group performance. Helping members to pay attention to basic energy sources within the group encourages the development of these resources and permits learned skills to be applied and structures to be reinvented for greater impact.

Group development is accelerated by the following five intervention approaches, which we will elaborate on in chapter 8:

1. Structure the environment to release and enhance energy sources.

2. Teach about the five energy sources of high-performing groups.

3. Mediate selected intervention points.

4. Model the five energy sources.

5. Monitor evidence and artifacts of selected energy sources.

The five energy sources, drawn from the work of Costa and Garmston (2002) and members of the Institute for Intelligent Behavior, are discussed below.

Efficacy

The group believes in its capacity to produce results and stays the course through internal and external difficulties to achieve goals. The group aligns energies within itself in pursuit of its outcomes.

Flexibility

The group regards situations from multiple perspectives, works creatively with uncertainty and ambiguity, and values and utilizes differences within itself and the larger community of which it is part. The group attends to rational and intuitive ways of working.

Craftsmanship

The group strives for clarity in its values, goals, and standards. It applies these as criteria for its planning, actions, reflections, and refinements. It attends to both short- and long-term time perspectives. It continually refines communication processes within and beyond the group.

Consciousness

The group monitors its decisions, actions, and reflections based on its values, norms, and common goals. Members are aware of the impact of their actions on each other, the entire group, and outside individuals and groups.

Interdependence

The group values its internal and external relationships. It seeks reciprocal influence and learning. Members treat conflict as an opportunity to learn about themselves, their own group, and other groups. The group trusts its interactions and the processes of dialogue and discussion.

Simple Rules Govern Complex Behavior

In this book we are attempting to frame the complex work of developing and facilitating collaborative groups. Although the frameworks, lenses, and tools we offer might seem a bit overwhelming at first, underneath them are some simple principles that guide our work.

This simplicity is illustrated in a story related by M. Mitchell Waldrop in his book Complexity: The Emerging Science at the Edge of Order and Chaos (1992). *Complexity is the study of intricate dynamical systems*. It is an integrative science in which economists, biologists, ecologists, meteorologists, and specialists from other fields connect to explore the underlying principles that govern natural and human systems. Much of the work is done using high-powered computers to simulate natural and designed systems.

Craig Reynolds of the Symbolics Corporation in Los Angeles is one such researcher. He designed a computer program that captures the essence of the flocking behavior of birds, the herding behavior of sheep, and the schooling behavior of fish. The elegance of his design was in not trying to build rules into the group. Instead, the rules resided within the individuals. He created a collection of autonomous, birdlike agents he called *boids*. Each "boid" was programmed with three simple rules:

1. Maintain a minimum distance from other objects in the environment, including other "boids."

2. Match the velocity of other "boids" in your vicinity.

3. Move toward the perceived center of the mass of other "boids" in your vicinity.

There was no superintendent of "boids." None of these rules said to form a flock, yet flocks formed every time the program ran. "Boids" would at first be scattered around the computer screen but would soon flock up. Flocks were able to fly around obstacles or break into subflocks to fly around objects, coming together again on the other side. On one occasion a "boid" banged into a pole, lost its bearings momentarily, then darted forward to rejoin the flock.

If simple rules govern complex behavior in groups, what might be some simple rules for group members to follow? We propose the following:

1. Take care of me. It is each group member's groundedness, resourcefulness, and energy that develops the synergy that makes high-performing groups possible.

2. Take care of us. It is our interdependence, interactions, and caring for one another and the group that motivates us to want to continue to work together.

3. Take care of our values. It is our values that drive our goal clarity about who we are, how we want to be together, and what we will accomplish for students.

In chapters 3 and 4 we explore these simple rules in action as we dicuss group-member capabilities, the seven norms of collaboration, and two ways of talking in groups.

Chapter 3 Developing Collaborative Norms

Working in groups is a natural condition of human life. Since the dawn of humanity on the plains of Africa, bands, clans, tribes, and families have collaborated for defense, food gathering, and ceremonial purposes. Work in groups is often difficult, filled with conflicts and tensions, but it is also absolutely necessary for achieving results in modern organizations.

Each group member must balance personal goals with collective goals, acquire resources for his or her own work, and share those resources to support the work of others. Navigating the tensions between part and whole—between personal autonomy and collaboration—is an ongoing feature of both the surface and the deep structure for any working group.

Many organizations try to control these tensions by using facilitators to shape and mold group energy and task focus. Although a person in such a role can often make a difference in a group's performance, a skilled facilitator is only one element of group success. (See chapter 7 for more on the role and skills of the facilitator.) Individual group members need consciousness and lenses for shaping personal decisions and behaviors in meetings.

All surface behaviors are driven by inner awareness and ongoing calibration of deeper values. Skillful group members monitor and adjust their behaviors to support the other group members and the group as a whole. To operate with sufficient flexibility, group members need self-awareness and self-monitoring skills to guide their choice making. Skillful facilitators increase this awareness by shining the light of reflection on group processes and by supporting group members in reflecting on the behavioral decisions they are making.

Four capabilities shape the self-monitoring system of high-performing group members. These in turn organize and drive seven norms of collaboration. The seven norms are the verbal working tools for both skilled group members and skilled facilitators.

The Four Group-Member Capabilities

We first realized the special power of focusing on capabilities as part of a group that was developing Cognitive Coaching[sm] with Art Costa and other colleagues from the Institute for Intelligent Behavior. A *capability* names what a person is able to do. It is different from *capacity*, which refers to how much one can hold. Capabilities are the metacognitive awarenesses with which people determine when to use, how to use, or not to use certain skills. Capabilities therefore organize and direct the use of skills; they influence the application and effectiveness of knowledge and skills.

The four group-member capabilities are as follows:

1. To know one's intentions and choose congruent behaviors

2. To set aside unproductive patterns of listening, responding, and inquiring

3. To know when to self-assert and when to integrate

4. To know and support the group's purposes, topics, processes, and development

To Know One's Intentions and Choose Congruent Behaviors

Clarity of intention in the moment and over time drives attention, which in turn drives the what and how of a group member's meeting participation. This clarity precedes and influences the three other capabilities. It is the source of impulse control, patience, strategic listening, and strategic speaking.

This capability is the foundation for flexible and effective behavior. If, for example, a person's intention is to positively influence the thinking of others, various behaviors can be used congruently with that intention: Under some circumstances, a paraphrase will convey an attempt to understand and open the door for reciprocal understanding; in some situations, direct advocacy will be more persuasive; in other cases, an inquiry into the thinking of another speaker might be more effective.

To Set Aside Unproductive Patterns of Listening, Responding, and Inquiring

For each meeting participant, there are two audiences. One is external, made up of the other group members. The other is internal, made up of the feelings, pictures, and talk going on inside each individual. Group members need to continually decide which audience to serve. Three major set-aside areas focus this choice and allow fuller and more nonjudgmental participation. They are as follows:

1. To set aside autobiographical listening, responding, and inquiring: "Me too!"

2. To set aside inquisitive listening, responding, and inquiring: "Tell me more!"

3. To set aside solution listening, responding, and inquiring: "I know what to do!"

The autobiographical frame leads to several problems in group work. The first is the filtering process that goes on when individuals try to hear another's story through the lens of their own experiences. Although this can be a source of empathy, it can also lead to distortion and miscommunication.

This type of listening, responding, and inquiring is a major source of wasted time in meetings. It can lead to endless storytelling in which everyone around the table shares a related anecdote. This is dinner party conversation, not productive meeting talk. Each member of the eighth-grade team does not have to relate a discipline horror story. The team should explore a collective understanding of the students and their needs and develop appropriate response patterns that elicit desired behaviors.

The inquisitive frame is sometimes triggered by the autobiographical. People inquire to see how others' stories compare to their own. Pure curiosity also motivates inquisitive listening, responding, and inquiring. A critical question at this juncture is "How much detail do we need to move this item?" This is an example of what we call a *naive question*. (See Appendix A for other examples of naive questions.) Such questions can be asked by any group member. The purpose is to focus attention on critical matters and avoid unnecessary specificity.

The solution frame is deeply embedded in the psyche of educators. Status, rewards, and identity are all tied up with being a good problem solver. The pressure of time in schools pushes people toward action and away from reflection. The downside of this pattern is that groups and group members get trapped in situations and action plans before they have time to fully understand the perspectives of others.

The solution frame also stifles the generation of new possibilities. It gets in the way of developing alternative ways of framing issues and problems, and it pushes groups toward action before clear outcomes have been created.

To Know When to Self-Assert and When to Integrate

In productive groups, each member must decide when to self-assert and when to integrate with the group. In one group, a member confided to us that she was concerned about the autocratic disposition of the new chairman. Although she valued the directness that he brought to the group's work, she was concerned that a collective ownership would gradually be lost if he were not sometimes challenged. Her issue, and the tension for each group member, was when to challenge and when to go with the flow. Self-assertion and integration are conscious choices only when group members have personal clarity about their own intentions as well as a knowledge of and a willingness to support the group's outcomes and methods.

Self-assertion does not necessarily mean self-focus. It can mean asserting oneself into the flow of group interactions to refocus the group on a topic or on a process. It can mean reminding others of the purpose of the meeting when the conversation strays off course. It can also mean speaking up and advocating topics and processes.

When individual group members integrate, they align their energy with the content and processes of the meeting. During dialogue they suspend judgments and counterarguments in an attempt to understand viewpoints different from their own. During discussions, they follow the flow of logic and reasoning as it emerges. In this way, solutions satisfying to the group as a whole are more likely to emerge.

Consensus decision making is the ultimate test of this capability. This procedure assumes that participants know when and how to self-assert and when and how to integrate, both during and after the decision-making process.

The next two chapters describe ways of talking in groups as well as principles and practices for successful meetings. In these chapters you will find many ideas and examples of places for self-assertion and for integration.

To Know and Support the Group's Purposes, Topics, Processes, and Development

All ongoing groups need to balance three simultaneous agendas. The first is *task focus*, which is the ultimate expression of the group's purpose. The second agenda is *process skills development*. Without continued attention to expanded repertoire and expanded skills, the group stagnates and does not expand its capacity for handling more complex work in the future. The third agenda is *group development*. All groups exist on a continuum from novice to expert performance. Experience alone is an insufficient teacher. Many longstanding groups operate at novice levels of performance. In chapter 8 we elaborate on our concepts of group development.

High-performing groups are adaptive groups. They learn from experience and improve the way they work. In supporting the group's purposes, topics, processes, and development, individual group members make a commitment to this shared learning and to personal learning.

The paradoxes of work in groups establish the essential tensions that groups and their individuals must continually resolve. The four

29

group-member capabilities supply metacognitive and emotional filters for decisions, choices, and behaviors. All this requires a tool kit for productive group work.

Promoting a Spirit of Inquiry

High-functioning groups and group members infuse their work with a spirit of inquiry. Inquiry is central to professional communities that produce stable gains in student learning. Learning at its root is a questioning process, and successful collaboration embraces the patterns and practices of inquiry. Inquiry presumes an openness to and an investment in the ideas of others. Physicist David Bohm has noted that thought is "largely a collective phenomenon." These thoughts, like electrons, are shaped by their interactions with others (Senge, 1990).

To inquire is to ask, be curious, invite the transmission of thoughts or feelings, confer, consult, wonder, request, examine, and investigate ideas. Richard Elmore (2000) points out that "the knowledge we need to solve problems [in schools] often doesn't reside close at hand; it has to be found through active inquiry and analysis" (p. 13). Such interactions are not always the norm in schools. Collaborative work is fraught with the tensions and the fears of being judged or of being perceived as one who might be judging others.

Teaching as a private practice has a deep cultural history. Breaking and reshaping the patterns within a culture requires both skill and commitment to the ongoing process of building community. Teaching is in many ways a "telling" profession. Teachers tell students what they need to know and how to do the things they need to learn how to do. This "telling" behavior often carries over into patterns of adult communication as we tell others our stories, thoughts, and opinions or wait for our turn to do so. This culture of advocacy defines much of the interaction in adult groups. We are often caught up in the tyranny of *or* (Collins & Porras, 1997). Things must be right or wrong, true or false, yes or no.

Dichotomous thinking leads to dichotomous questions, which in turn polarize group members. The art of asking invitational questions that avoid these dichotomies is the heart of collaborative inquiry. Invitational questions form connections between people and ideas as well as between ideas and other ideas.

All group work is about relationships. Relationships shape and define patterns of discourse. These relationships are shaped by who initiates a query and the form of that query. Who responds and how he or she responds is a direct result of the ways in which a topic is initiated. Form, function, and outcome are linked within an emotional and social system that, when handled with care, opens and expands thought and creates new possibilities.

The patterns of inquiry built with the tools of the seven norms of collaboration lead to deeper understanding and to better-informed action. This understanding and these actions can be internal for participants and external in their behaviors. As we grapple with ideas and perspectives we come to know others and ourselves more deeply. To do so requires us to reflect on our inner and outer reactions to data, information, and events. Purposeful inquiry helps us to interpret personal and collective values and the implications of these as we live them out in our organizations. Skillful inquiry also helps us to clarify our priorities for a topic on the table. Where does this issue fit within the bigger picture? In what ways is this topic important and in what ways might this topic be a distraction?

In the end, what we talk about and how we talk to one another is a way of acting out our beliefs about the world and the way it works, our beliefs about the group and its purposes, and our beliefs about our personal place in both arenas. What we talk about and how we talk also defines who we are and ultimately whom we become. By promoting a spirit of inquiry within our groups, we make an investment in our personal and collective futures.

The Seven Norms of Collaboration

Several years ago our friend and colleague Bill Baker commented that organizations have been training the wrong people. Instead of spending time and energy developing more skilled facilitators, he said, they should develop group members' skills as the way to improve practice and success. Our experience bears out the wisdom of this approach. When group members are knowledgeable and skilled, anyone with simple knowledge of facilitation principles and moves can facilitate constructive group work.

Drawing from the Cognitive Coaching[sm] model (Costa & Garmston, 2002), the work of Peter Senge (1990), and the work of Baker, Costa & Shalit (1997), we have adapted and refined this set of norms of collaboration as the tools for productive communication between group members. These are as follows:

1. Pausing
2. Paraphrasing
3. Posing questions
4. Putting ideas on the table
5. Providing data
6. Paying attention to self and others
7. Presuming positive intentions

Reflect on your typical behavior in some group with which you regularly work. Before reading the descriptions of the norms of collaboration below, do the following self-assessment. In the list above put a checkmark after the norms to which you pay conscious attention in most meetings with the group you have in mind.

There is a marked difference between skills and norms. A *skill* is something that someone knows how to do. A skill becomes a *norm* when it is normal behavior in the group. When this occurs, the behavior becomes normative for new group members, who model their own behavior on the standards tacitly set by the veterans.

When the seven norms of collaborative work become an established part of group life and group work, cohesion, energy, and commitment to shared work and to the group increase dramatically. The seven norms serve as guides and benchmarks in groups. As they become established within the working substrate, they teach and remind all group members, both veterans and newcomers, that this is the way we talk to each other around here.

In our follow-up work with clients, this

Intention, Attention, Linguistics

The norms of collaboration are driven by the following:

1. Intention to support thinking, problem solving, and group development

2. Attention of each group member, who attends fully with ears and eyes for the essence of others' messages.

3. Linguistic skills of the listener and/or responder

---

phenomenon is reported time and again. An assistant superintendent shared with us that when one or two people in a meeting practice the norms, the behavior of other group members becomes more effective.

A major tension is that all groups have more tasks to accomplish than time in which to accomplish them. Yet any group that is too busy to reflect on process is too busy to improve. The seven norms become goals for collective growth. In adaptive schools, individuals and groups select goals from among the seven norms. They practice, monitor, and reflect on the impact of the norms for themselves and for the group.

Each norm is deceptively simple. Most are skills that people regularly apply in one-to-one communications. The irony is that these seemingly simple behaviors are rare in many meetings. Inquiring into the ideas of others increases the capacity for group members to influence each other. Pausing and paraphrasing are often missing, especially when things get tense. Probing for details is forgotten when members presume to understand others' meanings. This can lead to later confusion and complication. Presuming positive intentions prevents members from judging others. Interpersonal judgments spawn blocked thinking and negative presuppositions. We offer the following explanations of the norms as a rationale for their importance.

Pausing

There is a vast research base on the positive effects of teacher pausing and silence on student thinking. The "wait time" research of Mary Budd Rowe (1986) has been replicated around the world. Thinking takes time. High-level thinking takes even longer. This research indicates that it takes from 3 to 5 seconds for most human brains to process high-level thoughts.

Not all brains work the same way. This is especially evident in meetings and group work. Some people prefer to think out loud and construct their ideas externally; others prefer to process ideas internally and reflect and analyze before speaking. The external processors often get in the way of the internal processors. This can be an alienating experience for deliberate, internal thinkers. The meeting topics move by before they have had a chance to contribute.

The members of one middle school team with whom we worked began to laugh at themselves after completing the Norms of Collaboration Inventory (Appendix B). When we inquired, they said they'd been working together for more than 2 years and had yet to make a decision. In their group, if you stopped to breathe while speaking, you lost the floor. Consequently, they all had tremendous lung power and claimed they could each talk for hours on a single inhalation. What they recognized was that without a norm of pausing, meetings became a competition for air space. They soon learned to monitor several types of pauses to increase their productivity and satisfaction.

Groups become skilled at four types of pauses. The first type occurs after a question is asked. This allows initial processing time for those being asked the question. The second type occurs after someone speaks. Human beings think and speak in bursts. With additional processing time, more thoughts are organized into coherent speech.

In the original wait-time research with students, when teachers paused after asking questions and after the students' initial responses, the length of the responses increased from 300% to 700%, depending on the socioeconomic status (SES) of the child. The lower-SES children had the greatest gains.

The first two types of pauses require the questioner and other group members to monitor and control their own behavior. These are pauses to give other people time to think. A third type is under the control of each individual who is asked a question. This is personal reflection time in which that person waits before answering. Sometimes one says, "Give me a moment to think about that before answering." At other times one acknowledges the question nonverbally, goes inside oneself to think, and then responds to the question. This is also a nice way to model thoughtfulness for others and can be an important normative behavior in groups.

A fourth type of pause in meetings is a collective pause. This can be formally structured or can occur spontaneously. These shared pauses allow ideas and questions to settle in and allow time for note taking and reflection. The intent of these breaks in the action is to create shared cognitive space for the group and its members.

Pausing begins a pattern that is followed by paraphrasing and questioning. Groups give themselves a powerful gift when they establish this pattern as a norm; pause, paraphrase, and probe for details; pause, paraphrase, and inquire for a wider range of thoughts; and pause, paraphrase, and inquire about feelings.

Paraphrasing

Paraphrasing is one of the most valuable and least used communication tools in meetings. Even people who naturally and skillfully paraphrase in one-to-one settings often neglect this vital behavior in group settings. Groups that develop consciousness about paraphrasing and give themselves permission to use this reflected tool become clearer and more cohesive about their work.

Try this experiment. Paraphrase, then ask a question. Do this several times. Now ask questions without preceding them with paraphrases. Since a well-crafted paraphrase communicates "I am trying to understand you, and therefore I value what you have to say" and establishes a relationship between people and ideas, questions preceded by paraphrases will be perceived similarly. Questions by themselves, no matter how artfully constructed, put a degree of psychological distance between the asker and the asked. Paraphrasing aligns the parties and creates a safe environment for thinking (Lipton & Wellman, 1998).

Mediational paraphrases reflect the speaker's content and the speaker's emotions about the content and frame a level of abstraction for holding the content. The paraphrase reflects content back to the speaker for further consideration and connects that response to the flow of discourse emerging within the group. Such paraphrasing creates permission to probe for details and elaboration. Without the paraphrase, probing may be perceived as interrogation.

The Structure and Flow of Effective Paraphrasing

Listen and observe carefully to calibrate the content and emotions of the speaker. Signal your intention to paraphrase. This is done by modulating intonation with the use of an approachable voice and by opening with a reflective stem. Such stems put the focus and emphasis on the speaker's ideas, not on the paraphraser's interpretation of those ideas.

For example, reflective paraphrases should not use the pronoun *I*. The phrase "What I think I hear you saying" signals to many speakers that their thoughts no longer matter and that the paraphraser is now going to insert his or her own ideas into the conversation.

The following paraphrase stems signal that a paraphrase is coming:

- You're suggesting . . .
- You're proposing . . .
- So what you're wondering is . . .
- So you are thinking that . . .

- Hmm, you're pondering the effects of . . .
- So your hunch is that . . .

Choose a type of paraphrase with which to respond. There are three broad categories of paraphase types (Table 3-1):

1. Acknowledge and clarify content and emotion. If the paraphrase is not completely accurate, the speaker will offer corrections: "So you're concerned about the budgeting process and ways to get input early."

2. Summarize and organize by offering themes and "containers" to organize several statements or separate jumbled issues. This is an especially important type of paraphrase to use when multiple speakers contribute to a topic: "There appear to be two issues here. One is resource allocation and the other is the impact of those decisions on student learning."

3. Shift to a higher or lower level of abstraction. Paraphrasing within a flow of discourse often moves through a sequence of acknowledging, summarizing, and shifting the focus to a higher or lower level of abstraction. Paraphrases move to a higher abstractional level when they name concepts, goals, values, and assumptions: "So a major goal here is to define fairness in the budgeting processes and compare those criteria to the operating values of the school." Paraphrases move to a lower abstractional level when concepts require grounding in details: "So *fair* might mean that we construct a needs assessment form for each department to fill out and submit to the site council for public consideration."

Learning Styles and Paraphrasing

Paraphrases that summarize or shift the abstraction level of discourse support and stretch the thinking styles of different group members.

Global thinkers appreciate paraphrases that separate and organize "thinking in progress." At other times the shift down in logical levels grounds global thinkers in specific examples and concrete details. Concrete, highly sequential thinkers learn from the shift up to higher logical levels. This helps them to explore a bigger picture and creates a wider context for thinking.

Posing Questions to Specify Thinking

Thinking is a biochemical process that engages the molecules of emotion and the molecules of cognition. We are wired to detect threat in the communications of others. Reducing the potential for threat in our questions means that how we inquire is as important as the topic of our inquiry. To keep others open and thinking, we need to pay attention to several important features in our communication.

Full Attention. The invitation to think begins with our giving full attention to others in the group signaling that our full presence is available for this conversation and that we intend no harm. This physical message meshes with several important verbal elements that form an invitation to think together and think about the ideas being explored.

Approachable Voice. Using an approachable voice is the first element of the invitation. This voice is well-modulated and tends to rise at the end of a statement, summary or question (Grinder, 1997). This tonal package wraps around our questions and comments indicating the intention to invite and explore thinking and not to interrogate or challenge.

Plural Forms. Two important syntactical choices invite colleagues to think with us and increase the options and possibilities for thinking. The first is to use plural forms: *observations* instead of *observation*, *options* instead of *option*. The use of plural forms sets aside the need for evaluation and the sorting of ideas.

Table 3-1. The Three Types of Paraphrases

Acknowledge & Clarify	Summarize & Organize	Shift Level of Abstraction
A brief statement in the listener's own words Metaphorically: a mirror	A statement that offers themes or containers Metaphorically: baskets or boxes	A statement that shifts the conversation to a higher or lower level of abstraction Metaphorically: an elevator or escalator
• You're concerned about . . . • You would like to see . . . • You're feeling bad about . . .	• You seem to have two goals here: one is about ____ and the other is about ____. • We seem to be struggling with three themes: where to ___, how to ____, and who should____. • On the one hand, we ____, and on the other, we____.	Shifting up: • value • belief • goal • assumption • concept • category • intention Shifting down: • example • nonexample • strategy • choice • action • option

Often group members need to hear their ideas aloud before they know which are most central to the issues before the group.

Exploratory Language. The second syntactical choice is to use exploratory phrasing in statements, paraphrases and questions as the second syntactical element. Words like *some*, *might*, *seems*, *possible* and *hunches* widen the potential range of responses and reduce the need of confidence and surety. Words like *could* and *why* may decrease the confidence of listeners by seeming to ask for premature commitment or a need to defend ideas and actions that are not yet fully developed.

Nondichotomous Questions. Invitational, mediational facilitators and group members frame their questions using the elements listed above. In addition, they frame their questions by using open-ended, non-dichotomous forms. These are questions that cannot be answered *yes* or *no*. For example, instead of asking a group, "Did anyone notice anything unusual in this data," "Will you," or "Have you," facilitators and skilled group members invite productive thinking and promote a spirit of inquiry within the group.

Positive Presuppositions. These language forms assume capacity and positive intentions. "Given your knowledge of . . . ," "As an experienced professional . . ."

Posing Questions to Explore Thinking

Using the elements of invitation, we pose questions to explore thinking by asking about perceptions, assumptions and interpretations, and invite others to inquire into their own thinking.

Examples:

What might be some of the assumptions we have about . . .

Given our concern and knowledge of this issue, what might be some of the observations . . .

What are some of the perspectives you are considering as you are reflecting on . . .

As we are considering the bigger picture, what might be some of the factors and . . .

What are some of our feelings about . . .

Questions for Specificity

Human brains are not designed for specificity. In a world swimming in details, brains form quick generalizations from fragments of information. Brains delete particulars from streams of data and distort incoming and outgoing messages to fit deeply embedded models of reality (Bandler & Grinder, 1971). These are all natural processes; they do not willfully occur. Generalizations, deletions, and distortions are survival patterns hardwired into the human brain. They are adaptations for the challenges faced by our hunting and gathering ances-

tors, who needed to make quick decisions for survival.

In modern times these same traits cause difficulties in human communication. Conversations go haywire when the various parties make different assumptions about the meaning of words and concepts and neglect to verify or correct those assumptions. Problem definition, problem solving, and solution generation all rely on specificity for success.

Five categories of vagueness inhabit human speech; these are described below.

Vague Nouns and Pronouns

Someone named "they" makes most of the decisions in organizations. "They" are joined by "the central office," "the administrators," "the union," "the parents," "the students," and a host of others as the source of mysterious messages, concerns, and directives. Unless group members know who "they" are, communication takes longer, and people do not always know how to treat the information.

When a speaker in a meeting says our students can't write, someone in the group should probe for specificity by paraphrasing and asking for details. It might sound like this: "So you're concerned about student writing. What's your hunch about how many of our students have writing difficulties?"

After the speaker answers, the logical follow-up question would be about which areas of writing are of most concern. If the group discovers that a small number of students have specific skill gaps, they can develop a remediation plan for this targeted audience. If the group discovers that a large number of students have fundamental issues as writers, this calls for a more in-depth look at the patterns of curriculum and instruction in the school. Without the details, the group does not know which problem to solve.

Vague Verbs

Planning and problem-solving sessions require specificity for targeted action. The verb *plan* itself means very different things to different people. Some think that it means scratching ideas on a napkin; others imagine timelines and flowcharts with names and dates attached. Groups have to define their verbs. Words like *improve, enhance, design, modify,* and *understand* are all examples of vague verbs used by working groups. Someone should serve the group by probing for specificity in order for the team to agree on concepts, plan for change, and act in concert.

A statement like "We want our students to be on time and prepared for class" easily produces surface agreement in most groups of educators. It is only when we probe for which students are not yet meeting these requirements and what the meanings of "be on time" and "be prepared" are that the issue can even be discussed rationally.

Vague nouns and pronouns and vague verbs often go hand in hand.

Comparators

"This meeting was much better than last month's session." Unless the group discovers the speaker's criteria for *better*, the members will not know how to repeat the improvement or, for that matter, whether the speaker's "better" is even desirable. Words like *best, larger, slower, more,* and *least* leave out the point of comparison and the standard for the comparison.

When undefined comparators are used, a group member should probe for criteria. "So you've enjoyed this meeting. What were some of the ways this was better for you?" The respondent here has been careful to ask the speaker for his or her criteria ("better for you"), which might not be important criteria to

other group members. The intention is to draw the speaker out and expand the meaning of the statement.

Rule Words

People operate with conscious and unconscious rules about how the world works and how they are supposed to operate in it. These rules appear in language when people say things like "We have to," "We must," "You shouldn't," and "I can't."

To clarify these rules and the ways that they govern behavior, other group members should probe for the rules behind the statements: "What would happen if we didn't?" "Who or what says we must?" "*Shouldn't?* Who made up that rule?" "What stops you?" Intonation is important here. The voice carrying the response has to be well modulated, friendly, and nonthreatening.

Universal Quantifiers

"Everyone knows that this program is great." Words and phrases like *everyone, all, no one, never,* and *always* are examples of universal quantifiers. Linguists use the term *deity voice* to describe this type of language. It is spoken as if the statement contains a universal truth of which "everyone" must be aware.

As most parents and middle school teachers know, universal quantifiers are the lingua franca of teenagers. "I need to go to the mall; all my friends will be there." The typical response pattern is "*All* your friends? I can't imagine that *all* your friends' parents would permit them to go."

By qualifying and clarifying a universal quantifier, group members ground their conversations in data and measurable details. When someone makes the statement that "These students never understand the assignments the first time," another participant can probe for the meaning of *never*: "Has there ever been a time when students understood the first time around?" This can be followed up with an inquiry into the qualities and conditions of the assignments that are an exception to the initial statement.

Putting Ideas on the Table

Ideas are the heart of group work. In order to be effective, they must be released to the group. "Here is an idea for consideration. One possible approach to this issue might be . . . " When ideas are owned by individuals, the other group members tend to interact with the speaker out of their feelings for and relationship to the speaker rather than with the ideas presented. This is especially true when the speakers have role or knowledge authority related to the topic at hand. To have an idea be received in the spirit in which you tell it, label your intentions: "This is one idea" or "Here is a thought" or "This is not an advocacy, I am just thinking out loud."

Knowing when to pull ideas off the table is equally important. "I think this idea is blocking us; let's set it aside and move on to other possibilities." In this case, continued advocacy of the idea is not influencing other group members' thinking. This is a signal to pull back and reconsider approaches.

Productive group work is driven by data, both qualitative and quantitative. Data about student learning, school climate, teacher satisfaction, parent satisfaction, and the like are important grounded ideas to put on the table. Collaborative work in schools requires data as well as impressions. In fact, important learning is possible whether or not the data align with the impressions of group members.

Providing Data

Data have no meaning on their own. Meaning is a result of human interaction with data. Many schools are data-rich and meaning-poor. Adaptive groups develop the capacity to dis-

cern what data are worth paying attention to and what collaborative practices help people to engage with data in ways that increase their ownership and willingness to act on conclusions.

Data can be quantitative or qualitative. Schools are difficult places to motivate and govern with numbers. A 6 percent rise in student reading scores is often not as compelling as a teacher's tale of the slow reader who makes a breakthrough. Reasoning by anecdote is often more common than reasoning with data. Interpreting and using data are learned skills that take time and practice to develop.

Knowledge, meaning and commitment result from dialogue and discussion about what story is told by the data. Without organized story making, people in organizations make up their own explanations for events. Part of the reason for this is protection from unwanted truths.

Three Point Communication

Third Point is a nonverbal strategy that comes from the work of Michael Grinder. It establishes a triangle, with the facilitator as one point, the group as a second point and the data or focusing information as the third point.

Third Points might include professional articles, text selections, samples of student work and displays of quantitative or qualitative data. The focus on the third point increases participants' psychological safety, separating the information from the facilitator and allowing group members to talk with and about the data without having to make eye contact with colleagues.

Skilled facilitators aid this process by depersonalizing the information under consideration. They do so by using impersonal language to describe the information—*the* data, *this* information, *that* chart, *the* article, *the* student work—instead of using personal pronouns to describe information—*your* students' work, *our* results, *your* test scores. The goal is to turn data and information into a "thing." It is much easier to talk about "things" than to talk about "us."

Data-Driven Dialogue Process

In their book *Data-Driven Dialogue*, Bruce Wellman and Laura Lipton (2004) offer a collaborative inquiry process to construct meaning from data. The three phases of the process are Activating and Engaging, Exploring and Discovering, and Organizing and Integrating.

In the *Activating and Engaging* phase, collaborative inquirers surface experiences and expectations prior to examining the data. Prompts for dialogue during this phase might be "What are some predictions we are making?" "With what assumptions are we entering?" "What are some possibilities for learning?"

In the *Exploring and Discovering* phase, collaborative inquirers observe and analyze the data. Prompts for dialogue might include "What seems to be surprising or unexpected?" "What are some patterns, categories or trends that are emerging?" "What are some things we have not yet explored?"

In the *Organizing and Integrating* phase, collaborative inquirers generate theory. Prompts for dialogue might include "What inferences/explanations/conclusions might we draw?" "What additional data sources might we explore to verify our conclusions?" "What are some actions we might take as a result of our conclusions?"

Paying Attention to Self and Others

Meaningful dialogue and discussion is facilitated when each group member is conscious of oneself and of others. Skilled group members are aware of what they are saying, how they are saying it, and how others are receiving and responding to their ideas. This includes paying attention to both physical and verbal cues in oneself and others. Since the greatest part of communication occurs nonverbally, group members need consciousness about their total communication package (Goleman, 2006). This includes posture, gesture, proximity, muscle tension, facial expression, and the pitch, pace, volume, and inflection in their voices.

One important skill to develop is paying attention to and responding to the learning styles of others. The earlier section on paraphrasing offers some tips for communicating with global and concrete thinkers. In addition to using those ideas, skilled group members should try to match the language forms of others. This occurs when the respondent joins in a metaphor offered by another. It also occurs when the respondent matches the representation system of the speaker by using visual, kinesthetic, or auditory words in response to hearing the speaker operate within one or more of those categories (Lankton, 1980). Here's an example:

> *Speaker*: I'd like to see us develop a workable action plan.
>
> *Respondent*: So you have an image of practical process that we can apply to our work. What are some of the features you'd like to have on view before us?

Presuming Positive Intentions

Assuming that others' intentions are positive encourages honest conversations about important matters. This is an operating stance that group members must take if dialogue and discussion are to flourish; it is also a linguistic act for speakers to frame their paraphrases and inquiries within positive presuppositions.

Positive presuppositions reduce the possibility of the listener perceiving threats or challenges in a paraphrase or question. Instead of asking, "Does anybody here know why these kids aren't learning?" the skilled group member might say, "Given our shared concern about

Table 3-2. Balancing Inquiry and Advocacy

The Structure of Inquiry

Ask others to make their thinking visible.

Use nonaggressive language and an approachable voice. "Can you help me understand your thinking here?"

Use a pattern of pause, paraphrase, pause, and probe or inquire.

Use exploratory language. "What are some of . . . ? How might you . . . ? What are your hunches about . . . ?"

Inquire about values, beliefs, goals, assumptions, examples, or significance. "How does this relate to your values, beliefs, goals, or assumptions? What are some examples of what you think might happen if we act on your proposal? In what ways does this relate to your other concerns?"

Explain your reasons for inquiring. "I'm asking about your assumptions here because . . . "

Invite introspection. "What questions do you have about your own thinking?"

Compare your assumptions to theirs.

Investigate other assumptions. "Would you be willing to have each of us list our assumptions, compare them, and explore if there might be other assumptions about this issue?"

Check your understanding of what is being said by pausing, paraphrasing, and inquiring. "So your main concern is the way our team is interacting and you'd like to see more cohesion and focused energy. What are some of your thoughts about how this might look and sound in action?"

Test what others say by asking for broader contexts and examples. "How might your proposal affect . . . ? In what ways is this similar to . . . ? Please share a typical example of . . . "

Reveal your listening processes. "I have been listening for themes. So far I've heard two. Are there others?"

The Structure of Advocacy

Make your thinking and reasoning visible.

State your assumptions. "Here is what I assume are the causes of . . . "

Describe your reasoning. "I came to this conclusion because . . . "

Describe your feelings. "I feel _____ about this because . . . "

Distinguish data from interpretation. "These are the data I have. I'll share them as objectively as possible. Now here is what I think the data mean . . . "

Reveal your perspective. "I'm seeing this from the viewpoint of . . . "

Frame the wider context that surrounds this issue. "Several groups would be affected by what I propose."

Give concrete examples. "To get a clear picture, imagine that you are in a new school and . . . "

Test your assumptions and conclusions.

Encourage others to explore your model, assumptions, and data. "What do you think about what I have just said? Do you see any flaws in my reasoning? What might you add?"

Reveal where you are least clear. "Here's one area that you might help me think through . . . "

Stay open. Encourage others to provide different points of view. "In what ways do you see it differently?"

Search for generalizations, deletions, and distortions. "In what I've presented, do any of you believe that I might have overgeneralized, left out data, or reported data incorrectly?"

---

student achievement, I'd like to examine our assumptions about what might be causing gaps in learning."

The first question is likely to trigger defensiveness. The second approach will most likely lead to speculation, exploration, and collective understanding. This is especially true when a speaker has strong emotions about a topic and even more important when the respondent initially disagrees with the speaker. Here's an example:

> *Speaker*: I'm really ticked off about the lack of communication in this school. We never find out about the important things until everyone else knows about them. In fact, I get more district news from the local paper than I do from internal sources.

> *Respondent*: So as a committed professional, you'd like useful information about our organization in a timely fashion and in a means convenient for you. As you think about such a system, what might be some important components?

In the example above, the respondent presumes that the speaker is a committed professional who wants to solve a real problem. People tend to act as if such presuppositions are true. The emotional processors in the brain hear the positive intention and open up access to high-level thinking (Ledoux, 1996).

Working With Grace in a Culture of Advocacy

In working groups that have not yet embraced a spirit of inquiry, round-robin or back-and-forth advocacy are often the prevailing patterns of discourse. People who are not talking are not necessarily listening; in fact, they might just be waiting to talk and are composing their thoughts and responses as they sit poised to pounce at the first opening. By applying the norms of collaboration, skilled group members, individually or together, interrupt this nonproductive pattern and establish more thoughtful forms of discourse within their groups. To do so, they must first break the pattern of matching advocacy with their own advocacy. Flexible group members and skillful facilitators learn to respond to advocacy with a pattern of pausing, paraphrasing, and inquiring.

We are influenced in this arena by the work of Peter Senge and his colleague (1994) at the Massachusetts Institute of Technology's Center for Organizational Learning. We have extended the concept and have refined specific language patterns for operating within this framework.

Matching advocacy with inquiry requires both emotional and cognitive resources. The balance is most necessary at the exact moment when many group members are least likely to want to inquire into the ideas of others. It is at the moment of greatest disagreement and discomfort that this pattern makes the biggest difference.

To balance means to spend equal amounts of time and energy inquiring into the ideas of others before advocating one's own ideas. To do both equally well requires the resources of the seven norms of collaboration. Inquiry and advocacy are built on the linguistic and perceptual foundation described earlier in this chapter. Table 3-2 shows how to balance advocacy and inquiry.

The power of this pattern became apparent to us in an experience related to us by our friend and colleague Diane Zimmerman, who was enrolled in a doctoral program in organi-

zational development. At the time, she was also a principal in Davis, California. Diane and her staff had taken on the norms of collaboration as a shared learning goal. As a skilled and congruent leader, Diane knew that she needed to apply the seven norms in her interactions with adults and students. To support her own learning, she continually sought opportunities to master and integrate these communication skills.

At an early stage in her graduate program, the professors organized a small-group learning experience. The students were placed in small groups and given a controversial topic to discuss. Most of the groups were soon at one another's throats with rising emotions, much heated talk, and little listening. Diane's group

Table 3-3. Transitioning From Inquiry to Advocacy

Signal your intention to shift from inquiring to advocating.

Gesture, posture, voice qualities, and silence have contextual meaning based on the setting and verbal message. Mark your intentions to transition from inquiry to advocacy with some of these forms of paralanguage. For example:

- Shift your body—to signal a shift in the direction of the conversational energy.
- Break eye contact—to momentarily break rapport.
- Pause—to "gently interrupt" the speaker and refocus attention.
- Employ a frozen gesture—to nonverbally hold the pause.
- Use an approachable voice—to maintain psychological safety.
- Use transition stems—to relate your new thought to the flow of the conversation.

The following are some transition stems:

- "Here is a related thought . . . "
- "I hold it another way . . . "
- "Hmmm, from another perspective . . . "
- "An additional idea might be . . . "
- "An assumption I'm exploring is . . . "
- "Taking that one step further . . . "

took a much different course. After a time, the professors gathered around in surprise, because the activity normally evoked the responses present in the other groups. Unable to resist their curiosity, they asked her group what was going on. Diane confessed that she had been practicing the habits of pausing, paraphrasing, and inquiring into the ideas of others before advocating her own ideas. Her behavior established this pattern, solely by example, within her group.

Skilled Advocacy

The intention of advocacy is to influence the thinking of others. Group members sometimes attempt to influence with volume and passion. Advocacy works through revealing logic and the chain of reasoning that supports assumptions and conclusions.

The power of advocacy increases when it is structured to influence multiple audiences. Global reasoners increase their impact when they learn to frame issues for concrete and sequential thinkers. Those who are driven by logic and facts increase their influence when they learn to frame their ideas within feelings and emotions. This ability to stretch one's own thinking preferences often makes the difference in group members being able to hear one another and be persuaded by the positions and stances of others.

Table 3-3 shows how to gracefully transition from inquiry to advocacy.

Developing Personal and Group Skills With the Seven Norms of Collaboration

Ballet dancers practice in mirrored studios to monitor posture and the subtleties of their movements. Groups also improve by reflection. The inventories in Appendixes B, C, D, and E

serve this purpose. Printable versions of these inventories can be found in the CD in the back pocket of this book.

For personal skill development as both a facilitator and as a group member, Appendix B serves as a starting point for self-assessment and goal setting. One useful approach is to select one skill at a time on which to work. Our basic mantra here is *Isolate, overlearn, and automatize*. By seeking opportunities in daily communication experiences to practice a particular norm, you will be able to overlearn that tool so that it is available to you when you need it the most in a meeting.

With groups in the early stages of development, Appendix C can be filled out by individuals. Once completed, the form becomes the basis for dialogue about skill development and baseline data for goal setting for individuals and groups. We encourage groups to master one or two of the norms at a time rather than attempt to take them all on at once.

For intact groups with some history of working together, the form is best completed by subsets of the group. In twos and threes they can work through the form, rating the full group's use of each norm. Each subset then compares its assessments with the other subgroups. Most groups discover that all members do not perceive meeting behaviors in the same way. This conversation leads to goal setting for individuals and groups.

The rating scale in Appendix D is a useful instrument for individual self-reflection after running or participating in a meeting.

The rating scale in Appendix E provides a useful vehicle for ongoing group assessment. Regular monitoring with reflective processing keeps the norms alive and motivates steady improvement. In addition, the round-robin reflection pattern described in chapter 8 is a powerful tool for increasing personal and group consciousness and skills.

The four group-member capabilities and the seven norms of collaboration are essential capacities and skills for high-performing groups. They operate within several practical frameworks that help groups to develop shared meaning and gracefully reach decisions. In the next chapter we describe two ways of talking among adults that make a difference for student learning. Both ways, dialogue and discussion, draw on group-member capabilities and norms.

Chapter 4

Two Ways of Talking That Make a Difference for Student Learning

Professional communities are born and nurtured in webs of conversation. What we talk about in our schools and how we talk about those things says much about who we are, who we think we are, and who we wish to be, both in the moment and in the collective future that we are creating for ourselves as colleagues and for the students we serve.

Group talk is the organizing ingredient of shared learning, yet it is dangerous and often counterproductive to put adults in a room without frameworks and tools for skilled interaction. The group-member capabilities and norms of collaboration described in the previous chapter supply part of the equation. What is missing is a map for two kinds of talking that make a difference for student learning (Garmston & Wellman, 1998).

An elementary school staff was struggling with the problem of reduced money for instructional aides. Although consensus and fairness were their goals, they reported that they felt like turkeys being asked to vote on the merits of Thanksgiving. No one really wanted his or her aide time cut. One first-grade teacher was adamant: She would agree to lose aide time "over my dead body." Six months later, as part of a schoolwide effort to support development of literacy and reading skills, this same teacher volunteered to share her classroom aide with a third-grade tutoring program "if it will really make a difference in helping those students learn to read."

What happened? In 6 months these teachers learned to distinguish and practice two different ways of talking: dialogue and discussion. They adopted the seven norms of collaboration, and individually they focused on their capabilities for professional discourse and openly reflected on these in order to improve personal and collective practice.

These capabilities form the core of a professional community. Such communities talk about hard issues; they honor cognitive conflict and minimize affective conflict (Amason, Thompson, Hochwarter, & Harrison, 1995); and they make decisions based on objective data, shared values, and deep examination of mental models. They measure success by increased student learning and adults' satisfaction with their work.

Developing a staff's capabilities for talking together professionally is no panacea, but it can represent one of the single most significant investments that faculties can make for student learning.

To develop shared understanding and be ready to take collective action, working groups need knowledge and skill in two ways of talking. One way of talking, dialogue, leads to collective meaning-making and the development of shared understanding. The other way of talking, discussion, leads to decisions that stay made.

Both forms of professional discourse use common tools. The four capabilities described in chapter 3 guide group members in selecting tools and help them to monitor the effectiveness of their participation.

Figure 4-1 shows the pathways of dialogue and discussion. First we will define the terms in the diagram. Then we will describe how groups use these concepts to guide their interactions. Finally, we will report the ways that we introduce groups to these maps, tools, and capabilities.

Dialogue honors the social-emotional brain, building a sense of connection, belonging, and safety. As a shape for conversations, it connects us to our underlying motivations and mental models. This way of talking forms a foundation for coherent sustained effort and community building. In dialogue we hear phases like "An assumption I have is . . . " and "I'd be curious to hear what other people are thinking about this issue."

Discussion, in its more skillful form, requires conversations that are infused with sus-

Figure 4-1. Ways of Talking

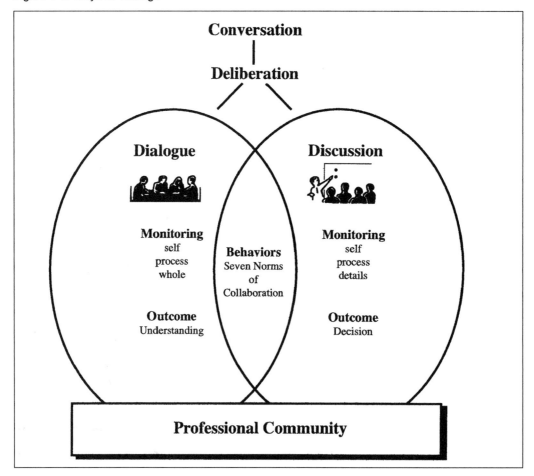

tained critical thinking, careful consideration of options, and respect for conflicting points of view. This way of talking leads to decision making that serves the group's and the school's vision, values, and goals. In a discussion we hear phrases like "We need to define the problem we are solving before jumping to solutions" and "I'd like to see the data that these assumptions are based on before we go much further."

Conversation and Deliberation

When groups come together, they "converge" and "converse." These words' respective Latin roots means that group members "turn together" and "associate with one another." Conversation is informal talking in which participants share information, anecdotes, and opinions to learn from one another or simply to enjoy one another's company. When the conversation takes on an organized purpose, to either deepen understanding or make a decision, a group that understands that there are two ways of talking acknowledges this point of deliberation and consciously chooses to engage in either dialogue or discussion. Deliberation, in its Latin root, *deliberare*, means to weigh, as in to evaluate, assess, or ponder.

Group members have this choice point available to them only when they have road maps for ways of talking and consciousness about group processes and group purposes. A significant part of this awareness is recognizing that culturally embedded patterns shape behaviors—patterns from the larger surrounding culture and patterns from organizational and group culture. Many groups default into the Western cultural habit of polarized discussion and debate. Our media-saturated world bombards us with arguments framed by commentators as point-counterpoint, pro and con, left versus right, and other polarities. These models transfer to conversations in working

groups; they then frame how participants listen to others and how and when participants speak. If group members are not careful, they end up listening not to understand but to hear gaps in the logic of other speakers, or they interrupt to make a point even before the current speaker is finished. Conversations then break down into verbal combat, with winners and losers.

All too often, valued colleagues become conscientious objectors, choosing not to participate in the fray. The group then loses perspective and potential alternative viewpoints. The loudest and most persistent voices become the policy makers, and in the worst cases, the process sows the seeds of passive noncompliance or sabotage in those who feel excluded or devalued.

When groups understand that they have more than one way of talking available to them, they can consciously choose to pursue the path of dialogue or to follow the path of discussion. Most important issues require explorations along both pathways. Many sensitive issues, especially those with high stakes for the participants, call for separate sessions in which the dialogue and discussion are separated in time and sometimes space. One useful facilitation technique is to explicitly label agenda items as either dialogue or discussion and offer language models to further mark the distinctions between the two forms of discourse.

As group members become more sophisticated with the ways of talking, the pathways become more malleable. For example, during a dialogue, a group member senses an emerging consensus on an issue. He or she then inquires if this is so and frames a proposal to move the item to a decision. In another case, during a discussion, emotions rise and the details become muddled. Someone then proposes that the group switch to a dialogue format for a set time to explore the feelings and underlying issues that are present.

The Path of Dialogue

Dialogue is a reflective learning process in which group members seek to understand one another's viewpoints and deeply held assumptions. The word *dialogue* comes from the Greek *dialogos*. *Dia* means "through" and *logos* means "word." In this meaning-making through words, group members inquire into their own and others' beliefs, values, and mental models to better understand how things work in their world. In dialogue, listening is as important as speaking. For skilled group members, much of the work is done internally.

Physicist and philosopher David Bohm (Senge, 1990) described dialogue as a process of eliciting and altering the "tacit infrastructure of thought." As a quantum physicist, Bohm draws an analogy between dialogue and superconductivity. Electrons that are cooled to extremely low temperatures dramatically change their behavior, operating more as a coherent whole and less as separate parts. In supercool environments, electrons flow around barriers and one another without resistance, creating very high energy. The same electrons radically change behavior in a new environment. At higher temperatures they operate as separate entities, with random movement and loss of momentum.

Dialogue creates an emotional and cognitive safety zone in which ideas flow for examination without judgment. Although many of the capabilities and tools of dialogue and skilled discussion are the same, their core intentions are quite different and require different personal and collective monitoring processes.

Monitoring Dialogue

Mindful group members pay attention to three essential elements during productive dialogue. They monitor themselves, the process of the dialogue, and the new whole that is emerging within the group.

Self

Dialogue is first and foremost a listening practice. When we "listen to our listening," we notice whether we are internally debating with the speaker, reviewing our mental catalogue of related information and personal anecdotes, or composing a response. Noticing these common internal processes allows us to switch them off so that we can hear others without judging.

Dialogue requires choice making. Typical choices include how and when to talk. Do we paraphrase prior comments to check for understanding and or synthesis? Do we inquire into the ideas and assumptions of others? Do we put a new idea or perspective on the table to widen the frame?

Suspension is an essential internal skill in dialogue. To suspend judgment, group members temporarily set aside their own perceptions, feelings, and impulses and carefully monitor their internal experience. Points of personal conflict can easily emerge when we believe that others are not hearing us or that they are distorting our point of view. Points of conflict also surface when our own values conflict with those of a speaker. These areas of discomfort influence our listening and our responses, which in turn influence the thoughts and behaviors of other group members.

Suspension also involves developing an awareness of our own assumptions and purposely "hanging them from the ceiling"—that is, suspending them in front of the group so that all can examine them. These assumptions are beliefs—often unexamined—about why we think things work as they do. Our assumptions drive our perceptions, simultaneously opening and blinding us to possibilities in the world around us.

Process

Dialogue as a process requires focusing on the goal of developing shared understanding. In our action-oriented work environments, this is often countercultural. Yet in every group with which we've worked, all the participants could recite examples of decisions that were poorly conceived, poorly communicated, simply ignored, or, in the worst cases, violated by many organizational members without consequence. At the root of all these stories were group processes that were not thought out but rather often hurried and inappropriately facilitated. The rush to action pushed unclear decision-making processes and timelines onto the group without sufficient attention to developing a shared understanding of both problems and solutions.

By going slow and honoring the flow of dialogue, groups can often go fast when they get to the choice points in decision making. When the assumptions and the implications of those assumptions have been explored during dialogue, group members don't second-guess the motives of others during discussions.

Meetings should be safe but not necessarily comfortable. When a group confuses safety with comfort, it sacrifices productive tension for the ease of conviviality. Humor and banter can be avoidance strategies as much as they can be social lubricants. A lack of comfort with discomfort weakens dialogue and undermines the learning possibilities in that moment.

Whole

Thought is both a personal and a collective process. We influence and are influenced in turn by others. During dialogue, the line between self and others blurs when we open ourselves to the possibilities within the communal thought space. This created whole is in itself a goal of dialogue. Communities move forward together. Collective understanding leads to shared goals and shared practices that tap the power of cumulative effect for student learning and for the adult learning community.

The whole is always greater than the sum of the individual parts. In many ways it is both process and product simultaneously. By learning to observe the processes, patterns, and results that emerge from our dialogues, we can more consciously participate and more consciously contribute to the whole of which we are the parts.

Understanding as the Outcome

Well-crafted dialogue leads to understanding. This is the foundation for conflict resolution, consensus, and professional community. Decisions that don't stay made are often the result of group members feeling left out or having their ideas discounted by the group. Dialogue gives voice to all parties and all viewpoints.

Misunderstanding lies beneath most intragroup and intergroup conflict. Dialogue illuminates and clarifies misunderstandings when the underlying values and beliefs are brought to the surface for examination. There is often alignment at this level; it is at the solution level that opinions differ. Working from a foundation of shared understanding, group members can more easily and rationally resolve differences, generate options, and make wise choices when they move to the discussion side of the journey.

The Path of Discussion

Discussion, in its Latin root *discutere*, means "to shake apart." It focuses on the parts and their relationships to one another: the causes, the effects, and the ripple effects of proposed actions and solutions. In its most ineffective forms, discussion consists of serial sharing and serial advocacy without much group-member inquiry into the thinking and proposals of others. Participants attempt to reach decisions through a variety of voting and consensus techniques. When discussion is unskilled and dialogue is absent, decisions are often low quality, represent the opinions of the most vocal members or leader, lack group commitment, and do not stay made.

Three elements shape skilled discussions: (a) clarity about decision-making processes and authority, (b) knowledge of the boundaries of the topics open to the group's decision-making authority, and (c) standards for orderly decision-making meetings. Most meetings are, in fact, structured discussions.

Monitoring Discussion

Mindful group members pay attention to three essential elements during productive discussion. They monitor themselves, the processes of skilled discussion, and the details of the problem-solving, planning, and decision-making processes in which they are engaged.

Self

Productive discussions require group members to have emotional and mental flexibility. When our goal is to influence the thinking of others and we give up the model of winning or losing, we are more able to notice our thoughts and actions and the effects of those thoughts and actions on others.

Mentally, this requires taking a balcony view. This perceptual position is neither *egocentric* (I am intensely aware of my thoughts, feelings, and intentions and know my own boundaries) nor *allocentric* (I am aware of how something looks, feels, and sounds from the point of view of another). The balcony view is a third perceptual position, a *macrocentric* perspective, in which with compassion and detachment we try to understand the nature of the situation the group is in at the moment. It is with this view, looking down upon the group, that we gain the most knowledge about our group, the group's interactions, and ourselves.

From the balcony we can make the most strategic choices about how and when to participate. Should I advocate or should I inquire?

At what points should I press? When should I probe for detail or let go? How might I phrase an idea for greatest influence? These are the same internal skills that teachers employ when they monitor and adjust in their classrooms.

Process

Skilled discussion as a process requires mindfulness about focusing on one topic and applying one process tool at a time. When topics and processes blur, group members lose focus. To maintain focus requires clear structure, purposeful facilitation, impulse control on the part of individual group members, and recovery strategies if the group strays off course.

Effective group members share responsibility with the facilitator for maintaining the flow of the discussion, for encouraging other group members to share knowledge and ideas, and for hearing and exposing points of confusion or murkiness.

When working groups stray from skilled discussion, they often move to an unskilled form of debate. This occurs when group members overlook the useful advocacy of ideas and proposals and start listening for and challenging the fallacies in the arguments of others. *Battuere*, the Latin origin of the word *debate*, means "to fight or beat down." When meetings descend to the level of street debate rather than academic debate, we focus on beating down the ideas of others. Scoring points becomes the goal, and winning comes from intimidation and intonation as much as from—or more than—logic or reason.

Details

Whereas successful dialogue requires attention to the whole, successful discussion focuses on the details, both in isolation and in their interactions. The path of discussion is also the path of decision. As such, groups need to identify any constraints under which they might be working, such as timelines, deadlines, budgets, product standards, nonnegotiable items, task assignments, and, most important, who they are in the decision-making process.

Groups skilled in discussion employ many intentional cognitive skills. There is no set sequence for these efforts. The task before the group determines the necessary intellectual tool kit. Groups need tools for the following:

- Generating ideas, including a repertoire of brainstorming and creative thinking strategies and protocols

- Organizing ideas, including both conceptual and graphic tools

- Analyzing ideas, including a variety of tools for illuminating assumptions and clarifying particulars

- Deciding among alternatives, including the clarification of decision-making roles and processes

Decision as the Outcome

Decision, in its Latin root *decidere*, means "to cut off or determine." In practice this means to cut off some options. The purpose of discussion is to eliminate ideas from a field of possibilities and allow the stronger ideas to prevail. Groups must learn to separate people from ideas in order for this to work effectively. If ideas are "owned" by individuals, then to cut the idea away is the same as cutting the person away. Ideas, once stated, should belong to the group, not to individuals. In this way they can be shaped, modified, and discarded to the serve the group's greater purposes. The next chapter will address decision-making issues in greater detail.

Professional Community

Professional community is both a cause and an effect of the two ways of talking. As a cause, being in a community provides the motivation and vision of ways of interacting and working together. As an effect, a strong professional community results from both what is talked about and how people talk. Such talk requires courage, confidence in self and others, and skillfulness in applying the maps and tools for developing shared understanding and strategic decision-making practices.

Table 4-1 (on page 52) shows an example of how to move from discussion to dialogue when this becomes desirable.

Consensus as the Holy Grail

Consensus is one form of decision making, but not the only form. Some groups get stuck trying to use consensus processes without a consciousness of the difference between dialogue and discussion.

There are two types of consensus: (a) opening consensus, which develops through dialogue, and (b) focusing consensus, which develops through discussion. Opening consensus involves the consideration of perspectives and possibilities. Focusing consensus involves winnowing choices by clarifying criteria and applying these criteria to the choices. Focusing consensus for complex issues depends on effective opening consensus.

Ultimately, consensus is a value and a belief system more than a decision-making process. Unless groups are willing to hang out with the process for as long as it takes, they are not usually ready for full consensus decision making.

Work at the Center for Conflict Resolution in Madison, Wisconsin (Avery, Auvine, Streibel, & Weiss, 1981) points to the following necessary conditions for effective consensus decision making:

1. *Unity of purpose.* There should be basic core agreement on what the group is about and how it operates.

Table 4-1. Moving From Discussion to Dialogue

Discussion
"These test data point to a need to change our spelling program."
"I don't think it's the program; I think it's the test."
"I don't think it's either one; I think it's attitude."

Transition
"Wait a minute. This is sounding messier than it first looked. Can we shift to dialogue and explore our assumptions about what is going on with our kids and spelling?"

Dialogue
"We seem to have three areas before us; the test scores, kids' skills, and kids' attitudes. I'm wondering if there are other elements in this mix?"
"Help us to understand what you think some of these other elements might be."

2. *Equal access to power.* Consensus cannot work in formal hierarchies. Informal power also must be equally distributed.

3. *Autonomy of the group from external hierarchical structures.* It is very difficult for groups to use consensus processes if they are part of a larger organization that does not honor this way of making decisions.

4. *Time.* Consensus takes time and patience. Participants have to believe in the usefulness of this method enough to follow it and not the clock or the calendar.

5. *Attention to process.* Group members must be willing to spend group time reflecting on process and modifying it as necessary.

6. *Attention to attitudes.* Group members must be willing to examine their own attitudes and be open to change. The key ingredients are trust and cooperation.

7. *Willingness to learn and practice skills.* Communication, meeting participation, and facilitation skills must be continually honed and refined to make consensus processes work.

Most groups with whom we work are better served by "sufficient consensus." This generally means that at least 80% of the group is willing to commit and act. It also means that the others agree not to sabotage. Sufficient consensus relies on both dialogue and discussion for its effectiveness. The norm of balancing advocacy and inquiry is essential. Any dissenting voices must be able to influence and persuade 80% of the group to carry the day. This also means that other group members can paraphrase and draw matters to a close when only a few voices line up on one side of an issue.

Norms and Values

Professional community is built on the bedrock of norms and values, which are both honed by dialogue and discussion. Strong schools have core values about how children learn, what they should learn, and how faculties should work together. Some norms about faculty work are philosophical (e.g., everyone can be involved in decision making, or no one has to be involved, but once decisions are reached they are binding on everyone). Carl Glickman

(1998) calls this a charter, or guiding rules of governance. This type of norm signals what is important to the organization.

Another type of norm specifies how the values of the organization can be achieved. Our work with schools emphasizes the use of the seven norms of collaboration described in the previous chapter. When school faculties make these seven tools into norms—that is, normal operating behaviors in formal and informal interactions within the school—adult relationships improve, groups work skillfully to explore members' mental models and assumptions, and both dialogue and discussion are served. These norms also have a tremendous payoff in the classroom for both teacher-student interactions and student-student interactions. In many cases faculties take them on with the dual agenda of enhancing both faculty and student performance.

Getting Started

The collaborative norms of the group have more influence on the possibility of success than do the knowledge and talents of the group facilitator. Thus, our staff development energies must go to groups, not to designated leaders of groups. We have found three components to be helpful in groups that achieve high levels of skills in the challenging talk that is required in professional communities.

1. *Overview*. Provide groups with a rationale and a map for the two ways of talking (see Fig. 4-1). Within this framework, we add key details about the seven norms, the four capabilities, the purposes of dialogue and discussion, and approaches to constructive conflict. This overview is intended to create dissatisfaction with the current state of team and working-group performance and to provide a glimpse of productive ways of working together.

2. *Inventory*. Inventorying members' perceptions of how the group uses the norms reveals beliefs about current operating practices (Appendix C). Groups can select one or two norms to develop and can establish monitoring systems to improve their use of the map and tools. Inventories can be simple rating scales, ranking personal and collective use of each norm, or more detailed questionnaires that explore the subsets of each norm.

3. *Monitor*. Any group that is too busy to reflect on its work is too busy to improve. Every working group has many more tasks to do than time in which to do them and so is naturally reluctant to spend time monitoring and reflecting on its working processes. Many groups commit themselves to a task-process ratio to overcome this tendency; they budget a protected percentage of each meeting for examining how well the group is working and what it might do to improve.

Reflection can take many forms. The least effective form involves a process observer—a special role for gathering data about the frequency or distribution of behaviors that the group believes are important. Because this places the gathering of data outside the group members, they ultimately become less accurate in gathering their own data and self-assessments. The most effective form is through reflection on the four capabilities described in chapter 3. This can occur through journal writing, round-robin reflection, and dialogue that is focused on personal and collective learning about the power of attention to process.

Human beings are a social species. Living and working in groups is an important part of our genetic heritage. It is ironic, then, that in many schools, professionals who are charged with preparing students to be successful collaborative citizens are themselves cut off from the rich resources offered by true collegiality. That we talk together in our schools is vitally important in these changing times. How we talk is just as important, for it is how we talk that influences the personal and collective satisfaction that motivates us to effectively talk together in our schools.

Chapter 5   Conducting Successful Meetings

Professional communication is at the heart of getting work done in schools. It occurs informally within disciplines as well as across disciplines, grade levels, departments, and faculties. It occurs in pairs, trios, and large groups. It occurs spontaneously and when planned. It happens in meetings. It is in meetings that teachers work together to improve instructional practice and performance. It is in meetings that teachers clarify policies, identify and address problems, assess standards, and modify schedules. It is in meetings that faculties respond to the changing needs of students, standards, and curriculum demands. It is in meetings that groups mature and manage differences, and it is in meetings that their working culture evolves—or stays the same.

Meetings have a greater effect on organizational success than initially meets the eye. First, effective and time-efficient meetings produce work that is important to the school. Second, well-conducted meetings promote member satisfaction, the capacity to collaborate, and a willingness to conscientiously contribute. Third, the more successful groups are at getting important work done in meetings, the greater their collective efficacy, a resource that is undeniably linked to student success. (We will explore designing for collective efficacy in chapter 6). Finally, members of successful groups ultimately become members and leaders elsewhere and enrich the quality of work done by units within the school and the district. For these reasons, knowing how to produce work through meetings has become an essential part of a professional portfolio, regardless of an individual's role.

This chapter describes what members need to know and be able to do to have meetings that are productive, time-efficient, and satisfying. As we described in chapter 4, two ways of talking are necessary in working groups: dialogue and discussion. Dialogue, which leads to understanding, is a necessary precursor to discussion, which leads to decisions that stay made.

Talking to Decide

Inquiry into the craft of meetings is fundamental for effective meetings. This inquiry should include questions on (a) how to distinguish the urgent from the important; (b) how to stay on track, on topic, and focused; (c) how to use conflict constructively; (d) how to orchestrate space and materials; and (e) how to make decisions that stay made. This is important for leaders and members, for, as we shall see, skilled members have more influence on meeting success than good facilitators do.

There are three organizing principles that guide meeting productivity and satisfaction: collaborative norms, positive relationships, and collective energy sources. These are described below.

Collaborative Norms

Meeting success is influenced more by the collaborative norms of the group than by the knowledge and skill of the group's facilitator. For a committee, task force, department, or faculty to be effective as a group, the members need to have the skills and knowledge of producing work in meetings. Counterintuitively, this is more important than the skills of a good facilitator. Imagine an athletic team playing without goals, knowledge of the rules of the game, an awareness of other positions, and some sense of common strategy. As much as a football team needs a coach, it also needs players who have a common understanding of the game and who are committed to achieving the goals and improving their individual and collective performance. Whether or not a group knows that it is directing its own dynamics, this is the most determining factor in accomplishing work.

Positive Relationships

The power of a group to produce results is rooted in the quality of the relationships among the participants. Becoming a learning community that is focused on improved practice and shared accountability is a goal for many groups. As evidence mounts that student learning is the result of such cumulative effort, teachers increasingly need the skills to conduct productive meetings in which they generate the know-how and the will to inquire into student learning, dialogue about data, assess and refine instruction, raise student achievement, and enhance professional community. To achieve this requires skillful collaboration.

Collaboration is not easy, nor has it been required in schools. It implies shared objectives, a sense of urgency and commitment, mutual trust and respect, intellectual agility, and the application of diverse skills and knowledge. Achinstein (2002) notes the following:

When teachers collaborate, they run headlong into enormous conflicts over professional beliefs and practices. In their optimism about caring and supportive communities, advocates often underplay the role of diversity, dissent, and disagreement in community life, leaving practitioners ill-prepared and conceptions of collaboration under explored. (p. 5)

Collaboration requires the development and exercise of social, emotional, and cognitive skills. To demand collaboration without providing training is like the government mandating a program without providing the money to implement it.

Collective Energy Sources

The third organizing principle comes from cognitive social theory. The culture of the workplace influences what teachers do and how they think more than their training, experience, or knowledge do. Cognitive social theory holds that robust social norms and behaviors exert an influence on the individual members of a group. The work culture inhibits or amplifies the learning of its members. Well-structured meetings are one way to influence the working culture.

In our work we have noticed that five sources of collaborative energy become self-organizing values for high-performing groups: efficacy, flexibility, craftsmanship, consciousness, and interdependence. We introduced these in chapter 2, and readers who are familiar with Cognitive Coaching[SM] will recognize them as the five states of mind held by individuals (Costa & Garmston 2002, p. 29). How groups take on collaborative energy is an important question because collective efficacy is consistently and positively related to increases in student achievement. Experts in any field look below surface behaviors to analyze the sources of successes and challenges. Paying attention to the flow and interchange of energy as much as to things is the key to successful school leadership. Chapter 8 describes how to detect the five energy sources and influence them. Here we describe their basic features.

Efficacy. Collective efficacy is consistently related to improved student achievement. Collective efficacy beliefs seem to influence group performance by shaping the behavioral and normative environment of schools (Goddard, 2001). Groups with perceived efficacy judge themselves to have the knowledge, skills, and will to meet goals and overcome obstacles to learning and behave accordingly. Efficacious groups use more creative approaches to problem solving, persevere longer, work more diligently, and achieve outcomes more successfully than groups without efficacy. The greater the collective efficacy of a school, the more that teachers persist in their pursuit of excellence. If most teachers in a school believe that the faculty can successfully teach students, it becomes the norm for teachers to help the students achieve high levels.

Flexibility. To inquire into data, to develop theories of causation and solutions for academic challenges, requires an ability set aside the first (too) easy answers and continue to delve from various perspectives. Groups who develop this energy source honor and value diversity inside and outside the group, attend to both rational and intuitive ways of thinking, collectively shift perspective, and utilize a wide array of thinking and process skills. Such groups can also navigate the internal tensions that are related to confusion and ambiguity and can get unstuck by generating multiple ideas for moving ahead.

Craftsmanship. Like the mindsets of expert performers—musicians, artists, teachers, craftspeople, and athletes—groups with craftsmanship take pride in their work and consistently strive to improve current performance. Craftsmanship—the drive for elaboration, clarity, refinement, and precision—is the energy source from which groups set demanding goals

for themselves and ceaselessly work to deepen their knowledge, skills, and effectiveness.

Consciousness. To be conscious is to be mindful—moving beyond habituated thinking to thoughtful choice. Consciousness is a prerequisite to self-control and self-direction. Groups that tap this energy source maintain an awareness of their values, norms, and identity; monitor the congruence of their espoused beliefs and their manifested beliefs; and stand outside themselves to reflect on their processes and products.

Interdependence. Interdependent groups value and trust the process of dialogue, have an awareness of their multiple relationships and identities with other groups, and regard disagreement as a source of learning and transformation.

The Four Success Structures

We now turn our attention to four success structures. We use the term *structure* to describe a system of order and organization. Effective social structures honor the dynamic relationship of parts and bring them together into a workable whole. Since any group brings a variety of mental models, cognitive styles, personal histories, and individual agendas to its work, the potential for chaotic interaction always exists. Providing structures permits a full and focused expression of these differences in a manner that is useful to the work and life of the group.

The following four structures, taken together, guide groups to continual success. Each addresses a significant question in the work life of groups.

1. Who decides?

2. What topics are ours?

3. What meeting room features (the surround) will support the work?

4. What are the meeting standards?

Deciding Who Decides

Who decides? Is a decision to be made by certain individuals within the group, by the group as a whole, by the person who convened the group, or by some person or group not present at this meeting? Groups are most effective and productive when they are clear about whether their role is to inform, recommend, or decide.

Ask any group to describe instances in which a lack of decision-making clarity led to confusion and poor implementation, and you will hear many examples. We worked with a group once whose members discovered that they didn't know who would make the decision on the topic they were discussing. Yet they vigorously continued to work within this conceptual vacuum.

Trust diminishes when a group is not clear about who is making the final decision and what decision-making processes will be used. When the group members lose trust, second-guessing, resistance, or lengthy and unproductive process arguments can occur. This robs time and, more important, saps group energy, efficacy, and motivation to persevere on important agenda items.

When curriculum committees understand that a final decision will be made by the school board, they can strategically plan their time. Thus 80% of committee time might be devoted to becoming as clear as possible about the recommendations they will make to the board. The other 20% of the time might be used to study and implement ethical systems of influence. Many a curriculum committee has been dismayed to have its recommendations denied because it had not brought the board along in the deliberations. The following are possible levels of authority for decision making:

- An individual or group above you
- An administrator unilaterally
- An administrator with input
- An administrator and staff by consensus
- A staff with input from administrators
- A staff by consensus
- A staff by a vote
- A subgroup of a staff with input from others
- A subgroup of a staff unilaterally
- Individual staff members, selecting from a menu of options

Clarity about decision making is so crucial that we suggest that facilitators name the ultimate decision maker(s) and decision process as many as 4 times. Why over communicate like this? When people are investing energy in topics important to them, they often forget that there might be other parties in the decision-making chain. Thus, while introducing an item, the facilitator could say, "On this topic, you will be making a recommendation to the curriculum committee, which has the final say." During the conversation about the topic, the facilitator could say, "As you consider how to structure your recommendation to the curriculum committee, . . . " At the conclusion of the meeting, the facilitator could summarize the action taken on each item, again stating on which topics the group made a recommendation or decision. Finally, if there are minutes for the meeting, the language should convey the level of decision-making authority possessed by the group.

One of us worked with a superintendent in an eastern state who was particularly adept at maintaining clarity with groups about decisions. On one occasion, he visited each school's faculty to seek its information on a decision he had to make. He said to each group, "Your job is to give me the best information possible. Your job is to inform me. My job is to make a decision. When I do decide, you will hear it first from me." He then asked questions and listened. When his decision had been made, he again visited the schools. He reported to each staff, "This is the decision I made. This is my rationale. Here is how your information influenced me." He then responded to questions.

Several months later another issue emerged in which the superintendent wanted input from the schools. He sent a memo describing the situation and saying that if the faculty wished to inform him, please send a representative to the central office for a meeting at a designated time. The teachers said to one another, "He really means it." They had learned to trust the process. Teachers went to the meeting and informed the superintendent.

Remember the principle that meeting success is influenced more by the collaborative norms of the group than by a skilled facilitator? Members, too, share responsibility for group consciousness about decision making. They can ask naive questions (see chapter 3 and Appendix A) such as "Excuse me. Who makes the final decision on this?" or "Where does this recommendation go after it leaves us?"

Asking a naive question is one way that group members can effectively offer a correction to group work. To communicate naively is to speak with innocence. It is to be artless, unaffected, and natural. Naive questions have an intonational quality of childlike inquiry in which the question being asked is truly open-ended. "Who will communicate this decision?" and "Who will be informed about this?" are examples of naive questions. They serve the group in developing awareness about process, and they sometimes serve leaders because the question has been overlooked in planning.

A principal from a large urban district complained about 30 years of attending dysfunctional meetings. After being introduced to naive questioning, he realized that as a group member he could make a difference. He began to ask naive questions and was amazed at the power he held as a group member to get meetings on track.

One of the best guides for clarity about decision making is a 12-step model (Table 5-1) offered by Saphier, Bigda-Peyton, & Pierson, (1989). They emphasize that the model's effectiveness comes from making it public.

We advocate sharing and teaching this information to all members of an organization through modeling and explicit discussion; this goal is critical to school improvement. We do not do the process "to" or "on" people, nor is it a Machiavellian model for working one's will on others. It is, rather, a set of guidelines for making good decisions that will stay made.

Defining the "Sandbox": What Topics Are Ours?

Groups conserve precious energy by focusing their resources where they have direct influence. When the "sandbox" in which a group is to "play" is clear to all the members, group energy can be powerfully directed at the items it can affect. This structure works in tandem with the first structure, deciding who decides.

As simple as these two concepts are, they become complex in organizations in which different groups have intersecting interests. After much deliberation, a high school's faculty members went on a school holiday believing that because they had voted for a change in the school schedule, it would be changed when they returned to school. They were stunned to learn that schedule adjustments could not be made until the classified staff had been consulted.

In another case, a teachers' union spearheaded a joint project with the administration for a site-based decision-making program. One provision was a district-level council to oversee the site work. The union published the responsibilities and functions of each participating group, describing "sandbox" topics and decision-making authority on some topics. Despite good effort, insufficient specificity led

Table 5-1. 12 Steps for Making Successful Decisions

Planning

1. Identify and explicitly state the issue, who owns it, and what the underlying goal is.
2. Find out and explain how much discretion you have to take action or not. *Must* this issue be dealt with? State how strongly your personally feel about it.
3. Every issue lands in someone's lap in the beginning. If it lands in yours, be sure to choose the proper path for who will make the preliminary and the final decisions.
4. At the beginning of the process, communicate clearly who will make the decision and identify any constraints that will affect the scope or content of the decision (e.g., staffing, budgeting, time).
5. State explicitly the values you want to maintain and why they are not negotiable, if that is the case (e.g., "Whatever proposals come forward, I want to hand on to small class size and the high quality of personal student-teacher contact we get from that").

Deciding

6. Identify and periodically check out with people what the full impact or full consequences of the decision will be and communicate them to all parties involved.
7. Involve all parties whose working conditions will be affected by the decision.
8. Make clear the timeline for deciding and implementing the decision.
9. Decide. Then make an explicit statement of the decision or recommendations, summarizing to evaluate it and revise it if necessary.

Implementing

11. Close the loop. Communicate the decision fully and clearly to all affected parties after the decision is made, including how people's input was used.
12. Plan how to monitor and support the day-to-day implementation of the decision and communicate these plans to everyone involved.

to confusion, which in each case required time and emotional energy to untangle.

An examination of site-council responsibilities (Table 5-2) reveals several areas for possible confusion. While the principal serves as co-chairperson on the site council, what is the relationship of this person to the responsibilies specified in the table? Site council responsibilities are to make decisions about budget (which parts, specifically?). A district council responsibility is to "review" site budgets. Does this mean approve? This uncertainty can fur-

ther muddy the intended relationship between the two entities and take unnecessary time and stress to unravel.

All groups have interests that intersect with other groups' decision-making authority. Considerations of collegiality, politics, and effectiveness must honor these overlapping areas of concern. Individual and collective vigilance is an essential ingredient of group success. At some time in every group's history, this structure becomes important to departments, curriculum task forces, advisory groups, grade-level

Figure 5-1. Decision Making

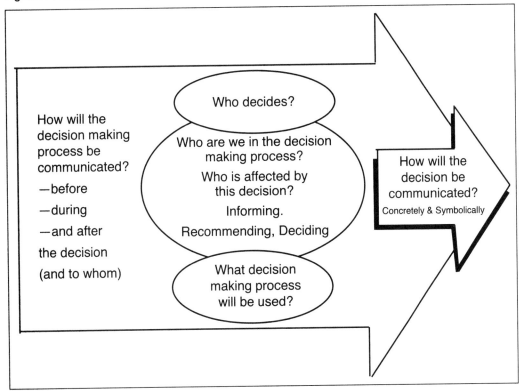

Table 5-2. Site Council Responsibilities

Participate in team training
- Develop a school site plan including goals, objectives, and ways to involve parents, staff development and an annual evaluation of the team's work.
- Make decisions about school issues such as budget, curriculum and safety.
- Establish/revise site level pupil idscipline plans and practices.
- Design and conduct site staff development.
- Develop procedures and communications that encourage teacher involvement in decision making.
- Make recommendations on staffing and the day-to-day operation of the school.

District Council Responsibilities
- Establish training schedule.
- Monitor site elections
- Review site survey—team membership, meeting schedule and focus of team.
- Review site budgets.
- Establish District Council training schedule.
- Provide system for communicating site concerns.
- Provide for site assistance.

teams, site councils, and faculties.

An issue common to many schools is who should be responsible for decisions about schoolwide policy and practices on student discipline. This seems like a simple "sandbox" question. However, even the briefest conversation will reveal that several related questions must be explored. (We have labeled these *naive questions* and listed examples in Appendix A.) Student discipline is necessary in what areas (gum or guns)? Within what parameters (state law or district policies)? At what level of authority (unilaterally or in consultation with the principal or parents)?

Suzanne Riley, a friend and colleague, was asked to consult with an elementary principal who was "under siege." The school technology committee, composed of parents and teachers, had written and received a technology grant from a community business partner. The initial elation at receiving the funding had been replaced by frustration. The committee had submitted a list of desired equipment to the principal. The principal submitted the requisition for the equipment but was then contacted by the district technology coordinator, who informed the principal that the desired equipment was not compatible with the district master technology plan. The principal informed the committee. The committee was very upset. One of the parents who was knowledgeable about computers said that the district plan was totally outdated. The committee argued that since it had secured the funding, it should be able to purchase the best available equipment for the students. The committee accused the principal of wasting its time and ignoring its recommendations. The disagreement escalated into a very unpleasant situation. Had the committee and principal clarified the "sandbox" issues at the beginning of the process, much unhappiness could have been avoided.

Designing the Surroundings of the Meeting Facilities

Consider the ideal meeting room. It is probably quiet, comfortable (but not too comfortable), and free from distractions. David Perkins (1992) defines these and other factors as part of the surroundings that mediate thinking and behavior. Although psychological, emotional, cognitive, and physical elements contribute to the surroundings, the facilitator has the greatest control over the physical arrangements in the meeting room (Figure 5-2).

Schwarz (2002) describes three principles for seating arrangements in meetings, and we have added a fourth. They are as follows:

1. All participants and the faciliator should be able to see and hear each other and any visual information presented (e.g., flip charts, projected images).

2. Arrange the seating to distinguish the participants from the nonparticipants.

3. The seating arrangement should be spacious enough to meet the needs of the group, but no larger.

4. The work-group space should accommodate physical movement, subgrouping with different partners, and personal ownership of the entire room rather than of a single chair or a table.

Arranging a room to accommodate the first principle is rarely a problem when the group size is about 20 or fewer. The semicircle, U-shape, or oval arrangements shown in Figure 5-2 will easily serve 20–25 participants. As the group size expands up to 40 or so in a council or decision-making group, arrange a series of tables in a herringbone pattern to allow all participants to see the facilitator and the flip charts. When the group size reaches 80–300 people, as it sometimes does for community forums, fa-

Figure 5-2. Room Arrangement

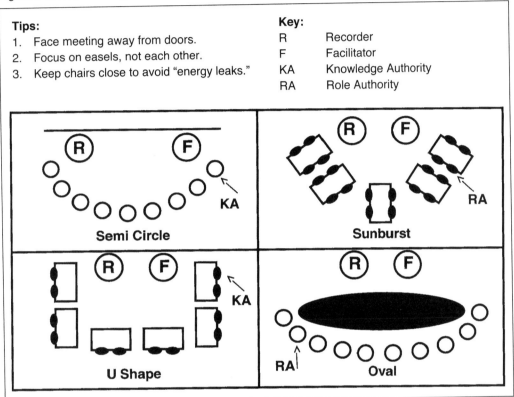

High-performing groups post charts that state outcomes for their tasks and charts that remind the participants of collaborative norms, meeting standards, and group-member capabilities. These groups chart for group memory during discussions. They choose strategies that include a visual component.

Tips:
1. Face meeting away from doors.
2. Focus on easels, not each other.
3. Keep chairs close to avoid "energy leaks."

Key:
R   Recorder
F   Facilitator
KA   Knowledge Authority
RA   Role Authority

Semi Circle

Sunburst

U Shape

Oval

cilitate from a set of risers. Position flip charts on the risers and use large markers like Avery Dennison's Marks-A-Lot® Washable Marker. Regardless of the size of the group, if the participants cannot hear one another at any time, they should call out, "Louder, please!" The facilitator should remind the group of this at the beginning of the meeting.

Specific tasks require conscious room arrangement and provision of materials. The room arrangement communicates and structures the desired interaction.

Keep in mind that if 11 million bits of information are bombarding the participants each second, 10 million come through the eyes, and only 40% of all that information is being processed consciously. Visual displays are more important for working groups than we have previously thought.

High-performing groups post charts that state outcomes for their tasks and charts that remind the participants of collaborative norms, meeting standards, and group-member capabilities. These groups chart for group memory during discussions. They choose strategies that include a visual component.

Group memory and graphic processes support learning and retention. Charting materials such as markers, tape, pads, and easels should be readily available. Wall space should also be considered. Blank walls without other artwork are best for meeting rooms. This lets each group craft the space to its own needs. When groups become fatigued, auditory functions are the first to go.

Many public bodies and decision-making groups work in settings in which others are present to observe, inform, or advocate. It is easier for the facilitator to monitor the moods, interactions, and energy of the members when the seating arrangements distinguish them from nonmembers. We've seen several arrangements for this. For instance, a council of 8–12 people is seated, facing one another, around a large conference table. Behind them are seated staff members and resource persons who may periodically be asked to "come to the table" to give a report, offer an opinion, or give information on a topic.

In another arrangement, involving a group of about 40 people, of whom 15 are resource people and guests, the entire group is seated together at tables during the dialogue portions of the meeting. The reason for this is to get a rich interplay of ideas and information from different perspectives. When the group shifts to a decision-making mode, however, the guests either leave or sit in a different part of the room. Policy boards sometimes formalize this in bylaws: "Decision making will be by 75% consensus of those present and voting. Only members shall advocate and vote in council meetings."

Facilitators and recorders usually stand or sit in a location that physically distinguishes them from the other group members (see Fig. 5-2). Like an orchestra conductor, the facilitator strategically uses space, tempo, posture, and gesture to keep the group moving together.

Two of the most important facilitator responsibilities are to focus the group on one topic at a time and one process at a time (see "Developing Standards," below). Space, flip charts, other visual displays, gestures, and the position of the facilitator's body become valuable tools

for focusing the group. In addition, all facilitator communications are enhanced when nonverbal signals are congruent with the purpose and the facilitation language. For example, people consciously direct their attention to an area at which someone points and unconsciously attend to where the person's eyes are looking. Thus, recorders who point to a flip chart and direct their eyes to the same spot not only focus group energies there but also ensure facilitator control of focus by not looking at the group.

Stand in one spot to give directions. Move to a new space to ask for clarification. This "visual paragraph" separates the intention of the two messages both verbally and nonverbally. Chapter 6 describes the facilitator role in detail and offers many nonverbal facilitation strategies to direct and hold attention.

Skilled groups develop a variety of seating patterns and room arrangements to support different types of social and cognitive interactions. Planning these setups is part of the meeting design process. Groups and meeting designers who lack this awareness can get trapped by the default furniture configurations of the rooms in which they work. Moving the furniture to support productive group work is an important part of a meeting's success.

One vital consideration is to remove any empty chairs from the work area. In both dialogue and discussion settings, empty chairs draw energy from the group and increase both the physical and psychological divide among the participants. The actual physical removal of unused chairs sends a powerful message to the group about the need for connection. This is reinforced when latecomers have to move a chair to join the group.

When people in meetings sit where they always sit, they tend to see what they always see and say what they always say. Group members will initially sit where they are most comfortable; let them. However, people unconsciously become territorial in meetings quite easily. You might have noticed that in groups that meet periodically, the members will take the same space that they occupied in the last meeting. There are two generic advantages for periodically changing the seating arrangements. First, it produces energy to move and sit with someone else. Group deliberations can be deadening, and thinking deadened, without physical movement.

Second, subgroup conversations that are always held with the same person or small group impose limitations on thinking. Conceptual boundaries are formed by these consistent relationships, backgrounds, cognitive styles, and positions. Moving members into different conversational subgroups brings fresh thinking. Occasionally, changing seating can serve other purposes as well, such as breaking up a clique or signaling a transition from one agenda item to another.

Certain tasks are done more effectively with special room arrangement and provision of materials. For example, planning, problem solving, and decision making require access to multiple kinds of data. Writing on charts and information posting on the walls become group memory devices. Many times we have witnessed a group fall silent while members scan what is on display, linking and relating information to the next task in their project.

Perhaps more important than serving memory, what is written becomes a visual voice—always in the room, never silent, interacting with group-member thinking. Many high-performing groups post charts to clarify tasks and remind members of working agreements. Some groups keep lists of collaborative norms, meeting standards, and group-member capabilities on permanent display. Furthermore, the act of composing language for public recording interacts with thinking, forcing greater specificity, economy, and consensus.

Developing Standards

Standards are agreements for ways of working together. Although each group is responsible for deciding what standards will guide its work, we advocate starting with the following simple set of standards, because whenever we have seen these standards in place, we have witnessed successful meetings: (a) maximum product, (b) minimum time, and (c) maximum member satisfaction. In addition, when effective groups implement these standards, their levels of efficiency, efficacy, craftsmanship, and satisfaction soar. When ineffective groups adopt them, their productivity improves.

Doyle and Straus (1993) initially discovered these standards for themselves in the form of success principles from attending and analyzing hundreds of meetings:

> We began to see that certain forces are common to all (successful) groups. A board of directors, a governmental task force, a student council, a citizen's committee, an administrative staff, [and] a radical political group may have different values and objectives, but they all face similar problems when they hold a meeting.

We have updated the principles to reflect current research. Our list of principles for this meeting structure is as follows:

1. Groups should address only one topic at a time.
2. Groups should use only one process at a time.
3. Meetings should be interactive and engage balanced participation.
4. Decision-making meetings should encourage cognitive conflict.
5. All parties should understand and agree on meeting roles.

Addressing One Topic at a Time

There is a limit to what any individual can

attend to in the moment. Groups are limited as well. If more than one topic is being discussed at a time, a group will lack focus, and confusion will reign. We often hear group members ask, "Which topic are we on right now?"

Multiple-topic discussions start because many issues are linked with others or because one idea stimulates an associated idea in another person. For example, a subcommittee is meeting to recommend new textbooks for adoption. One member says, "You know, I'm really pleased that we are working on this task because the old textbooks aren't that useful. In fact, I was in the supply room the other day and I saw several books just sitting on the shelf with dust gathering. I think some teachers are not using them at all." To this, another group member responds, "Supply room! I thought we asked that it be cleaned up. I was in there the other day; it's still a mess!" Another group member says, "Has anyone seen my microscope? I've been looking for it. It was in the supply room the last time I was there."

For the linear-minded among us, this type of conversation drives us crazy. Here are a couple of facilitator moves that can redirect the group to one topic.

Challenge relevance. Offer a relevance challenge by asking, "Please help us understand, Sam, how your comment relates to the topic that we are discussing." This request is made in an approachable voice, and sometimes, to the surprise of everyone, Sam

will indicate how his comment relates. At other times he will say, "You know, it doesn't fit right now. I'll save it for later," thereby monitoring his own participation.

"Cape" comments. Use the flip chart like a bullfighter's cape. Sam makes a comment (e.g., about cleaning the supply room), and the facilitator moves to the flip chart and writes "supply room" while saying to Sam, "Sam, I know there are several people interested in this. Let's put it here so we don't lose it. We'll come back to it later."

In this case, the facilitator has communicated respectfully, "Yes, it is important, but not now." Groups use a variety of strategies to accomplish this. They sometimes have a chart on the wall headed "Items to Come Back To," on which thoughts like this will be reported.

Using Only One Process at a Time

Group processes are vehicles for collective thinking. To brainstorm, to clarify, to analyze, and to evaluate require different mental operations. In order to use one process at a time, all group members must know what the process is, how it works, and why it is being used. The strategies in Appendix A can be of great help to meeting planners and facilitators. Doyle and Straus (1993) observe that facilitators who "go slow in order to go fast" can save meeting time by front-loading detailed

---

Brainstorming

Guidelines

- Allow silent think time. Don't hold back ideas
- The more ideas, the better.
- No discussion is allowed.
- No judgment or criticism is allowed.
- Hitchhike—build on ideas.
- Post ideas.

Sequence of Events

- Review the topic, defining the subject.
- Give everyone a minute or two to think.
- Invite everyone to call out ideas.
- One team member writes down the ideas on a flip chart.

instructions before they proceed.

PAG/PAU is one strategy for ensuring that members understand the process correctly. It stands for Process as Given, Process as Understood. The facilitator communicates each stage in three different mediums: space, voice, and language (Figure 5-3).

Figure 5-3. PAG/PAU

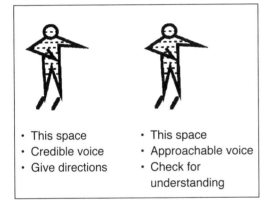

- This space
- Credible voice
- Give directions

- This space
- Approachable voice
- Check for
  understanding

The facilitator stands in the first space and, with a credible voice, describes a process. For example: "We are about to brainstorm [see Brainstorming sidebar]. As you will recall, the ground rules for brainstorming are to report ideas, phrases, and thoughts. These do not have to be in complete sentences. There are no criticisms or questions during this time. If you do not agree with something or if you have a brainstorming question about it, hold that thought for later. We will work for 4 minutes."

The facilitator then moves to a different space and, in an approachable voice, checks for understanding. "So, just to be sure I've stated this clearly, what are we going to do? What are the ground rules? George, if you have a criticism for an idea that someone has offered, what do you do with it?"

Stop and Redirect is another strategy. Here the facilitator has taken time to make sure that the group members understand the process and

now has permission to use hard facilitation skills with them. For example, if Sam forgets about the ground rules in the middle of brainstorming and raises a question, the facilitator can stop Sam and redirect him. This can be done by moving toward Sam, holding one's torso in a hugging motion, and saying in a credible voice, "Sam, hang on to that for a minute. We'll deal with that when we are finished brainstorming."

Holding Interactive Meetings With Balanced Participation

Groups can plan, share information, problem-solve, evaluate, make decisions, and define their boundaries. When you think of these purposes for working groups, it is clear that a pattern in which one person talks and the rest of the people listen is not productive. If you have 12 individuals in a meeting, you want 12 minds engaged. If you have 30 individuals, you want 30 minds engaged. Participants construct meaning and develop ownership interacting with ideas and each other.

Here are some examples of facilitator moves to balance participation:

- "Take a moment and jot down your ideas on this before we begin sharing."

- "Turn to your neighbor and generate a few more ideas. You've got 30 seconds."

- "In the context in which you are working, what is the difference between interrogate and inquire? Tell your neighbor (60 seconds)."

Facilitators can employ other strategies (all of which are described in detail in Appendix A). In Assumptions Wall, groups bring up and examine their assumptions. This requires recordable wall space for subgroups. In Corners, members vote with their feet, moving to a place in the room that represents their position. "In a moment," the facilitator says, "I'm going to ask you to move to a corner of the room. Stand there. When other people arrive, talk together about why you have selected that spot. Okay. Those of you who believe that option A is best, go to that corner; option B, to that corner; option C, to that corner; and option D, to that corner." After the group members have talked, the facilitator asks for reports from the corners.

Too often we have heard the statement that the purpose of participation in meetings is for "buy-in." We discourage the use of this phrase because it carries with it suppositions of manipulation and inferences that the leader has something to sell and the group has an opportunity to buy it. We find, instead, that the purpose of participation is to develop ownership. When ideas are owned, when values are articulated and owned, when beliefs are admitted, when plans and programs and strategies are posed by the group, commitment is high and the likelihood of successful implementation is great. As we shall see in the next principle, ownership does not occur without disagreements.

Balanced participation does not mean that every member must speak for an equal amount of time; it means that the door is open for member participation. There are two forms in which group members speak: to the entire group and to a partner or a small group nearby. Facilitate participation by asking individuals to share with a partner before speaking or to get together with a group of four and identify major criteria to be brought before the group. Moves like these richly engage everyone in thinking processes. They also offer a cloak of anonymity on when voices do not wish to be identified.

Encouraging Cognitive Conflict

Meetings must be safe but not necessarily comfortable. When a group's meetings are always comfortable, the group is probably not talking about the right things. Cognitive conflict—disagreements among group members about substantive issues like goals, values, and as-

sumptions—tend to improve team effectiveness, lead to better decisions, and increase commitment, cohesiveness, empathy, and understanding. Cognitive conflict occurs as teams examine, compare, and reconcile these differences.

The problem with encouraging cognitive conflict is that once it is aroused, it can be difficult to control. If cognitive conflict slides into affective conflict, then hostility, avoidance, cynicism, or apathy can result. Affective conflict focuses anger on individuals rather than ideas, and disagreement becomes personalized. It can occur when group members lack the skills to disagree gracefully. The greatest insurance against affective conflict is group-member skills and practice of the seven norms of collaboration (see chapter 3).

Conflict about ideas improves decision quality but can also weaken the group's ability to work together. Resolving this tension is especially important when consensus is valued and follow-through is required. Teams that encourage cognitive conflict without affective conflict are characterized by focused activity, creativity, open communication, and integration. They work close to the core of issues and are not distracted by trivial points. They encourage thinking beyond normal options, listen to the "minority voice," encourage dissenting opinions, synergize the thoughts and perspectives of different members, and approach problems from new perspectives (Amason, A. C., Thompson, K. R., Hochwater, W. A., & Harrison, A. W., 1995). The outcomes of conflict are shown in Table 5-3.

Conflict can be an asset to maintaining open communication. Members in groups with productive conflict challenge each other's assumptions. They make the fullest possible use of all their members, whereas in less effective groups there is often a disproportionate contribution from certain members. Good teams seek out the opinions of those who are less active

Table 5-3. Outcomes of Conflict

Cognitive Conflict	Affective Conflict
Disagreements about substantive differences of opinion improve team effectiveness and produce	Disagreements over personalized, individually oriented matters reduce team effectiveness and produce
• Better decisions	• Destructive conflict
• Increased commitment	• Poorer decisions
• Increased cohesiveness	• Decreased commitment
• Increased empathy	• Decreased cohesiveness
• Increased understanding	• Decreased empathy

and moderate the input of those who monopolize the conversation.

The conditions in which cognitive conflict exists without affective conflict call for cognitive, emotional, and social maturity. These attributes can be scaffolded with the understanding of meeting standards, the use of pyschologically safe protocols (strategies), and the application of the seven norms of collaboration.

Understanding—and Agreeing on Meeting Roles

Any team works most effectively when its members know one another's responsibilities. The shortstop can anticipate the first baseman's position in relation to first base; therefore his throw is effective. The second baseman knows that the center fielder will back him up on a long ball. Because he can count on his teammate, he stays close to second base to guard it. The same principle works for group meetings.

Although there are many possible meeting roles, we would like to identify four that are most typically found in working groups. These are (a) engaged participant, (b) facilitator, (c) recorder, and (d) role or knowledge authority.

Engaged Participant

Because meeting success is influenced more by the collaborative norms of the group than by facilitator leadership, we call the people who occupy this role "engaged participants" to illuminate the active and essential contribution they make to the group's work. Anyone, at some time, might be an engaged participant. Standing-committee members, participating guests at a special session, the recorder or facilitator before or after serving in those roles, and the building administrator can all at some time serve as engaged participants. What these group members know and do is critically important to group effectiveness.

In strong groups, engaged participants monitor their personal adherence to meeting standards. They notice and set aside comments they are about to make if the comment would violate the "one topic at a time" standard. They also monitor the group's adherence to standards with naive questions. Engaged participants use the seven norms of collaboration, seek and provide data, clarify decision-making processes and levels of authority, and perform gatekeeping functions for others.

Gatekeeping. Susan might say to Sid, "Sid, I'm aware that you haven't talked for a little while. Is there anything that you would like to add?" Notice in this interchange that Sid is not on the spot to respond. The gate, however, has been opened. Similarly, Todd might say to Teresa, "Teresa, I know you served on a committee like this last year. Do you have anything that you'd like to say?" Kristina says to Ken, "Ken, from where I'm sitting, your eyebrows look furrowed. Any comments you'd like to add?"

Setting and testing working agreements. Engaged participants set and test working agreements. For example, Jose sets a working agreement by saying to the group, "I'm requesting that we make an agreement to start our meetings on time. I notice that some of us are here on time and others are not. Frequently, I have to wait 15 minutes before the meeting starts." Discussion ensues. The group decides to begin meetings on time. Several weeks later, June tests the agreement by saying, "I'd like to talk about the decision that we made several meetings ago to start meetings on time. I notice that this is not happening. What do we need to do to keep our agreement?"

Testing consensus. Engaged participants informally test consensus by summary paraphrasing. Sometimes they say, "It seems that we may have agreement on this. Is that true?" or "Could we see a show of thumbs? Thumbs up if you are in agreement, thumbs down if not, thumbs sideways if you're not sure or it's not important to you."

Monitoring internal processes. Engaged participants monitor their own internal processes and listen to their own listening. They become aware of when they have stopped listening to others and are following a train of thought in their own minds. They recognize their emotional responses to other speakers. When they are irritated, they notice it, but instead of giving in to the irritation, they locate the probable reason. Then they set the feeling aside so they can stay fully engaged in the conversation. When they are listening to understand, yet find themselves offering counterarguments in their own minds, they notice this and suspend the unproductive mental activity.

Finally, engaged participants are conscious of the assumptions they bring to a conversation and notice how these influence their listening, thinking, and speaking.

Facilitator

A facilitator is a third party to a conversation and is responsible for process. As a director of process, the facilitator knows what kind of structures and strategies will be useful in helping the group do its work. When the facilitator asks the group to use certain procedures or intervenes with counterproductive behavior, it is on the basis of this process knowledge. A facilitator must be a person who is acceptable to all members of the group, who is substantively neutral, and who has no decision-making authority.

Although a facilitator displays no preference for any of the solutions the group considers, no facilitator is truly neutral. To be "substantively neutral" (Schwarz, 2002) means that facilitators give no verbal or nonverbal cues of their personal reactions to the ideas being discussed. Because the facilitator is serving the group, not certain members, this display of neutrality is important.

Roger Schwartz suggests that facilitators start by clarifying their own role with the group: "My job is to help you have a conversation about these topics in such a way that you understand one anothers' views and the reasoning that leads people to those views. In this way you have the information with which to make informed decisions. I will not share my own views on topics you discuss. However [this would sometimes be appropriate to add], as you know, I have some expertise in one of the topics on your agenda. Should you like information from me on that topic, let me know and I will step out of the facilitation role to provide that."

Schwartz (2002) also recommends that facilitators add another statement to their self-introduction in order to reinforce the group's understanding and proactive influence on roles:

"Please let me know if at any time you think I am acting inconsistently with my role. Does anyone have any concerns?" With groups that have no history of working together, the facilitator may go on to describe other meeting roles.

Chapter 7 details facilitator functions and tools in a meeting and describes how the facilitator focuses group energy, keeps the group on task, and directs processes.

Recorder

As groups tire, auditory acuity is the first modality to fade. Because many meetings are long and members begin to tire, or they are at the end of the school day and members are already tired, public recording is critically important for the group's short-term memory. The later in the day the meeting or the more fatigued the participants, the more public recording is necessary. At the best of times, humans can manage seven items of information (plus or minus two) in their working memories. Public recording keeps key data in front of a group.

Recorders, like facilitators, occupy a position of purposeful neutrality. Their function is to support the group by maintaining a clear visual representation of important ideas and data and to support the facilitator in managing processes as effectively and efficiently as possible. The recorder and facilitator also serve as behind-the-scenes custodians, arranging displays, clearing out unnecessary data, and arranging the room for special activities.

Because you want the faciliator to direct the focus of the group, it is advisable that recorders look at the charts on which they are working, or at the faciliator, instead of at the group. Because members' eyes go in the direction of the leader's eyes, recorders looking at the group split the visual—and cognitive—focus of the group.

A great deal of knowledge is emerging about the techniques and tools of public recording (Buckley, 2005). Following are several basics:

- Print rather than write.
- Use uppercase and lowercase case letters, not all caps.
- Use color—alternate green, blue, and brown for text. Never use red for text; it is hard to read. Reserve red for headlines and other organizers. Reserve black for boxes, arrows, or other organizers.
- Use only water-based pens.
- Write large enough for all members to read.
- Keep all charts visible at all times.
- Border charts for formal appearance.
- Use pictographs (see Buckley 2002 for traceable chart art).
- Keep your eyes on the chart when you are recording.
- Have the facilitator tell the group to direct corrections.
- Have the facilitator ask the group what not to record.
- Point to and/or stand by the items as they are being discussed.
- Remain still and nondistracting.
- Move your body to support the facilitator's use of space.

Role or Knowledge Authority

Leaders lead. Principals lead through modeling, and developing leadership in others is a critical attribute of improving schools. In the past, the principal has been expected to lead meetings, but this is changing. "Because of their positional authority and control over school resources, principals are in a strategic position to promote or inhibit the development of a teacher learning community in their school"

(McLaughlin & Talbert, 2006).

Many people lead meetings, of course. Leadership roles in meetings are called by many names: chairperson, convener, facilitator, leader, consultant, specialist, manager, and others. Because we see a critical leadership role in meetings that does not include running the meeting, we have been searching for a term that might be neutral, or at least unlike the other names we have for meeting leadership.

By what name can we designate such a leader in a meeting? The most descriptive term we've found so far is *role authority* or *knowledge authority*. The role authority might be the principal in a staff meeting, the vice principal if the principal is not there, the superintendent in a district office meeting, or the assistant superintendent if the superintendent is not there. The knowledge authority might be the literacy coach, at a task force dealing with the reading program; the science consultant, in a committee addressing a science curriculum; or an external consultant charged with making recommendations to the group on improving organizational effectiveness.

When the role or knowledge authority is in a meeting without a facilitator, this person typically manages the group processes. He or she sets the agenda, decides when to move to the next topic, recognizes those who want to speak, writes meeting notes to assist remembering, and summarizes actions to be taken. In managing all these procedural tasks, the role or knowledge authority limits, or at least diffuses, the attention given to meeting content and also limits group access to the special information resources that are part of this person's particular role or knowledge expertise.

Without a facilitator, the value of the role or knowledge authority's information is limited in two ways. First, because this leader has to balance attention between process and content, there is less time for interaction with the content. Second, and perhaps more important, it is extremely rare that a leader can maintain the neutrality required of the facilitation process and still give content information to the group. For this reason, leaders become more influential and the group matures and makes better decisions when a person other than the role or knowledge authority facilitates the meeting.

When leaders such as department heads or principals use the services of a meeting facilitator, they will often set meeting schedules, coordinate topics with faculty and others, arrange to have department members rotate through the facilitator and recorder roles, and codevelop the agenda design with the meeting facilitator. The role authority will also follow through to see that subcommittee tasks are clear, that resources are available, and that evaluation of processes and products is provided.

In many ways, the role or knowledge authority functions like any engaged participant in the meeting, but he or she is also available to inform the group about constraints, resources, and values related to the topic. Like other group members, the role or knowledge authority can advocate one's own ideas as well as inquire about the ideas of others. The primary caution is to remember that until groups have attained a high state of interdependence, actions in this role will speak louder than words.

Using the Four Success Structures

Every working group needs a declarative knowledge of the four success structures. This means that members can describe the four structures, their parts, and the principles on which they are based. As groups learn from their experiences, procedural knowledge will develop, and members will become skillful at exercising, monitoring, and self-correcting both themselves as individuals and the group. One way to increase both consciousness about and skill in applying the four success structures is to use the meeting assessment inventory found in Appendix L. Regular use of this inventory and reflective dialogue with group members about the results focuses attention on skill gains and sticking points for that group. This is especially useful when the group is discussing subjects about which there are strong emotions.

Mature groups eventually acquire a degree of conditional knowledge, allowing them to recognize when to break the rules and achieve their purpose even more effectively. Such powerful and cumulative knowledge can be, and

is, developed with faculties, committees, task forces, cabinets, advisory boards, and other groups. It does not have to be lost because of changing membership or environmental crises. We have facilitated a statewide group responsible for deciding how millions of dollars will be used each year to support technology. This group met for a full-day meeting 3 times a year. Because members were appointed as representatives from regions, membership constantly changed. Yet after a year and a half of facilitated meetings, the consensus of the group was that "we have become our values and operating

Meeting Inventory

Decide Who Decides

• We were clear about who we are in the decision making process.	1 - 2 - 3 - 4 - 5
• We were clear about the decision making processes being used.	1 - 2 - 3 - 4 - 5

Define the Sandbox

• We were clear about which parts of the issue(s) we explored live in our sandbox.	1 - 2 - 3 - 4 - 5

Develop Standards

• We adhered to one process at a time.	1 - 2 - 3 - 4 - 5
• We adhered to one topic at a time.	1 - 2 - 3 - 4 - 5
• We balanced participation.	1 - 2 - 3 - 4 - 5
• The degree to which I felt listened to.	1 - 2 - 3 - 4 - 5
• The degree to which I listened to others.	1 - 2 - 3 - 4 - 5
• We engaged in productive cognitive conflict.	1 - 2 - 3 - 4 - 5
• We were clear about meeting roles .	1 - 2 - 3 - 4 - 5

Design the Surround

• We managed the environment to support our work.	1 - 2 - 3 - 4 - 5

_____	_____	_____
Topic(s)	Date	Group

principles." Effective groups develop a commitment to practice and monitor their use of the four structures.

In any session in which planning, reflecting, or problem solving occur, the engaged participants—that is, the group members—are the ones who do the work of the meeting. In fact, as we have noted, the meeting's success is more dependent on their informed participation than on the skills and knowledge of a boss, a content expert, or a facilitator. This is especially so in small work teams. In large groups a facilitator is required to orchestrate and direct the contributions of group members. Group members should be able to distinguish between data and inference; distinguish relevant from irrelevant information, claims, or reasons; identify unstated assumptions; and interpret data.

Conclusion

In this chapter we've explored foundation knowledge for the art and science of meetings. Our definition of success for meetings is that they take minimum time, produce maximum work, and generate a maximum amount of member satisfaction. The ultimate goal is that meetings serve as vehicles to protect and support the primary mission of the school, which is student learning. At schools and in special district committees—McLaughlin and Talbert (2006) say it well—the goal is to study data on teaching and learning, and then agree to the next steps for changing instruction and for examining the effects of change on student learning.

Meetings are becoming as important a part of teachers' work as lesson design. For this reason, knowing how to produce work through meetings has become an essential part of a professional portfolio, regardless of one's role.

In the next chapter, we explore in detail the principles of facilitation, facilitator functions, and facilitation tools.

Chapter 6   Designing Time-Efficient and Effective Meetings

Agenda construction, like many other tasks that educators do, is first of all a way of thinking. There is simply no other activity that can economize time and maximize success and satisfaction as much as a well-formed agenda. The problem, of course, is that it requires time to develop one.

"Prepare more and meet less" is a motto for successful groups and effective leaders. By making a personal investment in agenda design, leaders reduce wasted time by tenfold and overall meeting time by as much as 30%. This in turn produces dramatic increases in productivity and group-member satisfaction.

When the organization values agenda design, department meetings become better run, ad hoc committees function more smoothly, and task forces and advisory groups feel better about their work and get more done. Being smart and proactive about meeting design pays off throughout the school and the district.

Thoughtful meeting planning is consistent with the adage "Plan first, then act." Leaders and facilitators should value meeting planning in the same way that high-performing teachers value planning for instruction because it influences the success of what follows.

How to Use This Chapter

We will describe the remarkable benefits of meeting design in complex nonlinear systems such as schools. Although protecting time to design meetings produces some tensions, and time-pressed leaders occasionally have to work extemporaneously, the majority of meetings, planned well, will produce benefits by the hundredfold. We will elaborate on some of these benefits. We will show how effective design takes into account and influences the greater context in which groups work. This chapter will also present principles of agenda construction with which you can confidently construct agendas for any situation, no matter how complex. We provide samples of agendas for various types of meetings, and we describe a template for delegating tasks to groups. Finally, we offer some general design and planning tips.

The sequence in which you will want this information depends on your prior information, personal history, present needs, and urgency. If you have an immediate need for agenda samples, move ahead to the section "Agenda Templates" or to the list of tips within it. If you want a rationale with which to persuade others to invest in design work, go to the section "Design Matters." If you are interested in design principles that capacitate you to teach others and to develop effective agendas in any setting, read "The Principles of Design." Should you want to delegate a problem to a group for its recommendations, go to the section "Posing Problems for Groups to Work On."

Design Matters

Consider the time you spend in meetings. At a modest 2 hours per week, you are spending more than 3,000 hours in meetings throughout the life of your career. If you translate that to a team of 12, then 4,500 eight-hour days are being spent in meetings. That's more than 12 years! All professions and industries tend to malign meetings as time wasters. This doesn't have to be so.

When meetings are not well organized, an abysmal cost occurs to an organization. Morale suffers, and the members grow less and less willing to invest their time in projects, committees, and teams. Frustration reigns in department meetings and ad hoc groups and insinuates its presence into school activities, including teaching. Many have experienced this and yet know that it does not have to be so. In many settings, meetings are well organized; what emerges there are well-run meetings, optimism, efficacy, successful results, and an increasing willingness to particpate in collaborative work.

What's talked about matters. What do you imagine people are talking about in meetings? One district collected and analyzed agendas from faculty meetings, school leadership teams, department meetings, and grade-level groups. From 60% to 80% of the meetings were devoted to "administrivia"—scheduling, announcements, event organization, discipline, compliance issues, or disputes—leaving only a small percentage of time for the discussion of teaching and learning.

This book reflects the dynamic systems principle that both things and energy matter. When meeting topics are matters of substance and the conversations are well organized, organizations receive both tangible and intangible benefits. The intangible products of meetings, though invisible in the meeting, translate to mindsets and behaviors. These must not be underestimated, for when the intangibles are positive, they provide the energy for productive work. Meetings that are well-planned and executed—and the planning is prerequisite to the execution—promote one of the most valuable

energy sources for groups, and the one most consistently related to school success: efficacy.

A report by Coleman and colleagues (1966) startled educators with the finding that socioeconomic status (SES) outweighed a school's efforts to produce learning. In the 40-plus years since then, no school characteristics, including an orderly environment or principal leadership—the darlings of the effective-schools movement—have been shown to contradict this. A recent meta-analysis (Waters, Marzano, & McNulty, 2003) reports promising correlations between certain principal responsibilities and student learning, using the measures of student success identified in the original studies. However, the authors note that the correlations must be treated cautiously when applied to real-world situations.

However, an even wider net is being cast by research on collective efficacy. *Collective efficacy* refers to the perceptions of teachers in a school that the faculty as a whole can execute the courses of action necessary to have positive effects on the students. These groups work harder, persist through barriers, are more effective, and employ a richer repertoire of teaching methodology than do teachers without a sense of efficacy. Students learn more and perform better on any test of academic achievement. Coleman and colleagues (1966), it turns out, were not quite right. Controlling for SES, three variables—collective efficacy, trust, and academic focus—were found to be predictive of academic success (Hoy, et al., 2006). In the things-energy scheme, these variables are energy sources. As Wheatley (1992) notes, the power to get things done in organizations is through relationships.

The purpose of this brief digression into school improvement history is to underscore the incredible influence that the energy source of collective efficacy has—and how productive meetings are resources for producing it.

Individuals and groups are not likely to initiate action without a sense of efficacy (Hoy et al., 2006). Student achievement and efficacy beliefs are inextricably intertwined. Positive associations of efficacy and student achievement have been found with three types of efficacy beliefs: the self-efficacy beliefs of students, the self-efficacy beliefs of teachers, and the collective efficacy of schools. The most important idea here is that collective efficacy is a variable that is amenable to change and that can affect teachers' beliefs about their own self-efficacy.

What happens in meetings is a manifestation of the degree to which the group is a learning community and will be a force for or a force against developing collective efficacy.

Thoughtful design can help to unify faculty perspectives and experience. Many schools experience too much fragmentation. Good meeting design can express and reinforce deeper organizational values—the beliefs about learning and the opportunities to model effective learning designs. Well-planned meetings link the project to the initiative, the immediate to the important, the short-range to the long-range, and the greater community to its subsets.

The Principles of Design

Because principles are generalizations, not rules, they offer elasticity, which rules do not. We will explore five agenda-design principles: (a) allocentrism, planning with the group in mind; (b) relevance, connecting to the members and unit goals; (c) information, ensuring that groups have the information they need to do their task; (d) interaction, keeping minds and voices active; and (e) congruence with organizational values and beliefs.

Allocentrism

Design with the users in mind. Put yourself in their place. Imagine how you will feel entering the meeting. Are there special needs that require attention? Will the group be tired or distracted? Are the participants informed about the purpose of the session? What knowledge do they bring to the table that does not have to be repeated? What would they need to know to encourage participation? What skills might have to be introduced or reinforced for them to do good work on the issues that will be addressed? Are there issues of mood that might run counter to receptivity? What seating is going to be comfortable, psychologically and physically?

We once conducted a meeting in a kindergarten room that was not going well. Finally, we realized the discomfort that people were feeling sitting in those itty-bitty chairs, so we corrected the seating, and the quality of the meeting imporoved. A simple matter of furniture placement can make an enormous difference in meeting success. We described practical models for room design and materials in chapter 5.

Relevance

The principle of relevance concerns membership, the internal fit of the agenda items, and the degree to which the agenda has some bearing on the larger contexts and goals within which the group works.

When an item is relevant to only part of the group, schedule it last and dismiss those who are not involved. Nothing is more frustrating and disrespectful of time than to make someone sit through agenda items that are irrelevant to them. Selective dismissals honor the group members and become part of a norm of appreciating their energies and time.

To what degree do the agenda items relate to one another? Cluster those that relate. Organize others using transitions activities that are described in chapter 7. Finally, and perhaps most important, what bearing does this meeting have on the larger contexts of the group's existence and work? Cognizance of this allows an opening in which the meeting is perceptually framed to help the participants make sense of the work. Groups often need a sense of their history to understand and embrace the work of a particular meeting.

Information

Three questions guide agenda construction related to information. The first of these is deciding what information is needed for the group to do its work. As mentioned above, sometimes this information is history and context so that the group members can start from the same place together. Groups might occasionally need policy information or research summaries on a topic in order to do informed work; the agenda planner can then provide for a paired reading activity from an appropriate journal. It is often important to know which players outside the group, or which other groups, have a say on the topic so that consciousness can be brought to the question of defining the "sandbox," one of the four meeting success structures described in chapter 5.

Second, and most important, groups need to know who they are in the decision-making process. Are they to inform, recommend, or decide? Third, if they are to inform or recommend, to whom are they relaying information and what are the next steps in the process? Display this information directly on the agenda next to the items.

Interaction

Assuming that the purpose of a meeting is for members to think, deliberate, or take action, interaction is essential. Any group that spends the majority of its time in full-group mode is keeping its brain activity surpressed,

encouraging lethargy, and reducing meeting achievement and the value for participants. Two essential questions must be addressed to plan for the degrees and types of interaction. What tasks will be asked of the group: comprehending, exploring, informing, recommending, or deciding? What cognitive actitvities will be required: generating, categorizing, analyzing, synthesizing, or extrapolating?

The thoughtful use of "conversation containers" fosters success. These essentially provide scaffolds for the talk. Skillful designers consider ways to start, structure, and sustain thinking in their meetings.

Starters

Just because people are sitting together does not mean that they are a group capable of working together. Recognize that groups do not arrive primed for work; they need to transition physically, socially, cognitively, and emotionally into the work space and topic. Wellman and Lipton (2004) refer to strategies that perfom this function as *conversation starters*. The key to conversation starters is that they are psychologically safe and pertinent to the task. Safety is important; it allows the risk of stating ideas when you are not sure, disclosing that you do not know, disagreeing, or being able to talk and not be overridden by highly verbal participants. Overcoming this risk is at the heart of effective meeting participation.

Protocols (both starters and structures) can be designed to minimize risk and maximize critical thinking. Avoid, at all costs, opening with "feel good" activities in which participants see no connection to their work.

Although safety is necessary to access the neocortex and the members' best thinking, comfort is not a requirement in meetings. In fact, if a group is always comfortable, it is probably talking about the wrong things.

Structures

Structures are strategies, or protocols, that shape and structure conversations, again providing psychological safety and maximizing time efficiency. Almost any strategy can be designed as a protocol that sets rules or instructions for a conversation.

Many are listed in chapter 7, related to facilitator tasks during different meeting stages.

We are using the terms *strategy* and *protocol* somewhat interchangeably. In diplomacy a protocol governs who greets whom first; in technology it governs the rules for two pieces of equipment to talk together. A meeting protocol provides a "container" for conversations that defines what is to happen and how it will occur. In meetings, protocols have the following three functions:

1. Establish topics, time for the activity, who speaks, and the sequence of the speakers, if any.

2. Provide challenge and limit discomfort.

3. Designate the thinking skills to be used.

Without a structure, conversations can meander, go off course, and take valuable time away from the meeting objectives. The thoughtful selection of strategies supports the efficient use of time by defining the total amount of time for a conversation and the time for each component. Protocols can also determine the type of thinking that is required, such as separating data from inference, analyzing, evaluating, or developing theories.

Some examples of structures are the paired-reading activities of Say Something, or the strategies Key Concepts/Key Ideas, Assumptions Wall, and Card Stack and Shuffle (Appendix A). Brainstorming is a structure because it specifies the thought processs to use and the order in which to use them, and because the facilitator is calling on people, determining who speaks when. It is our view that the steps in the brainstorming protocols always have to be reviewed and that facilitators should intervene immediately when violations or mutations occur.

Sustainers

Sustainers are strategies and tools that are used to maintain longer, focused conversations. How people talk to one another will either sustain or dampen communication. Sustainers are verbal and nonverbal tools used by group members to enhance their ability to deliver psychologically safe thoughts to one another even when they disagree. The seven norms of collaboration described in chapter 3 serve as the starting point for this set of skills. Learning the tools for inquiry described in chapter 3 represents an ongoing curriculum for many groups. Group size is an important sustainer. Paired activities require the least amount of time, compared to trios, quartets, or sextets. Pairs are psychologically safer units than larger groups are. Trios bring the valuable tension of three sets of experiences. It is also harder in a trio than in a pair to leave the task and enter social talk. Quartets are diverse yet small enough to be in the early stages of learning as they apply new communication skills. Quartets are an ideal size to dialogue about data posted before them on the wall. Groups of six are a good size for protocols like First Turn/Last Turn or Grounding (see Appendix A) and for activities that synthesize findings.

Individual reflection is the safest-size unit of all. Many strategies begin with private reflection, either mentally or in writing, giving members a chance to gather their thoughts before participating in a group.

Keep in mind that these are principles, not rules, and that the strategies named here are not limited to the group size suggested. Sue Presler, a colleague and friend, while working with a full faculty in Hawaii, once took a step from

Focusing Four (see Appendix A) and used it with the full group to have the members advocate lunchroom solutions that had been generated the week before. Never would we have considered it. Yet after just a few people talked, it became clear to the group which solution would serve it best.

Degree of structure is another sustainer. The planners decide when to select a tight or a loose protocol as a matter of scaffolding for success. A tight protocol is one in which members have little choice about when and how to participate and have maximum scaffolding for success. Examples are First Turn/Last Turn, and Futures Wheel. Designers will plan for tight protocols when the topic is complex or emotionally loaded or when the group does not have much experience working together effectively.

Loose protocols provide less scaffolding and leave more decisions in the hands of members. Examples are Paired Verbal Fluency, Around the Room and Back Again, and Most Important Point.

Group maturity, another sustainer, refers to the collective effectiveness of a group as it works together. A long-standing group can be immature; a recently formed group might be mature. The more immature a group is, the more need there is for tight structures and for carefully describing the reasons for and the structures of the strategies. Mature groups can work with either tight or loose protocols and, in fact, will sometimes ask for a tight protocol because they recognize that the topic is hard to talk about.

Congruence

Congruence with organizational values and beliefs is the fifth principle of agenda design. What happens in meetings is a manifestation of the degree to which the group is a learning community and will be a force for or a force against developing collective efficacy. Thoughtful design can help unify faculty perspectives and experience. Many schools experience too much fragmentation. Good meeting design can express and reinforce deeper organizational values and beliefs about learning and are opportunities to model effective learning designs. Well-planned meetings link the project to the initiative, the immediate to the important, the short range to the long, and the greater community to its subsets.

Drafting a Design

We now move from design principles to the hands-on activities of drafting an agenda you will use. We will explore whether a meeting is even necessary. If the answer is yes, what type of meeting will it be? To help answer this question, we present a planning template and samples of agendas that serve different purposes.

Is A Meeting Necessary?

Your first consideration is whether a meeting is even necessary. Ask yourself what you want to accomplish and if meeting together is the best possible use of your group's time on this topic. Are there alternatives, such as surveys, memos, focus-group interviews, or phone or video conferencing, that might serve just as well?

If you decide that a meeting is appropriate, examine the potential agenda topics. Does each item on the agenda concern at least three members of the group? If not, deal with it one-to-one. Is it clear what type of action the group is to take on the item? If not, clarify it. Can it be dealt with either initially or fully at a lower level? If so, reroute it to the appropriate group or subcommittee. Has the item for discussion been thoroughly prepared—researched, documented, and defined? If not, hold it over until the preparation is complete.

Once you've decided that a meeting is the best alternative and have screened the agenda items to determine which ones must be addressed, consider who should be there. Do the agenda items pertain to the entire staff or just some of them? As mentioned earlier, if some are for all, but others pertain to just a couple of departments, schedule two adjournment times, releasing those who are not involved before starting on the final items. Are the items under consideration important or urgent enough to be on the next agenda? If not, reschedule them for a later meeting.

Always reserve the last 5–10 minutes of discussion or dialogue meetings for the members to reflect on the meeting process. Developing groups is one of the highest callings of leadership. Using a meeting inventory reinforces paying attention to the success structures and meeting standards described in chapter 5 and helps groups to grow more skillful with each meeting (Appendix L).

Use the rule of one half: List the agenda topics, then cut the list by half. One reason meetings can be a source of dissatisfaction is that they attempt to cover too much. Slow down. Allow the time that the topics and the members deserve.

What Type of Meeting Will It Be?

The type of meeting will influence the type of outcomes that can be reached. Four meeting types common to working groups are musters, assemblies, discussions, and dialogues. Chapter 4 presented the purposes of dialogue (to understand) and discussion (to decide) as well as the structures for these meeting functions. Grade-level teams, department meetings, curriculum-council leadership groups, and full-facility meetings carry most of the important conversations about teaching and learning in dialogue or discussion formats.

Assemblies are routine meetings of very large groups like high school faculties, in which the large number of members limits the outcomes to receiving and clarifying "pass down" information and sanctioning or rejecting proposals presented by a leader or a subgroup. Another example of an assembly is union rallies, in which the purpose is to give information and get people excited. One exception to the limitation of assemblies is the 1-2-6 strategy, in which even a group as large as 200 can generate, clarify, advocate, and select a few items as most important to pursue (Appendix A). It should take no longer than an hour to accomplish this.

Musters are the regularly scheduled meeting of a department, an elementary faculty, or a special unit of workers such as bus drivers or principals. The function of musters is to communicate up, down, and sideways and to feel positive about the experience. They are a time for making announcements, coordinating calendars, and clarifying "pass down" information. Never use a muster meeting for "pass down" information in a group when a memo would do, unless members need to ask questions, raise issues, or agree to common approaches for effective implementation. Musters, like regularly scheduled faculty meetings, often reserve time for discussion or dialogue.

Clear Outcomes

We like to say that the three most important considerations in drafting an agenda are clear outcomes, clear outcomes, and clear outcomes. Creating clear outcomes is simple but not easy. Like a finely crafted lesson, a successful meeting will have outcomes that are behaviorally observable for each agenda item. Well-formed outcomes describe a product, not a process; a destination, not a journey.

"Discuss the proposal for nongraded primary" does not describe an outcome, it describes what members will do in pursuit of an outcome. "Identify the pros and cons of an ungraded primary here at Anderson School" is a statement of outcome appropriate to a discussion. "Explore the assumptions of an ungraded primary" is a statement of outcome for a dialogue. In each case, a specific, observable product emerges: in the first case, a list; in the second, articulations and inquiries about assumptions.

SMART outcomes is a useful acronym for planners:

S   *Specific*: To be specific, an outcome must describe the presence of some quality, not the absence—not, for example, "We want fewer tardies," but rather "We want more students to arrive on time."

M   *Measurable*: What will be seen or heard as evidence of achievement? This is stated as something that the participants will achieve, not that the meeting leaders will provide.

A   *Attainable*: Can the outcomes be attained within the time available and with the resources in the room? Time is most often the larger barrier to achieving success. Many groups discover that they are trying to "cover the agenda" as teachers try to "cover curriculum," by attempting to do too much. The result is surface treatment of many items rather than deep and longer lasting attention to a few. Groups that confuse urgency with importance often fall into this trap. The resources part of the question refers to information, skills, and attitudes. Are these sufficiently in place? If not, then perhaps some different meeting outcomes are called for that will deal directly with the affective domain.

R   *Relevant*: How is this outcome related to the larger purposes of the meeting and the organization's vision, values, and goals?

T   *Tactically sound*: Is it possible that achieving the outcome, or even just working on it, could backfire in some way and endanger people? An outcome in which all members of a department express their honest feelings about the department chairperson might in fact be ecologically unsound for the individuals and the group. We have found that whenever a well-intentioned outcome carries psychological danger, we must design approaches that take that into account, or members will unconsciously and inevitably sabotage it.

Agenda Templates

We've had much success in designing meeting agendas within our own organizations and for groups with whom we consult by asking ourselves, or the group, the following questions:

- What must happen at the opening of the meeting to provide an inclusion experience, define goals and roles, and adopt an agenda?
- What terms should be defined?
- What questions must the group address, and in what sequence, to achieve its desired outcome?
- How much time will be assigned to meeting topics?
- What processes and language will be used to maintain group-member efficacy, flexibility, craftsmanship, consciousness, and interdependence?
- What closing activities will ensure clarity on group decisions, and who is to do what by when as the next steps?
- What follow-up will be required?
- What will be communicated to others about this meeting, and how will it be communicated?

To further complicate the issue of having clear outcomes, we offer two final considerations. One is that high-functioning, intact groups should pay attention to their development as a group. Therefore, outcomes should be thought about not only in terms of cognitive, affective, and product goals for the meeting, but also in terms of how the meeting can be conducted in such a way that the group gets better at being a group.

Finally, regardless of your role within a meeting, or even the nature of the meeting, what, specifically, are your desired outcomes? As a group member, do you desire greater clarity about an issue, or is it your intent to influence the group on an item? If the latter, how will you know you've succeeded, and what might be some strategies? Mentor teachers often report to us with surprise that being clear about their outcomes has transformed one-to-one meetings with the teachers they are supporting.

In our own practice we often begin a consultation conversation with the following questions: "What do you want as a result of this meeting? How will you know if we have achieved that? What topics should be discussed for that goal? How much time should we allot, and in what sequence should we discuss them?" Helping the other party to think in outcome terms, whether the meeting is a parent conference or the start of a 30-minute session with two other colleagues, helps to focus time and strategies to get results.

The more one practices, the easier agenda construction becomes. Here are some final planning tips:

- Engage design help. In fact, part of developing your group is to increase group consciousness and skill in this area.

- Post outcomes in the meeting rooms. This forces you to construct clear language and observable goals and aids all members in knowing the reason for this meeting and how to best focus their energy. In addition, should group members get off topic, it allows the facilitator to gesture toward the posted outcomes and ask, "Please help us to understand how your comments relate to this outcome." Sometimes they will tell us; sometimes they will monitor their own contribution, saying, "I'll save it for later."

- Determine how much content and how much process will be required to achieve outcomes related to the agenda items. How much discussion, exploration, or dialogue might be necessary? How much information will be required? Remember that when goals are related to attitude and behavior change, more process time is required, not less.

- Estimate the time that each agenda item will take. Remember that if processes are involved, it takes time to explain them and to check for understanding.

- Place divisive items early on an agenda to minimize the possibility of members leaving at the end of the meeting in a funk.

- If the meeting purpose is singular and brief, remove the furniture. This signals a stand-up meeting—quick, focused, and everyone out in 15 minutes.

- When you are a meeting leader, keep the first hour after the meeting to write minutes and memos and do the necessary follow-up. Sending out a written follow-up to a meeting within 24 or 48 hours signals that you value the time people have invested.

- Consider what commitment will be made in the meeting to group development. What time, processes, and areas of group development will be addressed? At times, one of the seven norms of collaboration (see chapter 3) will emerge as important to strengthen; at other times, raising consciousness on the five standards for successful meetings (see chapter 5) will be useful. This attention to group development, often overlooked, is the secret to getting better and is the focus of the next chapter.

Agenda Formats

Tables 6-1 through 6-6 are sample formats for meetings of various lengths, from 70 minutes to a full day. Each specifies outcomes and processes. They are offered as idea stimulators for your situations. Obviously, these are not the only formats possible; you might have one that is working well for you.

Table 6-1. Superintendent's Cabinet Meeting

This format was developed by the International School Bangkok after one of the authors worked with them developing collaborative tools for instructional leaders. Members of these classes included the superintendent, associate superintendent for curriculum, all principals, some department heads, and teachers in informal leadership roles. The learning and the modeling by the superintendent was instrumental in spreading sound practices throughout the school. The cabinet also held its meetings in the round so that anyone could come and observe them at work, practicing meeting standards and employing norms of collaboration.

MEETING AGENDA

Meeting outcome: Revise and finalize the rubric for the common assessment.

Name of team or group: _____

Facilitator: _____ **Recorder:** _____

Other participants: _____

Starting and ending times: _____

Purposes: Understanding, Informing, Recommending, Deciding

TOPIC	PURPOSE	GUIDING QUESTIONS	BACKGROUND AND PROCESSES	PERSON AND TIME
Welcome and overview of outcomes	Inform	What do we hope to accomplish at this meeting?	Ann will review what has been done since the last meeting and explain the outcomes and topics for this meeting.	Ann, 3 minutes

Hear voices and celebrate learning	Inclusion	What learning can we celebrate this week?	We'll go round-robin to share a learning success with a student or an activity or strategy that worked.	Ann, 7 minutes
Rubric for the common assessment	Decide	• Does the rubric help students focus on the critical benchmarks for the unit? • Are the rubric's criteria the right criteria? • Does the rubric adequately discriminate among degrees of understanding?	We tried the writing rubric for the first time for the common assessment. At this meeting we will: • Look once again at the unit's benchmarks and determine whether the criteria are the right criteria • Share observations about using the rubric to determine levels of understanding and proficiency. In order to do this, please bring student papers that you scored at standard, as well as above and below, and any observations you made while scoring. • Make adjustments	Sandy, 60 minutes

Figure 6-2 illustrates an agenda that is designed to stimulate dialogue only, in which the purpose is to develop understanding, delaying decisions to another time.

Figure 6-2. Stimulation of Dialogue

MEETING AGENDA

Meeting outcome: Explore initiating a senior citizen volunteer service program.

Name of team or group: Site Council

Facilitator: _____ **Recorder:** _____

Other participants: _____

Starting and ending times: 3:30–5:00 _____

Purposes: Dialogue, summarize

Conduct a dialogue session to explore ideas related to initiating a senior citizen volunteer service program at Desert Sands School.

cont.

Assumptions:
We will reach a better decision on this topic if we have a chance to dialogue, then gather additional information from others.

Each of us learns from one another. We will test this assumption at the end of the meeting by asking for self-reports of shifts in assumptions and understanding regarding this topic.

Table 6-3 shows a two-and-a-half hour meeting to introduce and decide which of the seven norms of collaboration to develop first. Organizers are topic/time, outcome, and process.

Table 6-3. Meeting on Seven Norms

MEETING AGENDA – SESSION I

Meeting outcome: Introduce and decide which on seven norms to initiate first.

Name of team or group: Blissful Faculty _____

Facilitator: _____ **Recorder:** _____

Other participants: _____

Starting and ending times: 2:00–3:30 _____

Purposes: Assess, compare perspectives, decide

TOPIC/TIME		OUTCOME	PROCESS
2:00	Welcome Roles Outcome	Inform	Describe
	First paid job	Inclusion	Round robin – name your first paid job
2:15	Seven norms inventory	Assess	Distribute inventory to subgroups Subgroups rate full group Subgroups chart results
2:35	Analyze results	Analyze	Compare charted results Inquire about sources of differences (What do you see or hear that leads to those perceptions?) Dialogue for understanding
3:00	Select norm to adopt	Decide	Discuss and choose one

| 3:20 | Assess meeting and select next meeting's facilitator and recorder | Assess meeting and select roles for next meeting | Distribute meeting inventory: How did we do on success structures and meeting standards? Give to facilitator Request volunteers for next meeting |
| 3:30 | Adjourn | | |

Table 6-4. Follow-Up Meeting

MEETING AGENDA – SESSION II

Meeting outcome: Group development; generate faculty concerns about student writing.

Name of team or group: Blissful Faculty _____

Facilitator: _____ **Recorder:** _____

Other participants: _____

Starting and ending times: 2:00 – 3:30 _____

Purposes: Monitor, explore, summarize

	TOPIC	OUTCOME	PROCESS
2:00	Welcome Roles Outcome	Organize for work	Present and check for understanding (TAG-TAU) and (PAG-PAU)
2:10	Hear voices in the room and recall what happened at the last meeting	Inclusion Recall	Paired verbal fluency –"everything you remember about the last meeting"
2:20	Group development	Conscious commitment	Quartets review collated meeting inventory data "Given what we said about ourselves, what do we want to work on today?"
2:20	Select norm of collaboration	Consciousness for self- and group monitoring	Post the norm—generate what to attend to in oneself and in the group Pairs talk

cont.

2:25 Student writing	Generate	Members write observations or concerns about student writing Members mark two or three ideas in own writing
2:35 Student writing	Understand	Groups of six: First turn/last turn • First person names item he or she highlighted from own writing • Round robin – each person speaks to the item named • First person to name now gets final word on item • Repeat • No cross talk
3:05 Student writing	Synthesis	Groups of six: Chart summary paraphrase(s) of the conversation
3:15 Student writing	Inform	Carousel walk to summaries
3:25 Assess meeting Select next facilitator Announce that next meeting will decide on where to focus writing improvement efforts	Assess meeting and select roles for next meeting	Distribute meeting inventory: How did we do on success structures and meeting standards? Members complete Give to facilitator

Table 6-5. Meeting of Department Heads

Context: In this school there is a move to have departments, and the department heads in their own meetings, function as learning communities. This agenda is organized around questions the group needs to answer and processes to use in order to achieve meeting goals.

Prior to this meeting several journal articles on the topic have been read and commented on.

MEETING AGENDA

Meeting outcome: Define and adopt learning community resources to develop.

Name of team or group: Department Heads

Facilitator: _____ **Recorder:** _____

Other participants: _____

Starting and ending times: 7:30–11:00

Purposes: generate, select, code, decide, and delegate

	QUESTIONS	PROCESS
7:30	Welcome. What is our task today? What processes will we use?	Principal describes context, outcomes, and processes to reach these outcomes: 1. Create behavioral definition of learning community for this group 2. Decide which behaviors to adopt as group goals 3. Identify essential resources to acquire 4. Decide on next steps Facilitator leads a conversation to check for understanding
8:00	Inclusion. What's the worst, best…?	Table groups: What is the worst and best thing that could happen today? Brainstorm, chart one or two from each table, and agree to do a group groan if any on the list occur.
8:15	What will we see and hear when this group is operating as a learning community?	Pairs generate ideas and post on charts Report to full group Members add to posted group list
8:55	Of the above descriptors, which are necessary and which are nice?	Facilitator leads discussion and has items coded as either necessary or nice
9:15	BREAK	
9:30	Of the items coded as necessary, which few are most important?	Facilitator leads discussion in which members first clarify behaviors listed as necessary • Then advocate • Then each member uses sticky notes to "vote" Next, the facilitator leads a discussion in which patterns are observed and agreement reached on which items to list as most important
9:50	What resources (knowledge, skills, attitudes and energy sources) are necessary to attain the items listed as most important?	Designate three corners—members go to the corner they wish to work on: 1. Knowledge 2. Skill 3. Attitudes and energy sources Record on chart paper

cont.

10:10 Which of the resources will be most catalytic and therefore should be worked on first?	Carousel walk Facilitator-led discussion to identify which resources to work on first
10:40 Who will reflect on this information and bring a recommendation to the next meeting about how we might proceed?	Facilitator clarifies what is meant by this task Suggests table groups talk Asks for and charts names of volunteers
10:50 Summarize meeting Clarify who is to do what by when Assess the meeting	New facilitator and recorder guide this conversation and chart members' pluses and wishes about the meeting
11:00 Adjourn	

Table 6-6. Full Day Muster Meeting

Context: This is a group of about 40 people who meet 3 times a year. They have decision-making responsibilities for programs and the assignment of resources throughout the state to support instructional technology. Membership rotates so there are always new faces at a meting. Because of this, on every agenda, meeting norms and principles that guide our work are listed and referred to at the beginning of the meeting. A facilitator from outside the group manages the meetings.

MEETING AGENDA
Meeting outcome. Recommend amendments and adopt budget, adopt program outline for state board program, exchange and receive information reports.

Name of team or group: State-Level Council

Facilitator: _____ **Recorder:** _____

Other participants: _____

Starting and ending times: 8:30–3:00

Purposes: Receive, clarify, inquire, advocate, adopt

Meeting Norms

- Demonstrate Mutual Respect: Respect people and ideas. Such respect does not represent agreement.
- Employ Skillful Listening: Seek first to understand, then to be understood.
- Sufficient Consensus: Each person has an equal voice, the group works to understand all views, distinguish between dialogue and discussion, and 75% agreement of those present constitutes consensus.

Principles That Guide Our Work

- Make a commitment to collaboration and sharing of resources and work to coordinate the best solutions to common and differ needs across regions.
- Maintain a statewide perspective this is focused on student needs.
- Focus on making a difference in classrooms throughout the state.
- The council's actions shall be built upon respect, sharing, collaboration, and communication.

8:30   Organize Day
       Welcome
       Organization of Meeting
       Introductions
       Agenda
       Inclusion Activity

9:00   **Working Budget—Ms. Tappan**
       Receive recommended budget
       Respond to relate budget categories to today's agenda
       Check for understanding about processes

9:15   **Buying and Licensing Committee—Dr. Garcia**
       Receive report on committee meeting and budget recommendations
       Respond to clarify, inquire, and advocate
       Reflect to consider recommendations for later action

10:00 **BREAK**

10:15 **Information Stations—Dr. Garcia, Ms. Tappan, Ms. Roberts, Mr. Liang,
       Dr. Gordon. Ms. McCabe, Mr. Rodriguez**
       Initiate dialogue at information stations

cont.

12:00	**LUNCH**
1:00	**Budget: Adoption Phase** Receive process description Respond to check for understanding and adopt process Decide whether to treat budget as a whole or in parts Identify parts of budget for discussion Modify budget sections (if requested) Adopt by sufficient consensus
2:00	**BREAK** (Participants complete a written assessment of today's meeting before leaving)
2:15	**State Board Funds: $1.2 Million—Ms. Tappan** Receive requests from state board for administration of program for staff development and online resources Respond to clarify, inquire, advocate Act to adopt program outline
2:30	**Close Meeting** Summarize decisions Suggest topics for next meeting Confirm next meeting for Sunday evening and Monday, dates and location.
3:00	**Adjourn** Posing problems for groups to work on

Posing Problems for Groups to Work On

Much time can be saved when councils or other groups delegate tasks to subcommittees. Our experience is that 3 hours spent carefully posing the problem has saved literally hundreds of hours of committee work, eliminated false starts, and helped to keep morale and communications at healthy levels.

To delegate without clear directions, constraints, and other details often produces unsatisfactory results. Both parties feel bad, and sometimes the committee that developed the report is directed to repeat the work. It is in this type of work that clarity about decision authority must be at its most precise.

For any given situation, some of the questions in Table 6-7 will be more important than others. Decide which ones are most appropriate for a problem you are posing for a group to work on.

Table 6-7. Posing Problems for Group Resolution

Step 1. Leaders define the problem:
  (a) What is the problem or challenge?
  (b) Who is affected directly?
  (c) Who and what are affected indirectly?
  (d) What feelings may exist about the problem?
  (e) What time, personnel, and fiscal limitations apply to resolutions or resolving processes?

Step 2. Leaders develop resolution criteria:
  (a) What is the desired outcome?
  (b) What criteria must the outcome meet in order to reach a satisfactory resolution?
  (c) In what ways will the resolution contribute to organizational values or goals?
For example:
- The management team achieving and maintaining a common focus
- Employees knowing that they are cared about and can contribute to the organization's directions
- Development of five energy sources (efficacy, flexibility, craftsmanship, consciousness, and interdependence)

  (d) In what ways will the resolution procedures and processes contribute to the organization's reflection, continued learning, and systematically managed change?

Step 3. Leaders phrase the assignment for the task force or ad hoc group:
  (a) Determine the level(s) of decision-making authority the group will have.
  (b) Decide if the group is to present one resolution or three, with advantages and disadvantages for each.
  (c) Phrase the task with language such as "What might we do in order that. . ." or "In what ways might we provide the widest latitude to the task force and maximize potential for creativity?"
  (d) List the resolution criteria with language such as "In ways that increase group efficacy, sharpen the management team's focus, and do so within existing budget guidelines." This informs the group of organizational values and/or resolution restraints.

Step 4. Leaders present the assignment to the group and initiate processes for clarification and understanding of the task:
Example: This committee's task is to present to the superintendent of schools, by March 1, a recommendation regarding the issue stated below. The superintendent will take under advisement the committee's recommendation and will draft and recommend policy to the board of trustees. The board, after holding public hearings, will make a final decision at their June 8 meeting. Issue: In what ways might we develop teachers' capacity to teach for culturally proficient standards and authentically interact with families of minority cultures. The committee's recommendations must do this in ways that will:

cont.

(a) Bring us into full compliance with the law
(b) Maximize individual choice
(c) Work within the allocated budgets for professional and organizational development
(d) Contribute to collective efficacy

Chapter 7 The Confident and Skilled Facilitator

A facilitator manages processes so that a group can plan, problem-solve, share information, evaluate, and make decisions efficiently and effectively. A facilitator also works to improve group members' ability to work together effectively and helps groups to improve their processes.

Because facilitators are nondirective regarding meeting content, some misconstrue this to mean that the role is a passive one. Nothing could be further from the truth. The facilitator is the group's instrument for sound process choices that will lead to the full expression and understanding of relevant ideas and information. The facilitator supports access to the diversity of group resources, sound decision making, and problem-solving efforts.

A highly skilled facilitator is much like an accomplished dancer. One notices the dance but not the dancer. She directs process yet is supremely flexible. She follows principles, not rules. She improvises. She knows her own cognitive styles and stretches beyond them when it serves the group. She is comfortable with who she is and sets aside judgments about others. She is clear in the moment about her intentions. She thinks beyond activities to outcomes. She is reflective and learns from experience. She can direct or request, be firm or soft, serious or light, focus on task or on relationships. She has abundant knowledge about processes and groups. She is effortlessly competent with many facilitation moves.

Above all, the facilitator is an observer who helps groups to mediate tensions. Every system is influenced by demands that present mixed messages. The principal who responds to the demands of the central office can create the conditions for parents to demand a charter school. Teachers who are driven by student learning needs might work in opposition to the demands of the state assessment system. Parents and teachers look at a system through different eyes. Each day, there are different interpretations of the same data, and the stakeholders are responding from different perspectives. A facilitator serves the system by bringing the different perspectives to consciousness.

This chapter addresses the requirements for facilitators, the tasks during the various stages of facilitation, and ways to develop confidence. A special section is included on how a "citizen facilitator" solves the problem of maintaining facilitation services even in very small work groups.

Facilitation Compared to Other Leadership Roles

Facilitation is similar to but significantly different from three other leadership roles: presenting, consulting, and coaching. Groups need clear role definitions because what a role is called influences people's expectations. The most common error we've noticed is for the presenter and facilitator titles to be used interchangeably. A facilitator is not a presenter and a presenter is not a facilitator, just as a Ford is not a Honda and vice versa. In the latter case, both are vehicles. In the former, both are leadership functions with important differences.

In a professional community—an adaptive organization—leadership is shared; that is, all the participants play all the roles. All the participants must have the knowledge and skills to manage themselves and to manage others. Leadership is a shared function in meetings, in staff development activities, in research, and in projects. Recognizing what we have called the four hats of leadership (see chapter 2) and knowing when and how to change them becomes shared knowledge within the organization. When values, roles, and work relationships are clear, decisions about appropriate behavior are easy.

As described in chapter 2, four leadership functions are shared within systems of distributed leadership: facilitating, presenting, coaching, and consulting. The facilitator should rarely be the person with role or knowledge authority.

Facilitators are substantially neutral to content. We periodically witness meetings in which colleagues ask the group member who is facilitating to add to the conversation. Wanting to know this person's ideas is certainly understandable, but it is a disservice to the group to lose a content-neutral facilitator. The strategy Signal Role Change (see Appendix A) permits the facilitator to step out of the role to comment and yet protect the integrity of the role.

The Four Currents of Facilitation Management

Why facilitate? Facilitators manage four vital currents to maximize the value of meeting time: attention, energy, information, and logistics. Facilitators monitor and stimulate energy when necessary. Information flow must be clear, multidirectional, relevant, and comprehensible, and logistics for room arrangements, schedules, and announcements must also be clear.

Attention is the first current. In chapter 5 we presented five principles for developing meeting standards. The first two were to stay on one topic at a time and use only one process at a time. Facilitators use language, space, flip charts, and their bodies to focus attention on these standards.

Energy, the second current, is a primary resource of groups in accomplishing work. Productive energy is a side effect of productively charged human relationships. A facilitator's primary task is to amplify and direct emotional, cognitive, and physical energy to group goals. Facilitators manage energy through attention to three areas: (a) helping a set of individuals to work as a group, (b) engaging members in active participation, and (c) focusing group attention.

Information is the third essential current. Groups consume and construct information in order to plan, decide, solve problems, and take action. The facilitator's help in managing information is critical for several reasons. Information comes in a variety of packages: abstractions, examples, generalizations, details, thoughts, feelings, research, numbers, history, and dreams. There is typically too much data and too little time. Groups must select some data to study and others to ignore, and they must know when to look for details and when to examine themes and patterns.

The fourth current is logistics. "This is the 'ground' of group process—the most constrained and, when mastered, the most enabling flow because it frees up attention and energy for other things" (Sibbit, 2002, p. 55). This current carries the management of the meeting-room environment, equipment, materials, time allotments, schedules, and reporting procedures.

The Five Cs: The Qualities of a Good Facilitator

Facilitating a meeting is improvisational work, requiring a foundation of knowledge and skills, a clear sense of purpose, a juggler's gift of attending to everything at once, and knowing what to do when you don't know what to do. You don't have to be flashy to be a good facilitator, but you do need to be developing the five Cs: clarity, consciousness, competence, confidence, and credibility.

Clarity

Facilitators must be clear about their role, its boundaries, and its responsibilities, and they must be able to communicate this unambiguously to the groups with whom they work. They need to know to whom they are ultimately responsible. See Appendix F for the distinctions among contact, intermediate, and primary clients. Facilitators know the importance of language and strive for precision. The following list shows some examples of facilitator language:

- *To get attention.* "Look this direction."

- *To clarify purpose.* "Today's task is to ____ [approve, generate, select, identify, explore, resolve]."

- *To give directions.* "Identify some ideas you would like to explore as a team. Prepare to share your two most important ideas."

- *To encourage participation.* "Here are some suggestions for how to get the most value out of today's meeting. Be responsible for your comfort and learning. Don't wait for a break to make yourself comfortable. Be responsible as well for your learning. If you can't hear someone, say, 'Louder, please!' If someone is speaking too abstractly and you need a concrete example, please ask for it."

- *To enlarge perspective.* "Who is not in this room and can't speak for themselves on the topic? What do you imagine their concerns might be?"

- *To invite group awareness.* "How is the group doing on its norm of listening to one another? Tell your partner."

- *To foster understanding.* "Who can offer a summary paraphrase?"

- *To encourage agreements.* "Are you ready for a decision?"

Language can obscure or clarify. Precise language is a gift to the facilitator and the group. It saves time and frustration, eliminates ambiguity, conveys respect for the group, and fosters facilitator credibility. Attaining language precision can be a useful lifetime goal regardless of one's role. Strive to be organized, brief, and specific. Use words and phrases that have one meaning. Use nouns more than pronouns. Tell the group what it is to do, why or how that relates to the bigger context of its work, and the specific intention to be achieved at each stage. Use advance organizers like "There are three steps. Number 1 is . . . "

Consciousness

Facilitators are simultaneously aware of multiple events in the external environment and in their internal world. They work to hone their sensory acuity. Facilitators pick up cues that group members are engaged, socializing, fatigued, impatient, apathetic, curious, excited, or just going through the motions. Facilitators can detect nuances in voice tone and hear even when they are turned away from the group. They pay attention to breathing, room temperature, and sight lines. They shuttle from looking outward to looking inward. Facilitators maintain their own resourcefulness, take stock of their energy, notice when they might be making poor judgments, remind themselves of context, and assess their relationship with the group. The facilitator's internal focus must complement, not dominate, the external awareness.

Facilitators stay aware of multiple outcomes and contexts. Most meetings are nested inside other circumstances or initiatives. Perhaps most important, facilitators are aware of their point of view at any given time, and they press themselves to understand interactions from various perspectives. Facilitators know that success often depends on their ability to see things in new ways, gain new understandings, and produce new patterns of group interactions.

Competence

Competence is the third C. It develops with continuous learning, experience, and reflection on experience. Facilitators' competencies are grounded in a basic knowledge of effective meetings. This includes the distinction between discussion and dialogue (see chapter 4), a set of facilitation strategies (see Appendix A), and four meeting success structures (see chapter 5). Skills competencies include designing an agenda, reading a group, speaking with precision, paraphrasing, asking mediational questions, being comfortable with silence, and using a host of nonverbal strategies and skills. Competence also means realizing that a plan is only a map of the territory and having the wisdom to know when the plan is not working.

Confidence

Confidence is the fourth C. Extensive literature supports the idea that beliefs about oneself translate into actions and results. Facilitator self-confidence is a dimension of efficacy applied to the specific work of conducting meetings. As previously noted, efficacious people believe that they have knowledge and skills that, when applied to a goal, will overcome any

obstacles.

Such self-confidence derives from reflection on experiences, conversations with colleagues, and support from coaches or leaders. This chapter closes with the topic of ways to develop confidence.

No one who is beginning to facilitate is a blank slate. Each person begins the journey to increasingly effective facilitation with unique strengths and unique things to learn.

Credibility

Credibility, the fifth C, is a by-product of the other four; like permission, it is assigned to the facilitator by the group. Credibility does not live inside the facilitator; rather, it is a perception the group forms about the person. When a group believes that a facilitator is competent, confident, neutral, trustworthy, and fair, the group can say that this person is credible.

Credibility, like trust, can temporarily be lost. Being less than honest, not owning mistakes, or speaking disrespectfully about those who are not in the room will drive a wedge of discomfort between you and the group. One essential facilitator capacity is learning how to recover from mistakes. As a friend of ours says, if you step in it, know how to step out of it.

The strongest element of a recovery move is to step away from where you made the error. This strategy is called Visual Paragraph (see Appendix A). Acknowledge whatever you did that evoked discomfort. Take responsibility ("I'm sorry, I was supposed to bring that to you today, and I forgot"), apologize ("That was insensitive, please accept my apology"), self-disclose ("Did I say that?"—pointing to the space you just left), or direct some humor at yourself ("I always wanted to be skillful, now I realize I should have specified at what"). These are some unassuming ways to recover focus and direction.

Facilitation Stages

The facilitator's tasks involve not just the meeting itself but also what happens before a meeting and immediately after it. During a meeting, there are several stages with unique purposes and tools. Here we describe tips, strategies, and overarching goals for all the stages.

Before the Meeting

Talk with the group leader. Learn about the context in which the meeting is taking place. Is this part of an initiative in which the group has already worked? Will there be meetings to follow? Are other groups involved? Find out the leader's perception of the meeting goals. We've learned that you might have to be a consultant before you can be a facilitator in many situations. The meeting outcomes have often not been considered at the level of detail necessary to design an effective session. Explore the specifics. Find out if anything is happening in the group, or to the group, that could bring counterproductive energy into the meeting. Occasionally you might arrange to meet with a small planning committee or conduct a phone conference to get multiple perspectives. This is essential when you have been asked to facilitate conflict-related or problem-solving meetings. See Appendixes G and H for tips on contracting for facilitation services. Ask to see the meeting announcement; you want to know what information the participants have about the meeting.

Give instructions for room arrangement and materials (see chapter 5 for ideas on organizing the room for different purposes). Arrive at least 30 minutes early to make whatever adjustments are necessary. Get any clutter out of the room. Often there are too many tables or chairs to work effectively.

Opening the Meeting

An opening might take as little as 10 minutes or as long as 30 minutes, depending on your desired outcome, available time, group size, level of group maturity, and experience in working together. The first 3–5 minutes are critical in developing expectations, receptivity, and relationship with a group. During the opening the facilitator must get people's attention, focus their energy, acknowledge any resistance that might be present, be especially careful about pronoun use, provide for a public display of information and group memory, and clarify roles—the facilitator's, the participants', and the recorder's. Members want to know the topic, its relevance to them, if it will be worth their time (is it well organized?), and the credibility of the person facilitating. All these questions must be addressed in the first few minutes.

The following list is a typical order in which the opening activities are performed:

1. Focus attention and energy.
2. Clarify your role and receive permission.
3. Frame the work.
4. Acknowledge resistance.
5. Develop inclusion.
6. Arrange the charts.
7. Activate relevant knowledge.

Focusing Attention and Energy

Everyone knows the importance of attention, yet it is not unusual for a facilitator who is stressed or pressed for time to begin talking before attention is fully gained. This will backfire and become a cumulative problem, indicating to the group that full attention is not expected.

Grinder (2007) describes 21 nonverbal tools that people unconsciously use to enhance their speech. Since humans are influenced more by nonverbal communication than by the spoken

---

Attentive Facilitating

Carolyn silently observes the group. As she hears a dip in the volume of the small-group conversations, she says, "Please look in this direction." She stands silent and still until all eyes are on her. "You've just completed the first step in reaching a decision," she says. "Each group has listed criteria. Your next step is to code the ideas on your lists as either necessary or nice. As soon as you are finished, have a recorder from each group post the items on your necessary list on the chart in the front of the room." Carolyn asks, "Are there any questions about purpose or process?" She waits 5 seconds. "This step will take 5 minutes. Please begin."

As groups reengage, Carolyn scans to see that the work space is properly provisioned with chart pens, tape, and easel paper. She mentally rehearses the transition statement she will make when the lists are posted and decides how to structure the next step in the process.

---

word, it is necessary for facilitators to develop a nonverbal vocabulary. We have incorporated many nonverbal tools of communication in training facilitators and have had remarkable success in amplifying their effectiveness. Some of these nonverbal tools (see Appendix A) are the following:

- Attention First
- Break and Breathe
- Choose Voice
- Closing the Window
- Decontaminate Problem Space
- Finger Minutes
- Freeze Body
- Freeze Gesture
- Show, Don't Say
- Signal Role Change
- Third Point
- Visual Paragraph

*Clarifying Your Role
and Receiving Permission*

Don't assume that everyone knows what to expect of you. Take time now to specify that your role is to guide the process and stay neutral to the content. Encourage the group members to tell you if they think that you are stepping out of role. Have them direct you about the type of facilitation they desire: tightly directed by you or with greater allowance made for the group to guide the process. Facilitation is essential to maintain focus, efficiency, and energy as well as to conserve time and achieve results.

Groups allow themselves to be facilitated. If it has not given its tacit permission, a group will resist or subvert the facilitator's efforts to serve it. A group grants psychological permission to the facilitator to manage the meeting process and to place issues before the group to consider. These might be recommendations for ways of approaching a topic, directing perspectives to larger contexts, or intervening with the group to improve its effectiveness.

Permission is based on a number of intangibles. Among these are a perception of confidence, trust, and a belief that the facilitator can remain neutral and nonjudgmental. Confidence and credibility are perceived by congruent language—that is, the body says what the words describe. Confident facilitators breathe from the abdomen. Facilitators whose breathing is high and shallow signal their own discomfort, which affects the group's sense of ease. Wellman and Lipton (2004) describe a permission-getting process that signals responsiveness and permits the group to provide direction to the facilitation services:

> One approach to empowering a working group, whether it is at a novice level of performance as a group or at a more expert level, is to negotiate your stance as a facilitator. Stances may vary from hard to soft facilitation. An effective way to offer these options is to describe a physical continuum organized by metaphors, then ask group members to point to the spot on the continuum they believe will be most effective for that session. Some metaphors that we have used include facilitation stances that range from Rambo to Mr. Rogers; from Xena the Warrior Princess to Mary Poppins; or from a lion to a lamb. Presenting choices helps the group to gain or regain the power to control its own direction and purposes. This is especially true if individual group members are dominating the group's time and energies. Such a group will tend to select harder forms of facilitation and facilitator permission to intervene with problematic situations. (p. 15)

Framing the Work

As a noun, *frame* marks the boundaries within which an entire picture is displayed. As a verb, *frame* means to create a mental structure, or frame, through which people interpret or make sense of a situation. Facilitators frame tasks to set a tone for participation and productivity—to describe the purposes of the work, how it relates to a larger context, and how it benefits participant interests.

Groups perform at their best when they have clearly defined outcomes. You might start with an artfully vague statement such as "Today you will explore ways to save the after-school program." Broad outcomes maintain momentum because people relate to the intent and don't get bogged down by the details. Later, after framing and an inclusion activity, you should be more specific: "The purpose today is to identify what resources we could make available for the program. You will recommend some to consider. Next you will assess the costs to other school programs and, based on that, make a go or no-go recommendation on continuing the after-school activities." Working outcomes employ a verb that specifies what action is to be taken, such as *decide, recommend, inform, assess, explore, advocate, inquire,* or *identify.*

Acknowledging Resistance

Some of the people, some of the time, will want to resist, oppose, refrain from participation, or push back against proposals, programs, ideas, and even being in a meeting. Keep in mind that their resistance is just a way of taking care of themselves and is not about you. The resistance often has nothing to do with the meeting. One of the authors met with a group of principals and sensed apathy and fatigue. He asked what was going on. He learned that this was the fourth day that week that the principals had been out of their buildings. In addition, they had delivered reductions-in-force notices the day before. Given these circumstances, the proposed agenda made little sense, and as the group modified its task, energy returned to the room.

To resist resistance is futile. One cannot be reasoned out of resentment, hurt, anger, betrayal, blame, or discouragement, the typical sources of resistance. Only if you acknowledge the validity of the perceptions and feelings (which is different from agreeing with them) will the group have the choice to set them aside.

Here we identify three approaches to work with resistance. Each is a form of reframing. If resistance is present or anticipated, it must be addressed immediately at the start of a meeting.

The three approaches are as follows:

- Pace and lead. The facilitator acknowledges (by pacing) the legitimacy of feelings a group is having, then suggests the temporary suspension of those feelings in order to make the best use of this time.

- Use strategies that acknowledge the resistance as natural and that generate humor, such as Banned Words (see Appendix A).

- Choreograph an opening (Zoller, 2005). Imagine you are conducting a before-school meeting with teachers. They are attending because it is a workday at the beginning of the school year. Last year scores went up across the district. They were promised a classroom day, but the district office decided to send you to work with them instead. In choreographing an opening, the facilitator could describe the resistance in respectful terms and suggest that there are higher interests and benefits to come from the meeting.

Language precision is important. The resistance must be stated in vague terms so that people can identity with it. Table 7-1 offers language forms with which you can modulate the resistance description, using stems like *all of you*, *some of you*, or *a few of you*.

Table 7-1 Anticipating Resistance: Choreographing An Opening

Verbal	Nonverbal
Thank you for coming this morning.	Direct eye contact with group. A mix of credible and approachable voice with an open, palms-up gesture.
As if you had a choice!	Pause with the hands vertical. Stand still and wait for a laugh.
On the agenda are four topics.	Look at the agenda, use a credible voice, pause after each topic. With the last topic stated, turn to the group, freeze body, and count internally, 3-2-1.
Before we get started	Silently walk a few feet from the easel (facilitation space)
I imagine a number of you would rather be prepping your classrooms today and are disappointed that this has turned out to be a work day instead of a classroom day as promised.	Gesture outside toward the classrooms. Pause periodically. Use a credible voice. At the end, stand still, pause, and silently count 3-2-1. Then move halfway back to the easel.
There is good reason to want to be in classrooms, it is where our passion lies, supporting students.	Approachable voice. Palm-up gesturing to group. Inclusive language ("our").

cont.

As you know, there is the passionate part you have for your students' well being. You may be wondering how much information do I need to determine if would really serve my students. How long would you be willing to listen to determine if the information is useful. What would it take to see how useful the information might be?	Take a few steps toward the front center of the group. Approachable voice. Gestures of inclusion, palms up. Use downward beat gestures to accompany the words of your message like a maestro directing an orchestra. (passionate – part – of you – students). Pause, stand still, silently count 3-2-1 . . .
And out first agenda item is . . .	Turn and walk toward easel, point to first agenda item using a new voice pattern, pace, state the first agenda item.

Developing Inclusion

The first four opening activities—focusing attention, clarifying your role, framing the work, and acknowledging resistance—can take very little time. These tasks do not have to be done as separate entities but can be blended.

Developing inclusion, the fifth opening activity, can also be blended with the first four; for instance, it could be used in acknowledging resistance.

People always come to meetings from somewhere else—geographically, emotionally, and cognitively. Therefore, it is essential that you provide experiences that help them to make a transition into the new space and group. Plan for either full-group or subgroup inclusion activities. Full-group activities set norms, focus attention inside the room, generate energy, and help people to answer the question of who they are in relation to the group. They begin the process of moving from me-ness to we-ness. Subgroup activities also set a norm of active engagement and focus attention on the content of the meeting's work. Full-group strategies that accomplish these goals are Like Me, Grounding, First Job, Check In, and, to a degree, Corners (Appendix A). Grounding is particularly useful for groups that are experiencing conflict or that are talking about a topic that is hard to discuss.

With all strategies, it is desirable to name the purposes of the activity. This is especially so at the beginning of a session, when, if you are not already known, you are still establishing your relationship with the group.

Arranging the Charts

Visuals are indispensable for focusing attention. Most of our sensory information comes through the eyes. One major value of charts over images on a screen is their potential for permanence. People know that a screen image will disappear and therefore experience a muscular tension they don't have when looking at a chart. On a chart, information stays visible throughout the meeting, allowing the participants to know where they are on the agenda and the facilitator to refocus them on goals or norms. Charts are especially valuable if information is being presented that makes members uncomfortable.

A facilitator can use the strategy Third Point to direct attention to the data and away from him- or herself, providing a separation between the message and the messenger (Appendix A).

Color-code preprinted agendas or other data that has been prepared in advance. Use red for headlines; brown, blue, and green for text; and yellow and black for organizing or graphics. Always print in block letters, never in cursive—and, despite what some books advise, never use all caps. Any elementary teacher will tell you that printed upper- and lowercase block letters are the most readable.

Color coding is not advisable when you are recording during a meeting, because it can slow the flow of talk. Graphics aid memory and communicate complex concepts metaphorically. *ChartArt* (Buckley, 2002) is a series of images that can be traced onto a chart; they are considered useful by both experienced and novice facilitators. Buckley (2005) describes how to work with charts and graphics.

Activating Relevant Knowledge

Just as teachers engage students by helping them to elicit prior knowledge, the facilitator does this to generate energy and activate information that is relevant to the group's task. Doing it at the beginning of a meeting and each time new topics are introduced has multiple benefits. First, particularly at the beginning of a meeting, a norm for engagement is reinforced. It energizes the group members as they work and frees the facilitator to observe the group. Second, the relevant knowledge that is activated is instrumental in accelerating the pace of the meeting, for it brings information into play that is necessary to work on a topic. Sometimes this information is as simple as remembering what happened at the last meeting. Many meetings take unnecessary time getting started because group members do not recall what happened in earlier sessions.

Third, eliciting prior knowledge levels the perceived playing field within the group. This is especially true with mixed-role groups when the activity is preceded by a quick writing activity so that each group members has something to contribute. Finally, any initial task has to be structured so that group member feel psychologically safe, confident that they will not be demeaned, attacked, or ridiculed. The Sort Cards strategy serves this purpose nicely (Appendix A). Members privately respond to a prompt on 3×5 cards, then they display and organize the cards according to criteria that they invent.

Other strategies that activate relevant information while maintaining psychological safety are Paired Verbal Fluency; Know, Think You Know, Want to Know; Four-Box Synectics; Card Stack and Shuffle; and Give One to Get One (see Appendix A). Keep in mind that members must always feel safe but, as the meeting progresses, not necessarily comfortable. Discomfort is often a doorway to learning.

Engaging the Participants

After the opening comes the "show." This stage will engage group members in the first agenda item.

Meeting work is cyclical. The same functions—generating, organizing, and analyzing—can repeat, and complex strategies often have embedded in them several smaller ones. Focusing attention will be repeated many times throughout a session, along with framing the work and activating relevant knowledge. In addition, the following activities are involved: (a) giving directions, (b) offering guidelines, advice, and suggestions, and (c) leading the process.

Giving Directions

Precise directions conserve time and energy. As we will see later, personal pronouns can be problematic with this function and others. By saying things like "Here's what I want you to do next" or "Listen carefully to me as I describe this process," a facilitator conveys the idea that the group is serving him or her rather than the group's goals. Instead, use phrases such as "Your next steps are . . . " or "This process has three stages . . . "

These forms maintain focus on the group and on the task rather than on the facilitator. Directions, like framing statements, can be scripted. Charts and slides that hold directions visually aid retention. In the case of particularly difficult tasks, they focus participants' attention on the process-task interaction—which is where it is supposed to be—rather than on the person guiding the work.

Adopt a "what, why, how" pattern as a facilitation mantra. Even the most cautious or resistant group will be willing to participate when it knows the rationale for the work. Tell *what* the topic or task is, explain *why* it is important to the group, and describe *how* the group will work (i.e., give directions). The order can vary. Below is an example.

What. "Your next task is to determine what forces are in favor of the program's success and what forces oppose it. The strategy you will use is called Force-Field Analysis (Appendix A)."

Why. This concerns the benefits of this process. "A reason for using Force-Field Analysis is that you don't want to miss any significant factors. Each of you will be able to see the forces for and against, as people think of them, which has the effect of stimulating more ideas from the group. You don't have to explain or defend your ideas. This step is in the spirit of brainstorming, in which you want to get as many ideas as possible."

How. "You will work in small groups and use a strategy called Force-Field Analysis." The following procedure may be suggested:

- Table groups should choose a recorder.

- Members should brainstorm about the forces that are working in their favor to accomplish the goal. The recorder will chart the ideas on the left column of a T-chart.

- During brainstorming, members should look for perspectives that have not been used; for example, what would a student or a parent perceive?

- Then the group should brainstorm forces that are working against the goal happening. The recorder will chart the ideas in the left column.

Language matters. A facilitator's language choices will greatly influence success in giving directions as well as in offering guidelines and leading the process.

An often-overlooked yet powerful attribute of clear directions is pronoun use. Pronouns are substitutes for names. They label the speaker's place in any relationship and convey expectations of that relationship, such as compliance, affection, and whose group it really is. When a facilitator named Sarah says, "Please give me your attention," she might as well have been saying, "Please give Sarah, not somebody else in the group, your attention." One of the authors once heard a principal in a meeting refer to "our work this year," to which a teacher muttered, "No, it's not 'our work'; she's going back to the office, and we're going to be doing it." On another occasion a superintendent new to the job thanked one of us for coming to the district to work with "his people."

Who you are by position and relation to the group should influence your choice of pronouns. If you are a group member who has stepped up to facilitate a session, the work very well might be "ours." If you are external to the group in any way, referring to the work as "ours" can generate inferences that actually interfere with the group's work and/or its development.

It is usually wise to carefully plan and

script your comments. For an upcoming facilitation session, consider whether it is "our work today," "your work today," or "the work today." For work that is emotionally charged in any way, it is usually safest to apply the most pronoun-neutral forms and talk about "the work," "this task," "the data," or "the outcome." Neutral forms, which use articles and pronouns such as *the* and *this,* depersonalize the task and make it psychologically safer for group members to engage with the issue and not the person before them.

The neutral-pronoun pattern can be supported by the ue of charts and visuals that hold important technical, and perhaps emotionally laden, information off to the side (Grinder, 2007). This approach removes the emotion of the message from the facilitator, guiding the group's emotional energy to the information rather than toward the facilitator. Be sure to keep your eyes on the chart as you use neutral pronouns. If you revert to making eye contact with group members while framing difficult tasks, you run the risk of repersonalizing the task and drawing the emotional energy to the messenger rather than leaving it with the message.

Offering Guidelines, Advice, and Suggestions

When facilitators become fluent with the process tools the group is using, they are able to anticipate bottlenecks and common points of confusion. At these points, they succinctly propose targeted procedural tips and offer additional technical resources to move the group ahead. Again, these are situations in which careful pronoun choice can be important to the group's productivity. Given the wisdom of prior experience and an implicit desire for credibility with the group, you might be tempted to say things like "Here's what I've found with other groups at this point in the process . . . " or "In my experience the best thing to do is . . . " Such

phrasing has the effect of personalizing the advice or suggestions that follow.

The alternate approach is to drop the personal pronoun and cultivate a repertoire of phrases such as "Groups typically get stuck here and need to . . . " and "At points like this, productive groups tend to . . . " These more pronoun-neutral forms frame the notion of expertise as a capacity of some ideal group, not as a "gift" from this particular facilitator. In all facilitator functions, the intention must be to place the spotlight on the group, its development, and its task accomplishment—not on the facilitator.

Leading the Process

Facilitators facilitate—that is, they make work easier. Your awareness of the group combines with your repertoire of facilitation skills and knowledge to serve you as you maintain a neutral stance and guide the group through strategies and transitions.

Very small groups cannot afford the luxury of having one person stay in a neutral facilitation role, yet facilitation can still be present. We will discuss the concept of a citizen facilitator shortly.

Transitioning

We've explored opening a meeting and engaging the group with a topic on the agenda. Now, when the group members are ready to move to the next topic, to shift the focus from working to reflecting, or to take a break, a transition activity is needed.

A transition is a process of change from one state to another. Managing the shifts between activities or topics or between content and breaks is part of the art of facilitation. Without any warning, momentum can be broken. Group members can be so invested in the current activity that they feel resentment if the activity is suddenly broken off (Sibbit, 2002). Near the end of a process, help the group to anticipate a transition by announcing that you are beginning to move toward closure or are turning to a different stage in the process. Give people time warnings when they are engaged in self-managing activities. The strategy Yellow Light serves as a warning (Appendix A). Another strategy is to move quietly around the group and indicate the remaining time. A timer on the screen will also let people track the time for themselves.

If the topic is about a major issue the group is facing, use the 7-11 Conversation strategy, in which members mill about the room sharing what they would say to a colleague if they met in a convenience store over the weekend. Listen to some of the summaries—people will be surprised that they are reporting different things—and take care to help all the people leave with the same message. Closing the Window is a nonverbal strategy that signals that a full-group conversation is about to end. This often brings out those who have something to say before the time is up.

Because the group has not internalized the agenda sequence as you have, reminders about where they are now in relationship to the full agenda can be useful. Some form of transition is also useful to signal a shift in activity ("OK, that's it for brainstorming, the next stage is clarification"), pace ("The pace is going to slow down to open an opportunity for reflection"), and level ("Now the task moves from naming assumptions to exploring what inferences they might lead to").

Use transitions to have participants organize and integrate the work just completed when the ideas have to be carried to a next stage of thinking or when the content should be remembered for a future meeting. Some strategies (see Appendix A) that accomplish this are Journal, Most Important Point, Partners Report, Matchbook Definitions, Paraphrase Passport,

and Round-Robin Reflection. Strategies that engage the full group are Walk About and Stir the Classroom. Sound and Motion Symphony brings physical expression to the integration of information.

Closing the Meeting

After the meeting is opened, the stages of engaging and transitioning will occur several times, on most agendas. At the conclusion of the work, the group is ready to close the meeting.

High on the list of frustrations that people express to us is the feeling that at the end of a meeting, nothing was accomplished. A proper closing will eliminate this complaint. The following tasks should be accomplished at this stage:

1. Clarifying who does what by when

2. Testing commitments

3. Arranging for communications

4. Assessing the meeting

5. Arranging for the next meeting (date and facilitator)

Clarifying Who Does What by When

In the heat of conversations, the actionable part of decisions is often overlooked. Left overlooked, it is the cause of confusion, incomplete follow-up, and poor morale. The facilitator is responsible for seeing that this question is asked: Who is to do what by when? If no one else asks, the facilitator must. Names of the responsible parties should be recorded on charts and made part of the meeting minutes.

Testing Commitments

Everyone is busy. In the enthusiasm of the moment, some people overcommit. "I know you would never do this," the facilitator might say with a smile, "but under what conditions might you be tempted to violate these agreements?" Although it could be fairly easy—perhaps to go along with the group—to agree to a course of action during a meeting, real pressures can evolve later when one must choose between conflicting commitments. The facilitator's question brings an awareness of the realities and tensions associated with commitments. When these realities and tensions are articulated, the group has an opportunity to explore strategies that can overcome any barriers to the agreements.

Arranging for Communications

"What we have here is a failure to communicate" is a line from the movie *Cool Hand Luke*. When people are surveyed about the problems in their organizations, one of the top items mentioned is poor communication. Because work life is so hectic and individuals have interests and responsibilities in so many areas, it is critical to have a communication plan before people leave the meeting.

For leaders, as we've noted before, it is desirable to have a meeting summary in group members' hands within 24 hours. This signals that the group's work is important. Some facilitators and group leaders reserve 30 minutes after the meeting to develop a summary draft from the notes on the charts.

Other forms of after-meeting communication include scheduling reports at other meetings, e-mailing summaries to the entire staff, posting minutes in the staff room, or having each member speak to a few colleagues about what transpired.

Assessing the Meeting

Any group too busy to reflect on its work is too busy to improve. Taking a small amount of time at the end of each meeting to fill out a

meeting survey is a responsible form of professional development. Group members take 3–4 minutes at the end of a meeting to anonymously answer written questions about the group's effectiveness during the meeting. The data are collated by the facilitator or group leader and brought back to the group at the next meeting, with frequency distributions for each item. Small groups look at the data and then engage in a full-group discussion around the question "Given what we said about ourselves last time, what do we want to work on today?" This is a remarkably effective way to elicit concerns and rapidly improve group functioning (Appendix L).

Arranging for the Next Meeting

Many groups rotate the facilitation role so that all the members have a chance to develop strength and an understanding of meeting dynamics. This is the time to select the next facilitator and, ideally, arrange for this person to work with the group leader to design the next agenda.

The Role of the Citizen Facilitator in Small Groups

How can small groups, such as those with only three or four members, retain facilitation functions even without a designated facilitator who stays outside the conversation?

McLaughlin and Talbert (2006) describe how an elementary school using shared leadership for data-based inquiry redesigned staff meetings so that the teachers, rather than the principal, facilitated discussions on decision making, professional development, and the cycle of inquiry. Grade-level teams had full-day instructional meetings and would deliberate during common preparation times or at lunch. As such practices become more common, the need is emerging for small groups to view facilitation as a function rather than a person.

Three conditions are necessary for small-group collaboration in schools: (a) administrator clarity about the intention of working collaboratively, (b) understanding of group members' roles and responsibilities, and (c) the role of a citizen facilitator.

One of the authors recently worked with an elementary school in which grade-level teams met 1 hour a week to focus on instructional improvement. In each team, one teacher was designated to be the facilitator. Each team's charge was to set annual grade-level goals, develop units, plan lessons, and assess student work results. Yet by midyear, the teams were struggling. Many teachers were frustrated. Some teams had developed three goals for the year; some had none; some had just one. They were good people, smart teachers with time and resources, yet they were floundering.

The school in this example began its collaborative work without clear intentions. Of course, student improvement is a goal, but how does collaborative work help the group to achieve this? The school leadership established structures, roles, times for the group to collaborate, and a menu of tasks on which to work. These are valuable resources to help meet goals, but none answers the questions of what to do first; how much time to spend developing, implementing, or assessing goals; or where to focus group members' energy.

An administrator could provide the teams with an agenda of tasks and processes that would answer these questions, save time, achieve a faster focus, and help teams work more expediently, but giving people a prescription for work violates the very essence of collaboration, which is productive invention.

In conversations with facilitators, other administrators, and one of the authors, the principal began to articulate her intention in having groups work together to make systematic inquiries into the relationship between teaching and student learning.

In a sense, this is job-embedded professional development that supports continuing cycles of improvement in which the constant focus of conversations is student work and learning events. This intention is broad yet focused enough to inform facilitator and team decisions about how and where to focus energy.

A citizen facilitator, who may be designated for any amount of time (i.e., from one meeting to one semester to the life of the group), has three responsibilities:

- To serve as a two-way conduit between the team and the principal, informing the team of the principal's priorities and requests, and informing the principal of the group's ideas and recommendations.

- To serve as professional developer to the group—providing foundation knowledge about group processes, an awareness of the distinction between dialogue and discussion, and the tools for conversing, planning, and problem solving.

- To be the person in the group who maintains a macroperspective, using "helicopter" viewing to anticipate and assess when members are stuck or fatigued, and to be the person who initiates the processes to get energy and information flowing again.

Rather than having a neutral facilitator, the intention in citizen-facilitated meetings is to have facilitated conversations. If the designated facilitator will be an active voice within the room, then the group itself must take on the knowledge and skills base of the facilitator. It is imperative that group members acquire this knowledge, for in a small group led by a citizen facilitator, group members will want to suggest approaches to the group's work, take on charting responsibilities, or remind the group to get on task.

The following is a list of duties performed by a citizen facilitator:

- Develops the agenda either before the meeting or with the group
- Opens the meeting
- Achieves role clarification so that members can periodically and informally rise to facilitate or record
- Describes the task as a product—what the group will see or hear when done
- Calls on others to start the conversation
- Engages in conversation as appropriate
- Protects processes, especially one topic and one process at a time
- Watches for and initiates transitions
- Asks who will do what by when
- Calls for meeting assessment
- Closes meeting

Developing Confidence as a Facilitator

For citizen facilitators to be successful, it is often necessary to help group members increase their confidence in taking on the facilitation role.

At a preschool we visited, the teachers were showing videos of their "graduates" moving on to kindergarten. In each video, a teacher was interviewing a child. We watched as one 4-year-old answered the question "Who do you want to be when you grow up?" Without hesitation he answered, "I don't want to be anybody, I already am somebody." The audience laughed appreciatively.

You too are already somebody and have competencies and confidence in many areas. You can increase your confidence in the facilitator role just as you have done in other roles. However, because there are fewer opportunities to facilitate than to teach, you must invent ways to increase your skills. Gather information about conducting meetings. Isolate and overpractice essential skills like paraphrasing, pausing, probing, and inquiring. Use these anywhere and everywhere. The more you practice, the sooner these skills will move to a level of unconscious competence, so that you don't need to think about them anymore when you are facilitating.

Isolate and practice other skills as well. Listen to a group when your back is turned to them and record what you hear on a chart. Observe the group with diffused vision to get a sense of the group as a unit, to monitor breathing, and to assess energy levels. Select a small group of strategies from Appendix A and use them repeatedly until you are comfortable with them. If you are a teacher, most of the strategies can be used in the classroom.

The difference between experts and novices is that experts practice skills in large "chunks," whereas novices practice skills in separate units. For example, the Attention First strategy involves several elements: space, body, gesture, voice, and language choices. Experts, because they have overpracticed and internalized, can integrate the practice of these as one unit, freeing the conscious mind to attend to other things.

Practice in classrooms, in shopping malls, in conversations, in any settings in which you are interacting with other people. Of all the verbal skills, paraphrasing is the one to overpractice most. Use it when you need it least, then you will have this skill available when you need it.

Examine your own physiology of confidence. When you are confident, you hold your body in a certain way, your breathing is different from when you are not sure of yourself, and your voice takes on a certain tone or rhythm. When the body assumes a posture, the heart and the mind follow. You can, as it is said, fake it until you make it, at least for a while. Listen to your body tell you when confidence has left and has to be regained. Muscle tension, shoulders tightened and raised in the startle effect, and changes in voice quality are all signals of this.

Hold an object such as a pencil in your hand. For some reason, that helps many people to stay grounded. Focus on the group, not yourself. Focusing on yourself is a sure ticket to discomfort. Know that mistakes are your teacher.

Enlarge your repertoire. Pay attention to others' facilitation styles and language. Jot down phrases they use. Isolate certain language forms to practice. Jot down in advance any phrases you would like to incorporate into your next facilitation. Practice facilitation phrases when you are working with students. Keep in mind that knowing is different from understanding.

Seek vicarious experiences. It's been demonstrated that one way to personal efficacy is to watch someone who performs well (Goddard, et al., 2004) Talk with such people; explore their reasons for certain moves. Ask them to offer you ideas, suggestions, and support.

Skills Modeled [handwritten annotation in left margin]

The Seven Habits of Ineffective Facilitators

As you continue to develop your skills and confidence as a facilitator, watch out for the following errors, which are frequently made by novices:

1. *Inappropriate use of space*: staying rooted in one place; bouncing around the room; not establishing clear anchored space for input, direction giving, question answering, or attention moves.

2. *Identity confusion*: becoming a "parent" by wanting to protect or nurture the group; falling into the trap of expertise and being a magnet, not a mirror; being a "friend," for whom the highest priority is protecting the relationship and not pressing the group for excellence. Whatever identity you assume establishes a complementary role for the group members. If you play the parent, group members play the children.

3. *Wrong tone of voice*: using credible or approachable voices for the wrong purposes. An inappropriate voice tone confuses group members, and you lose believability and control.

4. *Skewed talk ratio*: too much facilitator talk compared to group-member talk. Keep in mind that whoever is doing the talking is doing the thinking.

5. *Lack of relevant interaction*: due to limited planning, lack of outcome clarity, or lack of repertoire.

6. *Inappropriate degree of structure*: too tight or too loose.

7. *Inappropriate paraphrasing*: wrong voice tone; too long; too frequent; not frequent enough; wrong pronoun.

Conclusion

Stakeholders respond from different perspectives. A facilitator serves the system by bringing consciousness about the different perspectives. As we work to depart from unproductive school cultures, the facilitation role takes on even more value than it did in the past. It remains as but one of four leadership roles played by all players in collaborative organizations, yet it might still be the one least occupied by teachers and classified staff. This is rapidly changing. Efficacious and craftsmanlike groups see their groups not as they are but as they might become. As we shall see in the next chapter, both design and facilitation play important roles in developing groups.

Everyone can improve
able + intellect

Chapter 8   Developing Groups

All groups are unique. Like their individual members, they have histories, personalities, norms, and aspirations. Groups develop when leaders and individuals within the group recognize and productively test the boundaries between group members and purposefully explore the boundaries between the group and its environment. As such, groups are adaptive when they actively engage with their larger contexts in a two-way interchange of energy, information, and ideas. Groups are also complex dynamical systems that embody the five principles elaborated on at the beginning of this book:

1. More data do not lead to better predictions.
2. Everything influences everything else.
3. Tiny events create major disturbances.
4. You don't have to touch everyone to make a difference.
5. Both things and energy matter.

Adaptive leaders of both large and small groups—no matter what their formal role in the organization—realize that developing a group is an ongoing, third agenda in their work. Groups that are stuck attend to the first agenda only, getting work done. Groups that are beginning to move also pay attention to a second agenda, enhancing group learning processes.

All groups, however, work at less than full potential. The best groups regard this not as a deficiency but as a healthy dissatisfaction with their current performance. They consistently commit their resources to working together more effectively. This is the way that research teams become better at researching, that basketball teams win more games, and that theater casts improve from performance to performance. All groups become better at their tasks when they reflect on their work, acquire new knowledge and skills, and practice the fundamentals of their craft. Any group that is too busy to reflect on its work is too busy to improve.

To help groups become more effective, policy makers and leaders often focus attention and effort on things: money, staff, curriculum, facilities, time, and materials. Investments in energy must also occur, by increasing knowledge and skills, which are clearly significant resources. Perhaps less obvious is the importance of paying attention to other types of energy resources that are less visible and harder to quantify: staff morale, core values, and a sense of mission. Adaptive groups also work on developing five energy sources for sustained high performance: efficacy, consciousness, craftsmanship, flexibility, and interdependence. We maintain that the greatest and most long-lasting effects of developmental efforts come from enhancing these five states of mind (Costa & Garmson, 2002).

Deep to Surface Structure

Figure 8-1 depicts the relationship between the surface structure of group members'

our paradigm impacts how we see the world

words and actions and the underlying factors that inform and shape them. This personal and collective "sense of self" defines who we are, who we think we are, and who we hope to be at any given moment. Neuroscientist Antonio Damasio (1999) describes these issues of identity in terms of simple and more complex forms of consciousness. Simple, or core, consciousness offers group members a sense of self in the present time and place. Extended consciousness shifts the temporal boundaries, reaching into the past and projecting members into an imagined future.

By shining the light of consciousness on the essential inner structures, skillful group developers help their groups to recognize the underlying mental models that might be limiting perspectives and possibilities. Some groups get stuck in beliefs such as "We work hard, therefore we are successful," "These kids can't learn because of their home environments," or "We value our autonomy and don't need to coordinate our efforts with others." A group developer's ability to paraphrase and inquire (see chapter 3) is an essential capacity for helping groups to open up their belief systems and ex-

Figure 8-1. Moving from Deep to Surface Structure

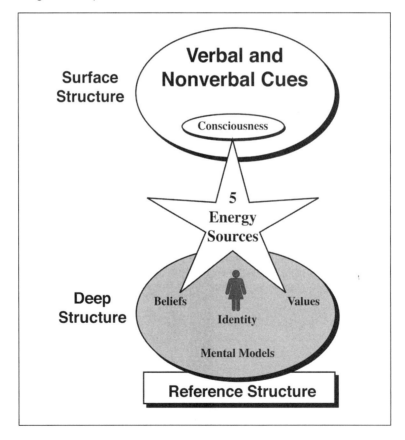

plore the positive and negative consequences of these mental models.

Reference Stucture

The deep structure rests on a foundation of reference experiences that individually and collectively inform mental models, beliefs, values, and identities. The reference structure houses initial experiences, which are stored in the kinesthetic, auditory, visual, olfactory, and gustatory systems through which they were transmitted. Individuals perceive and store data according to personal predispositions for assimilating data from different modalities and cognitive styles. These storage and interpretive processes begin before speech develops. A baby who is breastfed on demand, for example, records experiences and derives meanings about life from this early connection with his or her mother. A divisive teachers' strike and its aftermath affect emotional responses for many years—long after the school board members and the administrative teams have left or retired. These reference-structure experiences shape future interactions among the teachers, new administrators, and school boards.

Deep Structure

Mediating group members' thinking about energy sources is the conduit and catalyst for exposing and engaging the deep-structure elements that both constrain and energize the group's possible insights and actions. This deep structure holds personal and collective beliefs, values, identities, and mental models. It is here that the "rules" for how the world works or is supposed to work are encoded. Some of these meanings are held consciously, and some are outside conscious awareness, yet all inform and direct the choices and behaviors of the individuals and the group. Responses to change initiatives, problem-solving models, and the criteria

for effective solutions are all rooted in the deep structure of the group.

The actual workings and influences of the deep-structure elements are not always apparent to group members. Discrepancies between espoused beliefs and actions are in many cases the unconscious sources of tensions among group members or between the group and those it interacts with or serves. Schools that champion success for all and attempt to develop inclusive cultures can undermine their efforts with awards programs that recognize only a few high achievers. This is true for both student and teacher awards programs.

Surface Structure

The surface structure is the body of behavioral and linguistic expressions that are available to an individual or a group from the deep structure. This is literally what people say and do. These grammatical expressions are often incomplete; they reveal some meaning and values from the deep structure. Language is the medium for accessing and mediating deep-structure content.

Kegan and Lahey (2001) propose that work settings are language communities and that group leaders are leading language communities: "[Al]though every person, in any setting, has some opportunity to influence the nature of language, leaders have exponentially greater access and opportunity to shape, alter, or ratify the existing language rules" (p. 8). By attending to the verbal and nonverbal communication cues of group members, skilled group leaders frame their own communication patterns to positively influence the perceptions, choices, and decisions of their groups.

With this responsibility in mind, we offer Figure 8-1 as a lens through which to observe, assess, and frame interventions to help groups develop. Later in this chapter we will elaborate on the five energy sources and ways to assess and target interventions.

The Premises of Group Development

There are six basic premises of group development; these are described below.

Each Group Is Unique

History, cognitive styles, setting, mental models, and tasks all contribute to developing a group personality. Each group is not only unlike other groups, it is also different from the sum of its individuals. For example, a group might be composed of efficacious individuals who nevertheless believe that collectively they have little chance of making a difference.

Some Groups Mature

Some groups will mature along a continuum from novice to expert performance. Not all groups make this journey, just as not all teachers achieve a state of expertise. David Berliner (cited in Calderhead, 1996) speculates that the novice stage in teaching usually lasts for the first year and that most teachers reach the third stage (competence) within 3 or 4 years. Only a modest percentage of teachers moves to the next stage of proficiency, and an even smaller percentage, says Berliner, achieves the expert stage.

We believe that much the same is true for group development. Sternberg and Horvath (1995) note that expert teachers differ cognitively from novice teachers in terms of knowledge, efficiency, and insight in the following ways. Expert groups, like expert teachers:

- Have more knowledge
- Organize knowledge more thoroughly
- Integrate knowledge more thoroughly

- Have planning structures that are more complex and interconnected
- Have practical knowledge of the social and political context in which their work occurs
- Are able to solve problems more efficiently within their domain of expertise
- Can do more in less time with less effort
- Have automated well-learned skills
- Plan, monitor, and revise their approach to problems more effectively
- Use applicable cognitive processes with greater speed and accuracy
- Use think-aloud protocols that are richer and more interpretive
- Use higher order executive processes more effectively to plan, monitor, and evaluate ongoing efforts at problem solving
- Spend more time trying to understand a problem than trying out different solutions
- Are more likely to monitor their solution attempts
- Are more playful in their approach to problems
- Are more likely to be reflective and continuously learn through experience
- Use new problems as opportunities to expand their knowledge and competence
- Reinvest cognitive resources in the progressive construction of more nearly adequate problem models
- Are more likely to arrive at creative solutions to problems
- Reach ingenious and insightful solutions that do not occur to others
- Do better at distinguishing relevant data from nonrelevant data in problem solving
- Combine information in ways that are use-

ful for problem solving

- Apply information acquired in other contexts to the problems at hand

Attrition Does Not Have to Block Development

The disruptive effects of attrition on group dynamics can be minimized and in many cases overcome. Groups that emphasize developing group-member capabilities and norms of collaboration informally provide induction experiences for new members (see chapter 3).

Soft Variables Affect Performance and Performance Capacity

"Soft" variables, such as the collective energies of efficacy, interdependence, consciousness, craftsmanship, and flexibility, not only influence the performance of a group but also influence the group's ability to learn from its experience (Hennessy, 1998).

Learning Organizes Itself at Hierarchical Levels

Learning occurs through different mechanisms at the levels of environment, behaviors, capabilities, beliefs, identity, and mission. This learning is "nested," which means that interventions at some levels influence learning at other levels. The greatest benefits of group development efforts come from strategically intervening in these nested levels of learning. We describe interventions at the various levels later in this chapter.

Maturity Manifests in Six Domains

Group maturity manifests in the ways that a group manages its day-to-day work in order to deal with its external environment. How well it performs in six interacting domains, which are

described in the next section, will determine the group's achievement. Successful performance in each domain requires the energy sources of high performance and the application of domain-specific knowledge, skills, and structures. Each of the chapters in this book highlights the resources for developing these domains.

The Six Domains of Group Development

The six domains of group development are (a) getting work done, (b) doing the right work, (c) working collaboratively, (d) managing systems, (e) developing the group, and (f) adapting to change.

All groups struggle to achieve a successful balance between managing and adapting to external relationships and maintaining harmonious and effective internal relationships (Schein, 2004). In each dimension, the issues of task accomplishment and process skills development compete for attention. Although it is useful for groups to realize this macroview of their work, it is difficult to assess and intervene with group development at this level. To effectively build strong groups capable of maintaining their own identity and adapting to external environments, groups must be able to function skillfully within each of the six domains. Knowing the knowledge bases, skills, and structures of each domain is an essential first step. Knowing the assumptions held by the group about each domain reveals the mental models and drivers of group choices.

Before reading this section, think about a group with which you work, and ask yourself the following:

1. What are our strengths as a group?

2. What difficulties does the group encounter as it works?

3. How ready is the group to take on increas-

ingly complex or emotionally charged tasks?

4. What are some potential growth areas for the group?

Getting Work Done

Leaders and groups understand the dynamic relationship between task accomplishment and process skills development. The prevailing mental model in this domain is that the group assumes that its work is manageable. Essential knowledge includes mastering of dialogue and discussion (see chapter 4), conducting successful meetings (see chapter 5), designing efficient and effective meetings (see chapter 6), and using facilitation skills (see chapter 7).

Doing the Right Work

Leaders and groups plan work to realize their vision, values, and emerging goals. The organizing presupposition of this domain in that vision, values, and goal clarity focuses group energy. The necessary knowledge includes living effectively with conflict (see chapter 9), developing the capacities for change and adaptivity (see chapter 10), and creating community (see chapter 11).

Working Collaboratively

Leaders and groups work to create and maintain an effective environment for collaboration and interdependence. The dominant presupposition in this domain is that diversity is a necessary resource and that subcultures must connect with and value one another. The knowledge that is necessary to effectively work collaboratively and interdependently includes the four group-member capabilities and the seven norms of collaboration (see chapter 3), the mastery of dialogue and discussion (see chapter 4), successful meeting management (see chapter

5), facilitation skills (see chapter 7), and the ability to work effectively with conflict (see chapter 9)

Managing Systems

Groups develop new ways of looking at the world. An organizing presupposition here is that as systems become more complex, the ability to think systematically and know when to set aside linear logic is important. Critical knowledge includes working effectively with conflict (see chapter 9), developing the capacities for change and adaptivity (see chapter 10), and creating community (see chapter 11).

Developing the Group

Whatever the degree of accomplishment, groups can become better at their work. Individuals and groups need to develop resources for generating ideas and adapting to change. An important presupposition in this domain is that both individual and group orientations are necessary to produce innovations and implement them. The necessary knowledge includes information about group development (as described in this chapter), the ability to work effectively with conflict (see chapter 9), the importance of professional community (see chapter 2), and the principles of creating that community (see chapter 11).

Adapting to Change

An effective group relates to multiple communities that are external to the group. The agendas and resulting demands of these communities are often in flux and inconsistent with one another. The prevailing presupposition within this domain is that for groups to function effectively, they must constantly adapt to external environments. The more turbulent the environment, the more the energy must be focused outward. Critical knowledge includes working with conflict (see chapter 9), developing the capacities for change and adaptivity (see chapter 10), and creating community (see chapter 11).

Assessing the Six Domains

The six domains are inextricably intertwined; woven together, they make a whole. The knowledge for one domain is also necessary in another. As in all dynamic systems, what affects one variable affects the others. Because of this interactive nature, an assessment instrument that seeks detail about either the "things" or "the energy" in each domain would contain redundancies. Mastery of discussion and dialogue, for example, are requirements in the first and third domains. To be effective at dialogue, individuals must internalize the group-member capabilities and the norms of collaboration; these elements are also a prerequisite for managing conflict in the fourth, fifth, and sixth domains. To maximize discussion effectiveness, successful meeting skills are required, which is a focus in the first and third domains.

In contrast to the energies involved in assessing "hard data," the energies in system dynamics has traditionally been harder to measure, more prone to measurement error, and therefore less relied upon as a data source for group development. Nevertheless, "the importance of measurement error diminishes when the investigative focus shifts from concern over the system's current state to understanding the system's behavior over time, which is often the purpose of a systems dynamics model" (Hennessy, 1998, pp. 6-7). Measurement-error importance also declines when data are used to promote conversations about how a group might strengthen itself rather than being used for external evaluation.

We have found that a simple rating scale such as the following is useful for group self-assessment: 1 = Beginning, 2 = Emerg-ing, 3 = Developing, 4 = Integrating, and 5 = Innovating.

Organize a faculty group into subgroups of three or four members each. Have them discuss each domain using the descriptions above. Have them rate their group by loose consensus on each domain, using this scale. Suggest that a way of calibrating their place on the scale might be to locate, in general, where the group functions along a continuum of unconscious incompetence (they don't know they don't know) to unconscious competence (performing with effortlessness). Rate the major knowledge areas in each domain as follows:

Beginning	Unconscious incompetence
Emerging	Unconscious incompetence to conscious competence
Developing	Conscious competence
Integrating	Conscious competence to unconscious competence
Innovating	Unconscious competence

Now have the subgroups report their assessments to the entire group. Search for agreement among subgroups and set those aside. Locate areas of disagreement and seek to understand the differences in perception. Come to an accommodation in ratings. From this analysis, have the group select a domain for further study and development (Table 8-1).

A Systems Approach for Developing Groups

Like birds lifting off from far reaches in a meadow and flocking together in flight, ideas emerge from a variety of sources in a group, suggestive of a systems approach to developing groups. Within the literature on organizational development and school change, it is now taken for granted that teacher work and learning is largely influenced by socialization and that

Table 8-1. Assessing Six Domains of Group Development

	Low				High
1. Getting work done	1	2	3	4	5
2. Doing the right work	1	2	3	4	5
3. Working interdependently	1	2	3	4	5
4. Managing systems	1	2	3	4	5
5. Developing your group	1	2	3	4	5
6. Adapting to change	1	2	3	4	5

the culture of the workplace is significant in determining how teachers think, what they do, and how they express themselves (Newmann & Wehlage, 1995; Rosenholtz, 1991). From anthropology, cybernetics, psychology, and organizational science (Dilts, 1996) come conceptions of nested levels of learning in which learning at one level influences learning at another. In this model, a sense of identity organizes and informs other levels of learning.

For an individual, identity is a framework for understanding oneself. This framework is formed and sustained through social interaction. Identity is what makes a person a person; it is the consistently traceable thread that is "me" over time and that distinguishes me from other people.

People construct a set of essential characteristics to define their self-concepts. They interpret experiences and choose behaviors that are intended to maintain the continuity of those self-concepts over time. Group identity too is maintained by comparisons with others. Groups seek positive differences between themselves and other groups as a way of enhancing their own

self-esteem. Like individuals, they see themselves as distinct and act as if they were unique.

Albert and Whetten (1985) characterized organizational identity as a self-reflective question: Who are we as an organization? They concluded that organizational identity could be summarized in three major dimensions: (a) what is taken by the organization to be central to its work, (b) what insiders believe makes the organization distinct from other organizations, and (c) what is perceived by members to be an enduring quality of the organization.

The new sciences—quantum physics, complexity theory, and the study of fractals—portray a view of life organizing itself. Margaret Wheatley and Myron Kellner-Rogers (1996), articulate translators of the new sciences for leadership agendas, write the following:

> Identity, then, is another essential condition for organization. It is the self of the system that compels it toward particular actions and behaviors. . . . Organizational structures emerge in response to these imperatives of identity. Identity is at the core of every organization, fueling its creation. (pp. 85–86).

Therefore, in a quantum world, everything influences everything else. Individual efficacy influences group efficacy, and both influence a sense of identity for the individual practitioner and the group.

An Intervention Model

We have been working with a model of intervention conceived by anthropologist Gregory Bateson in which identity influences all lower levels of learning. Robert Dilts (1994, 1996) describes four operating principles in this model:

1. Any system of activity is a subsystem embedded inside another system, which is also embedded in an even larger system—and so on.

2. Learning in one subsystem produces a type of learning relative to the system in which you are operating.

3. The effect of each level of learning is to organize and control the information on the levels below it.

4. Learning something on an upper level will change things on lower levels, but learning something on a lower level might or might not inform and influence the levels above it.

We notice the congruence of these four principles with the understanding of systems as dynamic entities. The last two principles offer promise for group development. We've been testing applications with seminar groups, working teams, other individuals, and ourselves. We know others who are also applying these principles to individual and group development. The results of these efforts are promising.

Nested Levels of Learning

The brain, and any biological or social system, is organized into levels. To change behav-

iors, all levels must be addressed. Dilts (1990) observes the following:

> From the psychological point of view there seem to be five levels that you work with most often. (1) The basic level is your environment, your external constraints. (2) You operate on that environment through your behavior. (3) Your behavior is guided by your mental maps and strategies, which define your capabilities. (4) These capabilities are organized by belief systems. . . . (5) Beliefs are organized by identity. (p. 1)

Because the levels are embedded in one another, we call them nested levels of learning. Each level is more abstract than the next but has a greater degree of impact on the individual or group.

Identity. This is an individual or group's sense of itself; it organizes beliefs and values. This level answers the question "Who am I?" or "Who are we?" In chapter 1, we proposed this as the first of three self-reflection questions that groups could use for adaptivity (Who are we? Why are we doing this? Why are we doing this this way?).

Belief system. This is an individual or group's values, beliefs, and meanings. This system provides a rationale and gives permission to use or not use capabilities. Teachers who believe that they are more effective are likely to be more effective. When a group believes that its work is manageable, it will enlist the cognitive and emotional resources that allow it to persevere. This level answers the question "Why should we choose this course of action?"

Capabilities. Strategies, mental maps, metacognition, and the energy sources of efficacy, flexibility, craftsmanship, consciousness, and interdependence are all capabilities. The four group-member capabilities (see chapter 3) are examples of organization at this level. Capabilities guide and give direction to behavior choices. They answer the question "How should

121

we use the skills and knowledge that we have?"

Behaviors. Behaviors are what individuals or groups do. They represent the application of skills and knowledge to actions and reactions. Behaviors can be singular, as in a paraphrase, or in complexes, such as listening, which includes attending, paraphrasing, making meaning, and many other singular skills. This level answers the question "In what specific behaviors should we engage?"

Environment. Physical surroundings influence group and individual behavior. Room temperature, lighting, and access to tools and materials enhance or drain energy and focus. Attending to this level is always necessary but is not sufficient in itself for group success.

Without attention to these multiple levels of learning, professional development efforts ineffectively operate as activity-level thinking. We've observed staffs who dutifully perform collaborative activities—peer coaching, curriculum designing, serving on site-based councils—that is, going through the motions. Yet without engagement and learning at levels above these behaviors, they are only mimicking steps in a dance. No true collaboration—that is, the co-creation of ideas or practices by people who possess different resources but work together as equals—results. This could explain, in part, Richard Elmore's (1995) assertion that in restructuring schools, a direct relationship cannot be found between student learning and activities like site councils, decentralized budgets, and peer coaching.

The Indelible Importance of Identity

We don't see things as they are, we see them as we are.

—Anais Nin

Identity influences the incorporation of information at the deepest levels, responsibil-

ity for what one has learned, and commitment to putting it into action. Group development approaches that affect identity include the construction of metaphors that can lead to expanded senses of identity, processing questions designed to stimulate reflection at this level ("How does this activity compare with your image as an educator?"), and meeting practices that shift the spotlight from group members as information receivers to group members as constructors.

Who are you in this interaction? Whom do you need to be? Faculty members report that these questions help them to increase consciousness and choice in professional interactions. Offer a group the metaphors of identity information shown in Table 8-2.

Discuss how the group members know when they are responding to others from any of these metaphors. Explore the systems of interactions that metaphorical identities initiate. (If I respond to you like a parent, you are likely to respond to me like a child.) We find it interesting that the friend metaphor is a common barrier to collegiality in many school cultures. Colleagues must be willing to experience some discomfort in solving problems together, whereas friends have a primary commitment to protect the pleasure of the relationship. Although there is a time and a place for each of these identities, the identity of mediator (a person without judgment, in the middle) is the voice behind most successful school improvement efforts.

Identity is a major factor in personal change. A district office administrator in an eastern state talked to us recently about her superintendent's behavior in council meetings. On the one hand, the council values his leadership and contributions to the district. On the other hand, the council is frustrated because he takes phone calls during administrative council meetings and leaves the room to take care of business while a subordinate is talking. On

Table 8-2. Metaphors of Identity

IDENTITY	ORIENTATION	PRESUPPOSITIONS
Parent	Protector: I want you to grow up strong, healthy, and invested in my values.	1. Dependency 2. I am wiser and more experienced. 3. Reciprocated affection
Expert	Instructor: I will determine the correct and appropriate performance.	1. There is one right way 2. Authority is related to knowledge and skill.
Friend	Advisor or Colleague: I want us to be companions; we will provide comfort and affection for each other.	1. There is a relationship. 2. The relationship has value. 3. The relationship must be protected.
Sibling	Brother or Sister: A want you to be your best; I will support you; I might occasionally feel competitive.	1. Deep connection 2. I have permission to push you. 3. We have similar goals; we can work through adversity.
Boss	Authority: I expect compliance; I am responsible for success or failure.	1. I am responsible for you. 2. Power is hierarchical. 3. I am required to direct and control.
Mediator	Co-learner: We have an interdependent relationship in which you support my learning, and I yours.	1. Individuals have capacities to self-mediate and self-modify. 2. Resources are internal. 3. There is no one right way.

several occasions he has been gracefully told by council members that they feel a lack of respect in this behavior. They have asked him to stop, yet the behavior persists.

As they explored what seemed to motivate this behavior, a description of the superintendent's sense of identity emerged: He is a pragmatist. He takes care of things on the spot. He prides himself on providing solutions to problems without delay. All these orientations are valuable resources, but their shadowy effect is the disempowerment of the administrative council. The superintendent's behavior is un-

likely to change without a corresponding shift in his identity.

Identity is the way that insiders see the organization. This is in contrast to image, the way that insiders believe that outsiders see the organization. Beliefs, values, mental models, and assumptions are derived from experience interpreted through the lens of identity. They are held in deep structure and must be given form in language to be mediated (Garmston, Lipton, & Kaiser, 1998). Most people avoid questioning their own mental models unless they have evolved to a third stage of adult development that Kegan and Lahey (1984) call *postinstitutional*: work in a setting in which reflective dialogue is practiced and mediation of thinking is valued.

For a group, the problems of challenging its own mental models, beliefs, and values are compounded by the pattern of shared assumptions that its members develop over time. A group will tend to cling to existing models unless a crisis intervenes. One crisis example is a dramatic change in student population, rendering old assumptions and ways of working ineffective. For a group to shift, new assumptions must be shared. This means that they must be articulated and understood, though not necessarily agreed with. It is also not enough to understand new mental models; they must be acted on and put into practice.

The ways in which we view the world and our role in it derives from the metaphor of identity that we hold for ourselves in specific roles. Our beliefs, values, and behaviors are congruent with our sense of identity. Each of us, at different times, constructs meaning and makes choices based on this specific orientation. Usually our sense of identity is held at an unconscious level. However, the messages, both verbal and nonverbal, that we send to others emanate from our own metaphor of identity. These messages signal our intentions and our beliefs about our professional role.

Changing Beliefs and Challenging Mental Models

Conduct the Assumptions Wall strategy described in Appendix A. In this activity, group members nonjudgmentally illuminate and examine their assumptions about sources, rationale, values, and consequences. This develops a greater understanding of the presenting issue and of one another. A second way to challenge beliefs is to administer a principles assessment to help members see the degree of congruence between practices and espoused principles. Follow the assessment with individual and group analysis. This allows people to share their shock in learning that they are not living up to the principles they claim to hold (Weinraub, 1995). A third way to challenge mental models is to hold a values challenge seminar. Best done in a retreat setting, this is a conversation in which the group's core values are identified and then tested against a variety of increasingly complex scenarios.

Groups can challenge their own mental models by attending to different levels of data. The following strategies are common to systems thinkers who can move among multiple perspectives: (a) seeing discrete events, (b) recognizing patterns of behavior or trends over time, and (c) seeing the big picture of underlying structures (Kreutzer, 1995).

Most groups need to start at the level of discrete events. Any of the facilitation strategies (see chapter 7 and Appendix A) will help groups to focus on the concrete. Any conversation about facts will also carry emotions, values, and assumptions. Use facilitation questions to get these on the table, such as "What are your concerns?" or "What are you noticing about your reaction to this?" Any of the *who, what, when, where,* or *why* forms of questions can elicit this class of information. Principles of dialogue encourage a shared understanding of the data offered by group members.

The human mind excels at pattern detection, yet this mental tendency can lead to generalizations, distortions, and misinterpretations because patterns on the surface do not always have the same structures underneath. Several facilitation tools can direct attention to this deeper level of thinking.

An Issues Agenda

An issues agenda is a visual map to help

a group discover emerging assumptions that are useful to challenge. It reveals issues that are important to the group's work as well as the perceptions of those issues, it separates the important from the less important, and it displays relationships. To make an issues agenda, distribute 3 × 5 Post-It® notes to a small group. Ask the group members to respond, in four or five words per note, to questions such as the following:

• What are the most important issues, from your point of view?

• What ideas do you have?

• What do you think might be holding us back?

Place the notes on the wall sequentially. Have people explain their reasoning. As this occurs, have the group begin to cluster the notes in groups. Now draw a circle around the clusters and give each a name. The clusters most important to the group should be identified and will provide conscious direction to the group's work.

Causal-Loop Diagram

A causal-loop diagram displays multiple cause-and-effect loops. Start the process with Post-it® notes. Record the effects that the group is working to improve and the possible causal factors for the existing condition. For example, in dealing with the decline of fourth-grade math performance on standardized tests, a group might chart some data as described below.

After putting the notes on the wall, the group members look at the relationships among the items and discuss how they would rearrange the items. Clustering follows. Cause-and-effect loops are identified and drawn in with a chart pen. Causal-loop diagrams can reveal the non-linear nature of cause and effect. Many of the cause-effect relationships are not visible without some sort of graphic display. Without such a strategy, a group doing event-level thinking

might approach the issue of declining math performance by adding more minutes to the curriculum, bearing down harder on math facts, and slowing down instruction for students in lower tracks to ensure that they learn the basics. Such responses have tragic consequences for students and ultimately for public confidence in schools. Yet research in high schools reveals that most teachers use such traditional mechanisms to respond to changing student populations and changing curricula (McLaughlin & Talbert, 1993).

See the Big Picture

Step back from the patterns that emerge from the issues agendas and the causal-loop diagrams and search for the structures that lie beneath the patterns. Three approaches are useful: (a) Search for the variables, (b) ask transition questions, and (c) go to the source.

A variable is something that can increase or decrease. Assigning more, less, or different types of homework to students are variables that might affect the outcomes for learners. Sometimes key variables can be located by examining the most important clusters on an issues agenda and asking transition questions, such as the following, to shift the focus to an examination of the system:

• What do you really want?

• What would you see and hear if you got what you want?

• Who are the other key players?

• What might they want?

• How would they know if they got it?

• What would it mean to you if they got it?

• What are your key choices?

• What are the key uncertainties?

Once you understand a system, go to the source of people's behaviors within the system for the most elegant set of interventions.

An elegant intervention uses minimum energy, stimulates maximum results, addresses both short- and long-range outcomes, works at the level of deep structure, and is congruent with espoused principles and values. Of the nested levels of learning, capabilities provide the most direct organizing influence on behaviors. A special class of capabilities are the five energy sources for high performance: efficacy, flexibility, craftsmanship, consciousness, and interdependence. We have discussed these in earlier chapters and will describe them again in more detail later in this chapter.

Applying the Principles of Nested Learning

How might a group apply the principles of nested learning to its development? Let's say you have selected the first domain, getting work done. The requirements for this domain include being an informed participant in dialogue and discussion, being skilled in the seven norms of collaboration, being an engaged participant in meetings, and making good use of meetings. Choose one of these areas on which to concentrate.

Begin concretely. You can generate information by administering the Norms and Inventory (see Appendixes B and C). As the group reports its data, help it to seek an understanding of conflicting perceptions. Invite a search for patterns. Ask the group to relate, either verbally or graphically, the patterns in norm usage to satisfaction in meetings, quality of thinking, or impact on school programs. The group selects some norms to work on, identifies simple monitoring devices to keep itself conscious of usage and progress, and practices round-robin reflection or other metacognitve processing devices to strengthen the capabilities for the behaviors selected for improvement.

Later, you might ask processing questions at the level of identity and beliefs; for instance, "How does our use of the norms relate to who we are as a collaborative group?" This coordinates learning at the behaviors and capabilities levels with more potent organizers. The group's identity as a collaborative unit is sharpened or shaken as the members articulate their perception of the ways they interact. Another question might be "Does our use of the norms reveal any differences between our espoused and behaved beliefs about working with a common purpose?"

Strategic Processing Questions

Just as teachers work with taxonomies of both the cognitive and affective domains, group developers can also apply a taxonomy of intervention, seeking to direct training energies to the levels that will produce the most growth. One approach is to consistently provide processing questions that focus group members' conscious attention on multiple levels of nested learning.

Table 8-3 shows a facilitator inviting the group to reflect on a meeting.

Five Special Capabilities: Where to Intervene

Garmston and colleagues (1998) pose two questions related to mediating teachers' growth. First, are some filters of perception more important, or do they have different implications for cognitive coaching? Second, to what degree might some of the filters be developmental and therefore subject to mediation? The authors postulate that certain perceptual filters represent differences in preferences for the way one knows (i.e., learning modalities or cognitive style); they do not indicate one's competence or capabilities for knowing. "They are differences

Table 8-3.

Identify:
Given your sense of this being a true professional community, what were some of the ways that this guided your interactions today?

Belief:
Reflecting on your beliefs about the importance of collaboration, what were some things you noticed about the work today?

Capabilities:
In what ways did your understanding of the processes of dialogue and discussion influence your productivity with today's topic?

Behavior:
Given the emotional content of today's topic, what were some of the ways that you managed the internal process of the ways you listened to one another?

Environment:
What were some of the ways that this seating arrangement supported your work today?

in epistemological style, not epistemological capacity. They remain relatively unchanged. Capabilities do not" (pp. 242–286).

Our premise is that the five states of mind described in the cognitive coaching literature influence the capacity for knowing and are modifiable by mediated experience. These states of mind are related to stages of cognitive, moral, and ego development. Educators can therefore maintain a developmental view in working with individuals and groups.

The following discussion centers on what we regard as the developmental aspects of the states of mind. These are the energy sources of efficacy, flexibility, craftsmanship, consciousness, and interdependence.

Efficacy

Efficacy means knowing that one has the capacity to make a difference and being willing and able to do so. The RAND change-agent study (McLaughlin, 1990) found a staff's collective efficacy to be the most consistent variable related to school success. Efficacy is particularly catalytic because it is a determining factor in the resolution of complex problems. If individuals or groups feel little efficacy, then blame, withdrawal, and rigidity are likely to follow. Teachers with robust efficacy, however, are likely to expend more energy in their work, persevere longer, set more challenging goals, and continue in the face of failure. Efficacious groups regard events as opportunities for learning, are motivated by and committed to achieving shared goals, learn from experiences, focus resources where they will make the greatest difference, know what they know and do not know, and develop strategies to learn what is needed.

One study (Poole & Okeafor, 1989) that examined the relationship between efficacy and curriculum implementation showed that two states of mind in the teachers, efficacy and interdependence, significantly predicted the implementation of the new curriculum guides. Neither efficacy nor interdependence alone produced a significant difference in the use of the curriculum, but together they brought about change. Fullan (2001) regards teacher efficacy as a vital factor for the successful implementation of change. Rosenholtz (1991) also found that teachers' efficacy influenced students' basic skills and mastery. The more certain teachers are about their technical knowledge, the greater the students' progress in reading. The more uncertainty that is suffered by the teachers, the less the students learn.

Flexibility

As groups develop cognitively, they value and more consistently view situations from multiple perspectives. Piaget called this overcoming egocentrism. Flexibility allows one to see others not as representatives of a role nor in regard to the degree of agreement with one's own views, but from a broader perspective in which oneself and others are all players in a larger drama in which they are simultaneously the central characters and playing only walk-on parts.

The peak performers that Garfield (1986) studied displayed an ability for flexible attention that he called microattention and macroattention. Microattention involves logical analytical computation and seeing cause and effect in methodical steps. It is important in problem analysis or curriculum planning. It encompasses attention to detail, precision, and orderly progressions. Macroattention is useful for discerning themes and patterns from an assortment of information. It is intuitive, holistic, and conceptual. Macrothinking is good for bridging gaps, and it enables one to perceive a pattern even when some of the pieces are missing.

Groups that develop this energy source

honor and value diversity within and outside the group, attend to both rational and intuitive ways of thinking, can collectively shift perspective, and utilize a wide array of thinking and process skills. Such groups can also navigate the internal tensions of confusion and ambiguity and become unstuck by generating multiple actions for moving ahead.

Flexibility is a prerequisite to demonstrating respect for diverse perspectives. Flexible teachers are empathetic. Flexible groups listen with their ears, eyes, heart, and mind. They are cognitively empathetic with students, which enables them to predict misunderstandings and anticipate the most useful learning experiences. Flexibility, like efficacy, is related to risk taking. David Perkins (1992) describes creative people as living on the edge, always pushing the frontier, generating new knowledge, experimenting with new ways, and constantly growing into new abilities.

Craftsmanship

Studies from the League of Professional Schools (Glickman, 1991) found that in schools where teachers are the most successful, they have the highest dissatisfaction with the results of their work. Success, for craftsmanlike groups, produces self-imposed higher standards in an ongoing cycle of improvement. In a study using cognitive coaching with university professors, Garmston and Hyerle (1988) found that as craftsmanship increased, the professors grew in their ability to be critically self-reflective and effective in producing self-analysis and evaluation.

To appreciate this energy source, consider the mindset of expert performers such as musicians, artists, teachers, craftspeople, and athletes. They take pride in their work and consistently strive to improve current performance. Craftsmanship—the drive for elaboration, clarity, refinement, and precision—is the energy source from which people ceaselessly learn and deepen their knowledge, skills, and effectiveness. Groups that access this resource invest energy in honing and inventing better ways to do their work, honor in themselves and others the arduous journey from novice to expert, manage time effectively, and continually improve inter- and intra-group communications. They create, hold, calibrate, and refine performance and product standards for their work.

Consciousness

To be conscious is to be aware of one's thoughts, feelings, behaviors, and intentions and their effects. Csikszentmihayli (1993) notes the emergence of consciousness as "one of the most momentous events that happened on our planet. . . . For the first time, it was possible for people to emancipate themselves from the rule of genes and culture . . . [and] the illusions of the ego" (p. 76-77).

Consciousness is high-performance energy source with particular catalytic properties. It is a prerequisite to self-control and self-direction. Although all group members are capable of reflective consciousness, many do not practice this skill regularly or with equal vigor. Consciousness means that we are aware that certain events are occurring, and we are able to direct their course. Everything that we feel, smell, hear, think, see, touch, taste, or remember is potentially a candidate for entering consciousness, but the nervous system has definite limits on how much information it can process at any given time. Groups that use this energy source maintain an awareness of their values, norms, and identity; monitor the congruence of their espoused beliefs and their manifest beliefs; and stand outside themselves to reflect on their processes and products. Such groups are also aware of their criteria for decision making and

of how their own assumptions and knowledge might interfere with their learning.

Interdependence

Interdependence is a recognition of the interconnections among individuals, schools, communities, cultures, and all aspects of the planet. Interdependence includes a sense of kinship that comes from a unity of being, a sense of sharing a common habitat (a class, school, or neighborhood) and a mutual bonding for common goals, shared values, and shared conceptions of being. Sergiovanni (1994) tells us that the German sociologist Ferdinand Tonnies called this way of being *gemeinschaft. Gemeinschaft* is a community of mental life. In some respects, Sergiovanni says, these values are still central to indigenous people in Canada and the United States. *Gemeinschaft* contrasts with *gesellschaft*, in which community values have been replaced by contractual ones. This is the case in most modern organizations. Interdependent people's sense of self is enlarged from a conception of *me* to a sense of *us*. They understand that individuality is not lost as they connect with the group; only egocentricity is.

Interdependent groups value and trust the process of dialogue, have an awareness of their multiple relationships and identities with other groups, and regard disagreement as a source of learning and transformation. They regard knowledge as fluid, provisional, and subject to new interpretation with additional experience. Perhaps most important, interdependent groups see the group not just as it is but also for its potential.

Group Development: Ways to Intervene

Group development is a shared responsibility. People with role authority have a prime responsibility to be purposeful group developers. Along with supporting the skill development of a group's facilitators and recorders, planning, monitoring, and at times intervening with the group as a whole should be the leader's focus. With this intention in place, facilitators can then work with those with role authority to develop the group as a group while also accomplishing important tasks. Group members share in this responsibility, for ultimately it is the group's group, and the members should own the processes and the outcomes.

Data about a group, its inner workings, its overt ways of working, and its results are vital reference points for framing conversations that increase the group's capacities in the five energy sources. In this section we offer several lenses and approaches for helping group members to see themselves as a group. If these data are posted on the wall or are out on the table for everyone to see, a group developer can then act as a coach or a consultant to shape growth-oriented conversations with the group.

Group developers use at least five intervention strategies to support growth and learning: structuring, teaching, mediating, modeling, and monitoring.

Structuring

To structure is to manage the physical environment, the agenda, the tasks, and the grouping of participants in ways designed to promote certain levels of learning. This intervention acts on the nested level of environment. Stategically modifying the environment can increase the likelihood of learning at the levels of behaviors, capabilities, belief system, and identity. Some examples are as follows:

- Arrange the room so that the visual focus of members is on a chart, not one another, during problem-solving conversations. This helps to put problems "out there"

and not in the participants. (flexibility and interdependence)

- Use the Learning Partners strategy (see Appendix A) to break up cliques. (flexibility and interdependence)

- Use role diversity as a criterion for forming subgroups. On a school site council, for example, place a parent within each small cluster of teachers to list experiences on a topic. One typical by-product is a respect for one another's experiences that leads to universal perceptions of being a valued member of the group and being able to contribute. (flexibility, interdependence, and efficacy)

- Organize the agenda so that subgroups work on specific tasks during the meeting. (craftsmanship, efficacy)

Teaching

The intervention of teaching is best suited to the nested levels of behaviors and capabilities. Exposition and story, as forms of teaching, can influence learning at the levels of belief system and identity when combined with mediated experiences. Ultimately, this form of intervention includes the entire repertoire of good instruction: assessing, explaining, giving examples, scaffolding, practicing, reading, and so on.

Self-assessments provide a starting point for an adult learning experience. This notion is very much in line with the growing literature on the influence of formative assessments as guides to student learning (Stiggins, 2007). To focus on specific energy sources, group developers might share descriptions of the five energy sources and ask group members to share their impression of which ones are strength areas and which ones are stretch areas for this group. Use these impressions as starting points for planning group growth goals.

A CD-ROM group inventory has been developed by our colleagues Carolee Hayes and Jane Ellison, co-directors of the Center for Cognitive Coaching. (For ordering information, go to www.cognitivecoaching.com).

Mediating

Mediating makes its greatest contributions to learning at the levels of capabilities, belief system, and identity. Mediating is a form of coaching in which the intention is to support a group in achieving the goals that are important to it while also extending its capacity for goal attainment and self-directed learning. Ultimately, this is one of the four roles played at some time by leaders of groups in an adaptive school. To mediate is to shine a judgment-free "flashlight" on internal or external data in order to lead to self-directed learning. The verbal tools of mediation include six of the seven norms of collaboration: pausing, paraphrasing, putting inquiry at the center, probing for specificity, paying attention to self and others, and presuming positive intentions. Mediation most often occurs in relation to reflecting about prior experiences, planning, or problem solving. Costa and Garmston (2002) offer detailed maps for how to coach in these three dimensions.

Modeling

Leaders and group members practice modeling when they display exemplars of specific skills (like paraphrasing) or complexes of skills (like balancing inquiry and advocacy) in work settings with colleagues. Two refinements add to the potency of modeling as a learning device. One is to talk out loud about one's rationale in order to have metacognition about the particular behavior being modeled. Second is to practice public modeling, in which you announce to a group that in today's meeting you are going to work on improving your use of pausing. Reveal your reasons and ask the group members to be prepared to share their perceptions on the effectiveness of your application of the behavior.

Monitoring

Monitoring involves collecting data on a dynamic of interest to the group and reflecting on how this informs the group of its working patterns and how the group might improve its effectiveness. A critical mindset is that the group is gathering and examining data to improve, not prove or judge, a level of performance. Groups may gather information on their use of the norms of collaboration, the degree of congruence with meeting standards, an assessment of the operating energy sources, the inclusion of members, the value placed on diverse perspectives, and other subjects that interest them.

We have learned that the use of a process observer, a member who gathers data on participant behaviors while the group is working, might generate more negative effects than positive ones. A pattern of externally provided data will often lead a group toward a greater dependence on outside assessment, reduce the capacity for accurate self-assessment, and diminish the capacity for self-directed learning. Work with both students and adults has confirmed this (Sanford, 1995).

A strategy that employs both monitoring and mediation involves asking two questions of group members for their private reflection: "What are some of the decisions you made about when and how to participate in the preceding conversation? What are some of the influences of your decisions on yourself and others?" After silent reflection, the members might write a response, share and interact with a neighbor, or practice a full round-robin reflection as follows:

1. Person A speaks.

external data gather is less effective

2. The group pauses.

3. Any person paraphrases and inquires.

4. Person A elaborates.

5. The group pauses.

6. Repeat process with persons B, C, and so on.

Expert groups are more likely than novice groups to be reflective. The more reflection, the greater the learning from experience. Nonreflection dooms a group to repeat the same behaviors over and over, regardless of whether they are producing desired results.

Every working group has far more task than time. This contributes to a natural reluctance to take any precious time for monitoring and reflecting on the group's working processes. Some groups resolve this tension by committing themselves to a task-process ratio. They budget a certain percentage of each meeting to their own learning, exploring how well the group is working and what it might do to improve.

Perhaps no topic is as important as dealing with conflict, which is the focus of the next chapter. The skills that are developed in the norms of paraphrasing and inquiry are the most important verbal tools for addressing conflict.

Chapter 9   Using Conflict as a Resource

onflict and collaboration are the two faces of the coin of community. In a sense, the previous chapters have led us to this point. Getting the right work done successfully and learning to fight gracefully about important things require the capabilities, skills, and tools described in the previous chapters. This chapter offers frames, approaches, and additional tools for seeing and using conflict as a resource for group and personal development.

As the current generation of teachers and administrators struggles with the deep cultural shift from working in isolation with entrenched norms of autonomy and independence to working in more collaborative ways, conflicts of all type are inevitable. For many administrators and staff members, conviviality and surface harmony mask underlying tensions and differences about the purposes and processes of learning and teaching. Accountability pressures, sophisticated data management systems, and rewards for student performance amplify these differences and expose disagreements, both overt and covert (Newman, King, & Rigdon, 1997).

How groups work with and learn from their conflicts says much about who they are and who they wish to be. Betty Achinstein notes the following:

> Communities that can productively engage in conflict have a greater potential for continual growth and renewal. Conflict is a critical factor in understanding what distinguishes a generic professional community of teacher colleagues from a *learning community* engaged in ongoing inquiry and change. (p. 11)

In this chapter we describe the workings of conflict in complex nonlinear systems such as schools, and we present ways to increase your CQ (conflict quotient) by learning to see and respond to conflict as trapped energy.

You need two types of information to be at your most effective in situations with conflict: (a) an understanding of conflict, its dynamics, its dangers, and its opportunities, and (b) knowledge of a variety of conflict tools and ways to use them skillfully.

The sequence in which you will want this information depends on your learning style (abstract or concrete), urgency (are you thinking about conflict in general, or are you in the middle of one), and personal history. If you have an immediate need for learning new tools, move ahead to the section "10 Energy Traps." If you aren't hurting at the moment, begin here with the definition of conflict, and read on.

What Is Conflict?

The definition of conflict varies, and each variation illuminates a different and useful understanding that provides a framework for living and working effectively with conflict. Here are five definitions of conflict:

1. Conflict is just energy in the system— nothing more, nothing less. People bring

not personality
∗ Cognitive conflict — source fights
— effect healthy

meaning to conflict. The way they do so is influenced by personal history, cultural norms, family patterns, and the practices of the group within which they work (Crum, 1998).

2. Conflict is a situation in which interdependent people express differences in satisfying their individual needs and interests and experience interference from one another in satisfying their goals. These differences can be open or hidden.

3. Conflict is a situation that presents both danger and opportunity. The Chinese character for *crisis* combines these symbols and, like conflict, draws attention to each dimension. Danger emerges with the violation of personal needs. Opportunity emerges when clarifying the issues and generating workable solutions remain the focus of interaction.

4. Conflict stems from a perceived competition for limited resources: air, water, land, food, time, money, or power.

5. Conflict has different meanings to different individuals; therefore, multiple meanings exist within a conflicted group.

The truth about conflict lies somewhere in the vortex of these definitions. Becoming smart about conflict and having it work for you requires an understanding of conflict from all these perspectives as well as an understanding of yourself and of schools as complex nonlinear systems. It also requires being clear about your personal goals and values.

One useful distinction is affective versus cognitive conflict. Amason and colleagues (1995) developed these frameworks from their work with teams. *Affective conflict* is another name for personalized conflict. These are disagreements, either person-to-person or group-to-group, that involve antagonism. Such interactions sap energy, derail tasks, and

Affective – personality driven
Personality driven – antagonize personality flid

block much group work. They can be on the surface or buried in the substrata of group processes and outcomes. *Cognitive conflict* is disagreement over ideas and approaches. These "healthy fights" are one of the hallmarks of high-performing groups. In these groups, ideas and issues are separated from personalities. Ideas belong to the group and can be held up to the light of critical examination and analysis (Kolb & Associates, 1994).

Groups need productive cognitive conflict to produce good work. The absence of any type of conflict often leads to apathy, with decisions defaulting to leaders or those with the loudest voices. One major goal of group development, therefore, is to amplify cognitive conflict and minimize affective conflict.

Addressing the Sources of Conflict

empathy also listen below emotion

Scarcity, power, change, diversity, civility, emotional needs, values, task avoidance, and norms of privatism can all be sources of conflict. Connected to each of these are perceptions and assumptions based on personal history and mental models. Be empathetic but listen below the emotion. Help others to state their outcomes in several different ways. Doing so reveals the structure of mental models and opens possible avenues for satisfaction. Groups decrease the potential for conflict when they proactively educate themselves and develop norms for living with them.

Scarcity

Even friends can become protagonists when fears are stimulated about scarcity. The belief that there is not enough time, money, personnel, resources, or space stimulates survival impulses and limits creative thinking. Skillful groups confront their fears by naming and clarifying the details of the scenarios they are imagining as a prelude to considering and generating options and imaginative solutions.

Power

Develop your group's knowledge and skills in conducting successful meetings (see chapter 5). Overcommunicate the processes of decision making and influence. Clarify roles and responsibilities. Assist the group in understanding the larger contexts in which local decisions are being made.

Change

Changing environmental conditions inevitably disturb confidence, competence, and comfort. Change is unavoidable, however, so we must help teachers, parents, and students to learn to cope with change. The most practical resource we know is the work of William Bridges (1980, 1991). In a transition process, individuals and groups go through three stages: endings, the neutral zone, and new beginnings. It's often helpful to identify where people are and how they're feeling. You can use Bridges' three stages to help groups discuss what's happening and how they feel about it. Bridges also has specific recommendations about what to do at each stage to support individuals and groups through the change process. This helps the group to honor and let go of past practices and successfully adopt new ones. We describe the transitioning stages in greater detail in chapter 10.

Diversity

Humans are comforted by sameness and predictability, yet schools are increasingly multidimensional in color, culture, religion, generation, cognitive style, and community composition. If you proactively teach, touch, model, and value any of these differences, ben-

efits will accrue to the rest. Start anywhere. One school's core value is to respect human dignity. Teaching is continual at that school about what it means to be human and about ways to interact humanely with others.

Civility

Create workplace cultures of civility. The seven norms of collaboration (see chapter 3) are an excellent foundation. Be sensitive to cultural differences in affective and communication styles. "Why does the teacher yell at me?" asks an English language learner, interpreting the teacher's intonation as disrepect.

Emotional Needs

Feeling is first. When emotional needs are not addressed in problem solving, tensions persist at a subterranean level, affecting everything else. People have emotional needs for influence, approval, inclusion, justice, self-esteem, autonomy, and affirmation of personal values. Listen with your heart and your eyes and with the language skills of the seven norms. Groups that practice reflective dialogue will be successful at this. Many schools that use Cognitive Coaching[SM] (Costa & Garmston, 2002) in their instructional programs find an increase in teacher efficacy and satisfaction with the teaching profession (Edwards, Rogers, & Sword, 1998).

Values

Address values, not wants. Listen to determine an adversary's hierarchy of values. Show how helping you to gain your outcome will also satisfy an important value of his or hers. Genie LaBorde (1984) reports three universal classes of human values: identity, connectedness, and potency:

> These needs seem to be natural processes that
> push for fulfillment. If you do not feel potent,

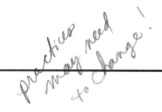

you will be attracted to doing things to express your potency. If you do not know who you are, you will continue to test various traits, searching for the ones that are yours. If you do not feel connected, you will search for a partner or a cause, a religion, or a group with which to feel connected. (p. 163)

Listen in the moment for what is most important to a person about his or her identity. Is it reputation, self-respect, success, integrity, creativity, generosity, or being "a professional"? Connectedness can be about love, honor, friendship, students' respect, religion, attractiveness, or unselfishness. Potency might be about influence, status, intelligence, choice, success, or uniqueness.

Task Avoidance

Some groups and group members use task avoidance as a means of conflict avoidance by diverting and dissipating energy through endless process debates, engagement in peripheral topics, or structured conviviality. These distracting activities waste a group's productive worktime and in the process postpone the confrontation of substantial differences and the decision making that might divide the group or upset one's friends in the group. The practices of dialogue and discussion (see chapter 4) and the standards and tools of successful meetings (see chapter 5) greatly help with breaking these counterproductive patterns.

Norms of Privatism

Teachers' work cultures are steeped in well-established norms of privatism (Lortie, 1975). Teaching space, both physical and psychological, is personal, idiosyncratic, and often fiercely protected. In a profession with low material compensation, the psychic rewards of personal accomplishment have historically been touted as virtues. Teacher-of-the-year awards reinforce the expectation that teaching is a solo act and not a collaborative performance. There are typically no awards for team of the year, grade level of the year, or department of the year.

The patterns and practices of collaborative work—especially conversations centered on student work, teaching practices, and assessment results—amplify the tensions between the desire for personal autonomy and the possibilities of shared collaborative efforts. As colleagues analyze the causes of student learning gaps and develop solutions to support immediate student needs and to address the curricular and instructional practices that produce the gaps, the boundaries between colleagues become ever more fragile. The ways of talking described in chapter 4 greatly help when groups engage with topics that are hard to discuss.

Learning From Social Psychology

Social psychologists study efforts to resolve human conflict through case histories, through mathematical models of rational thought, and by testing theories about conditions and outcomes of negotiations (Pruitt & Carnevale, 1993; Thibaut & Kelley, 1959). Advice found in the popular press often has its origins in social psychology. In our explorations of conflict from the perspective of this field, we have identified the following three principles to be of value to educators who work with any form of conflict:

1. Define fairness.

2. Identify and label the social norms for preventing conflict, regulating conflict, and finding solutions to conflict.

3. Address the sources of conflict.

Defining Fairness

Agreement is more likely and can be reached more quickly when a single standard of fairness applies than when a group uses multiple standards or no standards. It is best to negotiate the fairness criteria early in the process. Groups usually select from three definitions. Test the working definition of each with "what if" scenarios.

Equality

Everybody benefits or contributes equally. Three variations of this criterion have been observed: (a) equal outcomes, (b) equal concessions (i.e., all parties make the same degree of movement toward the middle), and (c) outside precedent (e.g., What are other districts paying their teachers?).

Equity

Benefit is proportional to contributions or work done. Merit-pay systems operate with this principle. Ideally, such systems should be based on student learning data and on a teacher's contribution to the greater good through skillful collaborative engagement.

Needs

Benefit should be proportional to need. Federal funding formulas for grants to schools with high populations of low-income children represent this line of thinking. It is striking to us that most local and state governments have left it to the federal system to apply this definition and have chosen not to do so with local funding.

Identifying and Labeling Social Norms

People will often attack the process when they are not happy with a resolution. Prevent this by identifying and labeling ahead of time the norms that the involved parties will agree to use.

Norms for Preventing Conflict

The norms for preventing conflict are either productive or destructive. Destructive patterns include being excessively polite, avoiding issues,

using humor as a distraction, and emphasizing congeniality (i.e., making nice) over professional collegiality. Overregulating the process for resolving issues with an avalanche of policies, forms, and detailed chains of command is a counterproductive approach used by some large organizations. We know of a school overseas in which conflict is "managed" by banning all employee organizations. Such approaches drive expressions of conflict underground, affect relationships, and ultimately destroy personal and collective efficacy and morale.

Productive patterns for preventing conflict include assigning resources and responsibilities on the basis of some agreed-upon definition of fairness (e.g., all teachers rotate yard-duty responsibilities except Mrs. Smith, who runs an after-school tutorial clinic). Interactive patterns for conflict prevention include the seven norms of collaboration and an agreement to trace rumors back to their sources.

Norms for Regulating Conflict

To talk first with one's adversary before going to a third party is an example of a norm for regulating conflict. Groups define what constitutes fair fighting. Agreements to address issues, not personalities, or to ignore certain behaviors (e.g., knitting during faculty meetings) are examples of ways in which groups might define fair fighting. Agreements to discuss the undiscussable, personal feelings, values, or student achievement in the math department constitute norms for regulating conflict. Groups make regulatory agreements about language. Instead of saying, "You're wrong," they agree to say, "I see it another way." (See the strategy Disagreement Grid in Appendix A.)

Norms for Finding Solutions

Agree first about solution criteria and solution processes (Who will decide?). Identify and explore the assumptions that underlie the different positions. Raise questions like the following to help groups confront conflict:

- What is the worst possible outcome of addressing this?
- What is the best possible outcome of addressing this?
- What are the worst and best possible outcomes of *not* addressing this?
- What outcome do you imagine that your adversary has?
- Would it be okay if your adversaries achieved their outcomes?

Addressing the Sources of Conflict

The traditional working culture of schools challenges the effectiveness of much of the established knowledge about conflict. Adaptive leaders know that schools are living paradoxes, operating simultaneously as thing models and energy models. In the spirit of "thingness," schools have been organized for more than a century as machines, a collection of smaller units making a part-to-whole universe: objectives to lessons and units to curriculum, a racecourse of relatively standardized ground that students must cover in their journey to the finish line (Tyler, 1949; Wiggins & McTighe, 2005; Zais, 1976).

In this model, principles of cause-and-effect prevail, values are formalized into contracts, event-level thinking is the norm, and tacit rules govern daily behavior. Transactions tend toward formality and politeness (Sergiovanni, 1994). A teacher once told us that each year students were coming to her without requisite skills, but she would be hesitant to bring up the problem with the students' prior teachers for fear of offending them.

Schools are also quantum systems—"bundles of energy in motion," more like com-munities than businesses. Drawing from the science of chaos and complexity theory, we get a different picture of the organizing energies of the planet (Gleick, 1987). Using sophisticated mathematical modeling, scientists who study complex systems provide us with images of different and often nonlinear patterns of organization. Such systems are best understood by studying the behavior of the complex whole rather than the behavior of the parts (Gharajedaghi, 2006).

Complex systems organize around "strange attractors." For schools, some of these strange attractors are the core values, vision, and mission of the school or district that draw people together like magical magnets in a common purpose. In these schools, the staffs energetically work to provide children and young adults with more than a sense of artificial belonging; the principles, passions, and conflicting energies of living systems apply.

Our central premise is that schools are enterprises of both things and energy, yet "thing" mental models dominate most approaches to conflict. When educators learn to see their schools as dynamic systems of energy and information, they are liberated to practice more effective ways of working with conflict. To understand how behavior operates in these systems, we have identified 10 energy traps that serve as lenses for analyzing and responding to conflicts.

10 Energy Traps

Certain ways of perceiving conflict limit possibilities and constrain energy in increasingly destructive loops. Energy traps establish counterproductive, recursive patterns throughout a system. Microphone feedback is an example: The closer the microphone is to the speaker, the louder is the squeal as the signal cycles repeatedly through the sound system, grating on the nerves of the listeners. The summer sun beating down on Death Valley, California, produces waves of energy that heat the rock walls of the valley, trapping energy that builds up throughout the day. A similar phenomenon occurs over cities on warm days and nights with cloud cover; heat is trapped beneath the clouds, making the air sticky and uncomfortable. One person who is being grumpy sets up an energy trap if other people respond by matching the grumpiness. A teacher who talks above the volume of the class to get attention simply leads to the students increasing their volume so they can hear one another.

Recognizing traps in order to release energy is the first step in problem resolution. When they detect energy traps, skilled group leaders can open emotional and cognitive space by establishing new frames for viewing situations for themselves and for other group members. "Frames are mental structures that shape the way we see the world. As a result, they shape the goals we seek, the plans we make, the way we act, and what counts as a good or bad outcome of our actions" (Lakoff, 2004, p. xv).

These frames, or mental maps, have two critical features that apply directly to working with conflicts (Kelly, 2006): (a) Faulty maps lead us to faulty actions, and (b) it takes purposeful effort to modify or change a map once it has been established.

Ten common traps, which can be reframed to provide fresh perspectives and additional solution options, are as follows:

1. Operating metaphors, like the "war on drugs"

2. Time orientations that confuse past, present, and future

3. Time horizons that are too short or too long

4. Nominalizations: naming processes as things

5. The illusion of human separateness

6. A focus on production to the detriment of production capacity

7. Fixing what shows, not what is broken

8. The myth that problems require solutions

9. Personalization of conflict

10. Being emotions rather than having emotions

We were once asked to consult at what we will call the Unhappy Elementary School. The school's difficulties had reached such proportions that the school board had threatened to remove the principal unless she could "turn the school around" before the end of the year. We were contacted in March.

The previous principal had been at the school for 18 years and was a laissez-faire leader. The current principal had been there for 18 months, bringing a strong background in curriculum and instruction and a more directive leadership style to the role. We decided to conduct information interviews with each staff member in preparation for a full-day staff meeting.

Our private interviews revealed that the teachers were not only complaining about the principal, they were also complaining about each other. We learned that many individuals made disparaging remarks about fellow teachers to colleagues, certified staff, and parents. Privately, a stream of vicious communication existed. "We're shooting at our wingman instead of working together," one teacher confided. Publicly, the staff wore polite faces to one another and discharged their negative feelings on a common irritant, the principal. Some staff members had pipelines to board members and regularly reported their versions of events at the school.

Several classical features of conflict are present in this example. First, conflict was perpetuating itself, ricocheting around in the energy traps of time orientations, nominalizations, fixing what shows, and personalizing conflict amid a labyrinth of underground communications. Second, conflict is always contextual. In this case, the school's history, a hands-off principal, and a building organized into pods contributed to separate and disconnected units of teachers, with each unit unique in identity, norms, and team leaders. Third, the teachers were bright, highly verbal, and passionately committed to action. The mix worked reasonably well with a laissez-faire principal who left each pod free to do its own thing, but it became an obstacle when the school was faced with a common crisis.

To release trapped energy, first you must identify the trap. Understand it as a conceptual shape that holds energy within certain configurations. One way to identify the frames through which you are viewing a conflict—whether you are directly involved or simply on the periphery as an observer—is to free-write for a set amount of time about the conflict. Resist the temptation to analyze as you write; keep your pen moving until the time is up. Then read through the descriptions of the 10 traps below to see which ones might be operating in your situation. Consider ways to release the energy by changing the frame and opening the trap, allowing the possibility of new resolutions into the situation.

Operating Metaphors

The human conceptual system is primarily metaphorical in nature. Concepts structure what people perceive. Language labels concepts and directs perception. A group's metaphorical language provides containers for thinking that hold unconscious assumptions, beliefs, goals, and values. The "reading wars" or the "war on poverty" are examples. Listen to groups or leaders in groups. Those who think in war metaphors

will use words like *fight*, *position*, *shoot down*, *bomb*, *attack*, and *defend*. Sports metaphors drive groups into "winning" against an adversary. Other types of metaphors challenge each person to do his or her individual best. What if we never had a war on drugs but instead had a rally for health? Changing the language puts the energy in new containers and opens fresh possibilities for resolution.

You can either extend concepts within a metaphor or change the metaphor. All metaphors illuminate some portions of reality and hide others. Search for unstated images within a prevailing metaphor to reframe group thinking. For example, if a committee is intent on "battling illiteracy," focus attention on "training the soldiers" rather than on "gathering weapons"— or change the metaphor. Why not a ship instead of a war, a journey instead of an attack, a garden rather than a field or a battle? What people name a thing determines their perception of it and hence their choices and behaviors. Below are some suggestions for reframing operating metaphors.

Listen for the overt and implied metaphors within the language that group members and group leaders are using. Illuminate and extend the unstated images within the metaphor. If we are a "family," who are the parents? Who are the children? What responsibilities flow from this equation? Does Daddy protect us from danger? Does Mommy soothe our hurts? If we are a team, what sport are we playing? Who is the coach? Who are the star players? How and what do we win or lose? If our students' parents are our customers, what are we selling? What if they're not in a buying mood? Is the customer always right? May customers return items to the seller?

Change the metaphor either by offering options yourself or by inviting group members to propose alternatives. Instead of arguing about "raising the bar," offer the idea of "developing springboards." Rather than "rallying the troops" and giving "marching orders," offer the metaphor of conducting an orchestra of skilled musicians. In the place of talk about investing in our children's future, propose a conversation about nurturing them today and tending to their growth.

Identify and label the assumptions, values, beliefs, and goals that are contained in the metaphors the group members are using. "You frequently use the term *teaching artistry*; what are some of your assumptions about the ways that this value might influences the choices and behaviors of people in this school?" or "You've been using the phrase *staff harmony*; what are some of your beliefs about what makes a staff harmonious?"

Time Orientations

The comment "We've always done it that way" identifies a speaker who is focusing on the past. Present-focused individuals tend to be concerned with the details of the moment or with quick fixes. Future-focused individuals prefer the big picture and care little for discussions about past hurts. Energy becomes stuck when groups focus exclusively on past, present, or future events or when conversations jump randomly across all three time dimensions. Free the energy by address-

---

In Time and Through Time

One way to use time in negotiations is to pay attention to whether the opposition lives *through* time or *in* time (LaBorde, 1984). In-time people remember the past so vividly that it is as if the past were the present. Through-time people bury the past so that previous experiences are not terribly important to the present moment. This applies equally to last year and to yesterday. For through-time people, the way you behaved yesterday will not affect today's negotiation.

Through-time people forget yesterday and start over each morning. In-time people will remember yesterday's argument as if is just happened, and their feelings about yesterday will affect today's negotiation.

Being aware of how people process time and how they relate the negotiation process to their experience of time gives you valuable insight on presenting your information and structuring your outcomes.

---

ing one temporal zone at a time. In general, we find that in problem-solving conversations, energy is most freed up when it is directed toward the future. Help groups to describe the desired state. Then back up to the present or the very near future to determine what must be done to achieve the envisioned future.

Some groups become stuck in the past. Free them by providing a vehicle to tell their stories. Our friend and colleague Suzanne Bailey teaches a timeline strategy to help groups become unstuck. The group designates eras in its history: the year the new superintendent came, the years of declining or increasing enrollment, the period of a major reorganization. Chart paper is hung on the wall in the form of a timeline, and icons are used to illustrate the different eras and the significant events that occurred. Groups of people complete the timeline with words and icons, and they recount their memories to one another as verbal histories.

As a result, people hear about the same event from different perspectives and form a more complex history with a greater understanding of conflicting perceptions. What is expressed and understood is released.

Time confusion occasionally causes meeting energy to career off the walls like a rubber ball in a racquetball court. In such cases, a facilitator can use the following methods for clarifying time orientations:

1. Focus group members on one temporal zone at a time. Say, "First we will address what outcomes we want, then we will explore the strategies that might help us to achieve those outcomes."

2. Adhere to the meeting standard of one topic and one process at a time.

3. Apply facilitator interventions to keep the energy focus of the group on the topic and process at hand.

4. Try the following strategies (see Appendix A): Existing State–Desired State Map, to bring in the future and link it to present actions; Outcome Mapping, to link the present to the future; Futures Wheel, to provide images of the future effects of issues and innovations; Histomap, to honor the past and bring it forward to the present.

Time Horizons

The time horizon—the unit of time within which a party plans to resolve a conflict—limits the solution options. Negotiation literature advises that everything is negotiable, including deadlines. Our friend and colleague Laura Lipton intuitively knows this and frequently moves to extend deadlines on projects. In return, she is released from deadline stress, has more time for reflection, can put finer detail into her work, and ends up with better products.

Many time horizons are taken for granted because of past practices. Take, for example, the habit of assigning teachers to students for a single year. The moment a teacher decides to follow a class from second to third grade, or from fifth to sixth grade, everything changes. Perceptions of student development expand from a 9-month window of growth to 2 years; diagnostic and relationship-building time at the beginning of the second year is practically eliminated; the social norms of the class are understood and can be utilized more effectively; and parents' relationships with the teacher carry on into the second year.

Either lengthening or shortening the time horizon modifies energy. A group of parents in a Colorado school wanted the principal removed. Extending the period for seeking a resolution to this controversy would have stirred up more problems as more people became involved and rumors multiplied. Keeping the processing time tight kept the attention focused on the facts and the issues and not on hearsay. Extending a time horizon sometimes provide benefits, however. A multiyear curriculum revision allows full communication with all the parties, reliable baseline data, and judiciously set expectations. Leaders' personal time horizons relate directly to their professional success and the success of their organizations. Extrapolating from the work of Jaques & Cason (1994), we have concluded that effective principals need at least a 5-year time horizon to make sustainable changes in their schools. Superintendents need a 10-year time horizon.

To clarify a time horizon for a project, assess the consequences of a longer or shorter time horizon. Lengthen the time horizon when deeper dialogue will allow the group members to work through options, emotions, and obstacles to change. One middle school principal we know ran a yearlong process for reconfiguring the grade-level teams in that school. Shorten the time horizon when issues are of lower order importance. For the question "What color shall we paint the staff room?", take exactly one meeting for participants to inform the principal of their preferences. (See chapter 5 for related information on decision making.)

To clarify a time horizon, try the following strategies: Outcome Mapping, to carefully calculate the time requirements for implementing the necessary strategies for goal achievement,

verbs
use -ing
respecting

and Futures Wheel, to offer images of ripple effects, both positive and negative, that might emerge from the issue or innovation under consideration.

Nominalizations

Speakers nominalize when they talk about a process as a thing or an event. Teachers at the Unhappy Elementary School said that the principal didn't "respect" them. *Respect* can be a noun that is static, or unchanging, or a verb, a process that is active in time, with observable manifestations. Verbs, especially gerunds (the *-ing* form, such as *respecting*) are process words and imply active participation by a subject. As such, they imply choice and direct attention to behavior.

Some groups tell us that trust is missing in their organization. Groups cannot improve trust; they can only increase trusting behaviors. We've learned to ask what people will be doing and saying when they are "trusting."

Conflict is another nominalization. With conflict—as with love, anger, happiness, fear, or any emotion we tend to nominalize—there is a starting point, various levels of intensity, a cooling off, and a transition to another emotional state. In each case the language that labels these processes as things freezes these dynamic flowing activities into static conceptual abstractions. When groups act on the abstraction instead of the real issue, they experience failure and frustration.

Conversely, the more groups use the language of logic, emotion, and process, the greater is their awareness and ability to direct and control conflicting energies; for instance, "We have two opposing views; let's distinguish between the data and inferences supporting each" or "I am feeling some despair over the progress we are making."

To open traps caused by nominalizations, change words like *conflict* to *conflicting*, *disagreement* to *disagreeing*, *relationship* to *relating*, and *responsibilities* to what the person is actually doing.

To denominalize language, try the following:

1. Notice the nominalizations that people are using in their oral and written language, such as *respect*, *trust*, *department*, *conflict*, *relationship*, *engagement*, *friendship*, *professionalism*. Ask questions like the following for each one: What would you expect to see or hear if people were showing you respect? How will you know when they are trusting you? What are the behaviors in that department that are upsetting you?

2. Create a "see and hear" T-chart to publicly denominalize a critical term. At the top of the chart, list the term to denominalize; in the left-hand column, list behaviors that the group says it would see if this attribute were present, and where they would see these behaviors; in the right-hand column, list the things they would hear if this attribute were present.

3. Ask group members to free-write about an issue, then swap papers and identify the terms that might have to be denominalized.

The Illusion of Separateness

During intense periods of Middle Eastern shuttle diplomacy, then Secretary of State Henry Kissinger used to say that he would remind himself of three things. First, he would remember to forget his culture; second, he would remember to forget his agenda; and third, he would remember his humanness. From such perspectives, conflicts remind people that they are irretrievably connected and that any sense of separateness is an illusion.

Rusty Swigert, an astronaut in the Apollo

program, tells this story about one mission. For several days the crew orbited Earth until the conditions were right for reentry. With relative leisure, he had time to gaze from the spaceship at Earth below. As they hurtled over the Pacific Ocean, the west coast of the United States suddenly appeared below them. Swigert was aware of a visceral reaction, a sense of joyful belonging as he recognized his "home." Then a little later, Cape Canaveral appeared, and he had another gut reaction of connection as he viewed the place from which the spaceship had been launched. Soon he noticed that he began to anticipate the view of the west coast and the launching site, and his sense of connection grew.

Around and around the globe he orbited, each time anticipating the joy of recognition a little earlier, until finally he realized that he was connecting with the entire planet. It was years before Swigert could put this experience into words. When he finally did, it was in a speech in which he talked about his experience in the third person. He came to realize that all the lines that separate us on Earth are artificial.

To release energy from the trap of the illusion of separateness, help groups to recognize the ways in which their members are connected. All the teachers were connected at the Unhappy Elementary School in purpose, in profession, and in humanness, but they were focused instead on their disconnectedness from one another and from the principal.

To overcome the illusion of separateness, try the following:

1. Use inclusion activities to help group members discover the ways that they are connected, such as sharing stories about first jobs, a job they might have taken if they had not become educators, or things the participants have in common that might not be obvious.

2. Structure fishbowl conversations, with ad-ministrators in the center and teachers in an outer circle. The inner circle describes desired outcomes while the outer circle listens without commenting. The groups then switch positions and tasks.

3. Share stories orally and in written form.

4. Share information, interview transcripts, or recordings from representative others, such as single parents who are just making ends meet, who have two jobs, and who are intimidated about coming to the school to deal with issues concerning their children.

A Focus on Production

Schools operate in demanding environments. Faculties sometimes press so hard for achievement that they forget to take care of themselves. A school in California was in crisis. Overnight the school population had doubled. Flooded with new students and staff, conflicting program demands and inadequate facilities, the faculty worked hard to address these issues. They ran communication-skills courses after school for two semesters in which 90% of the staff participated. The skills that were learned there helped the group members to manage tough conflicts with the board, the teachers' union, themselves, and, a few years later, a districtwide strike. This staff recovered faster and better from the trauma of the strike than any other unit in the district.

Groups avoid the trap of focusing on production to the detriment of production capacity when they honor and protect time for reflection. Adults do not learn from experience; they learn from processing their experiences. Any group that is too busy to reflect on its work is too busy to improve. Knowing this, some groups set task-process ratios. For every 60 minutes of meeting time, for example, 10 minutes is spent on reflecting about the meeting processes. Other schools use the first 5–10 minutes of faculty

how are we connected?

meetings for journal reflections.

To develop production capacities, do the following:

1. Teach, apply, monitor, and reflect upon the two ways of talking.

2. Introduce, inventory, develop, and monitor the seven norms of collaboration.

3. Introduce, adopt, and monitor the five meeting standards.

4. Train and rotate facilitator and recorder roles within meetings.

5. Institutionalize processes and programs that support self-directed learning, such as Cognitive Coaching[SM], mentoring, peer coaching, data-driven dialogue, lesson study, and action research.

6. Develop a process tool kit.

7. Design meeting agendas with both topic and process outcomes. Save time for reflection on both types of outcomes.

Fixing What Shows, Not What Is Broken

One common energy trap is a tendency to fix what shows rather than what is broken. Ours is a quick-fix culture. Television mysteries are solved in 30–60 minutes, minus time for commercials. Daily newspapers headline new solutions for school improvement, poverty, and crime. Legislative bodies adopt simple fixes for complex problems, and in many cases the answers have nothing to do with the problem.

Teacher evaluation systems are another case in point. As a profession, we've spent millions of dollars and as many hours learning and applying teacher evaluation systems, yet there is no clear evidence that such efforts improve instruction.

Test-preparation cram courses, mandatory summer school, grade retention, and remedial after-school programs all fail to address the core issues in the existing curriculum and instructional programs that are producing the learning gaps that these "fixes" attempt to address.

When groups fix what shows, it often leads to new problems. Fixing the new conflict that then shows merely leads to another. Since work is being done only at the level of appearances, the underlying tensions are left unattended and will erupt again at the next fissure.

The airlines' decision to monitor and report on-time schedules resulted in air carriers padding their flight times between cities to produce a higher percentage of on-time arrivals. Air traffic efficiencies, ground-crew turnaround procedures, baggage handling, and the like could then be ignored. What showed was the on-time arrival data.

Fixing what is broken requires a deep understanding of the interacting energies that are creating the undesirable conditions. Experienced problem solvers in all areas of expertise spend the bulk of their time on problem clarification, not on solution generation. School staffs that are skilled in dialogue have the tools for this (Garmston & Wellman, 1998).

At the Unhappy Elementary School, the board and teachers were bent on fixing what showed: complaints about the principal. Deeper than that, however, were artificial separations of the staff, communication by rumor, leadership tugs coming from multiple and uncoordinated directions, and feelings of being disempowered and disrespected. Fixing those areas could and did lead to substantive changes.

To avoid being ambushed by fixing what shows, look below the surface manifestations of a problem. Suppose fourth-grade math scores drops. On the surface it might look as if number facts are the issue, calling for more drill and memorization. Underneath, however, we might find that the language of mathematics is under-developed and is affecting performance as the

problem to solve vs polarity to manage

math curriculum becomes more abstract.

To fix what's really broken, do the following:

1. Paraphrase to understand and clarify how others in the group are framing an issue.

2. Try following strategies (see Appendix A): Assumptions Wall, Causal Loop Diagram, Existing State–Desired State Map, Fishbone Diagram, Issues Agenda, and Energy Sources Team Survey.

3. Structure conversations about data (see Appendixes I and J).

The Myth That Problems Require Solutions

After more than a century of movie watching, most of the world uncritically assumes that most problems have solutions. However, many situations exist in which no clear resolution is possible. In these cases a wise person follows the words of the Serenity Prayer: "God grant me the serenity to accept the things I cannot change, the courage to change the things I can, and the wisdom to know the difference."

Skillful leaders and savvy group members recognize the inherent tensions in the conflicting pressures of attending to both things and energy in their work. Turf issues in departmentalized settings are an example of a problem that will never go away. They are deeply rooted manifestations of territoriality, self-interest, and survival. The most useful question to ask is: How can we work together compatibly, holding service to students as our first priority while recognizing and honoring the needs of individual departments?

Management consultant Barry Johnson (1996) offers a set of principles and tools for identifying and working with the natural tensions that individuals and groups encounter in their lives and their work. He calls these tensions *polarities* (see Appendix J) and defines them as the persistent, chronic issues that are unavoidable and unsolvable. Groups must learn to recognize the difference between a problem to solve and a polarity to manage. How to get all the students in and out of the cafeteria on time is a problem to solve. Balancing the needs for personal autonomy and purposeful collaboration with others is a polarity.

Conflict within and between groups will always be a problem. We cannot wish it away, avoid it, or pretend that there is some ideal organization that experiences no conflicts. Furthermore, there will never be enough time or resources to do all the things that schools are asked or want to do. All these problems have no permanent solutions. They are conditions of life in organizations.

To avoid the trap of thinking that every problem has a solution, and to live with life's dilemmas with grace and dignity, frame problems in the following manner: What do we need to do to get the best of the upside of a dimension (e.g., productive change) and the least of the downside (e.g., fear and resistance)?

To live gracefully with problems that can't be solved, do the following:

1. Recite the Serenity Prayer.

2. Structure dialogues to explore "What do we need to do to get the best of the upside of this situation and the least of the downside?"

3. Use the following strategies (see Appendix A and Appendix L): Polarity Mapping; Futures Wheel, to explore the positive and negative ripple effects of any action or inaction; and Fishbone Diagram, to explore the forces working for and against any action or inaction.

Personalization of Conflict

A wise person once said that you will never grow up until you stop thinking that your parents' life was about you. To ruminate on childhood memories, pretending that we were the central character in the play, is natural but is only one version of the story. We fall into a similar trap when we assume that the conflict is about us personally. Many of our personal conflict responses are rooted in childhood memories, which can be triggered by current events and the behavior of others. Learning to recognize these personal response patterns and detach our sense of self from the surrounding energies produces flexibility and resourcefulness in an emotionally charged situation.

A wise and experienced principal we were working with was once late to an after-school meeting. When she finally appeared at the session, she shared with us that an angry parent "who needed to yell at someone" delayed her. The principal shrugged off the event and joined the meeting in progress with the statement "The parent came, the parent yelled, the parent left, and I'm here."

A thoughtful department chairman told us that when he is involved in conflicting situations, he mentally steps aside and imagines how he would explain his behavior during the conflict to his beloved grandson if he wanted to be the hero of the story.

Conflicts are hardly ever about you. They most often arise from some surface interference with another person's needs or desires. To release yourself from the personalization trap and depersonalize conflict, do the following:

1. Adopt a calm and centered body posture, monitor and release tension in your shoulders, and remember to breathe.

2. Go to the mental balcony. Look at the interaction as a system. What does the other person or group want and need? What might the other person or group be feeling? What might possibly be going on that could open up feelings of threat, uncertainty, or anger?

3. Paraphrase to diffuse the emotional tension for yourself and others.

4. Ask yourself what is the most generous interpretation of the other person's or group's behavior.

5. Ask yourself if it would be okay with you if the other person or group achieved his, her, or its desired outcomes.

6. Ask yourself how old you are feeling at the point of conflict and how old you need to feel to be resourceful.

7. Ask yourself how you would explain your behavior to someone outside the conflict if you wanted to be the hero in the story.

Being Emotions Instead of Having Emotions

Recall a recent experience of intense feeling. Were you happy, or were you feeling happiness? Were you angry, or were you feeling anger? Were you upset, or were you feeling upset? Language can lure us into the energy trap of being at the cause of another person's behavior. All emotions spring from choices. "The school board makes me angry" is an inaccurate expression of reality. You become angry all by yourself. The board has better things to do than to irritate you.

When you shift language from *I am* to *I am having* or *I am feeling,* you notice that you are not your feelings, you are not your thoughts, and you are not your point of view. Rather, you *have* feelings, thoughts, and points of view. It is freeing to discover that whatever you are conscious of, you can direct and control. With consciousness, we can become more resourceful and draw on a range of coping strategies.

During conflict it is essential to monitor and adjust one's oxygen level to restore and sustain mental and emotional resourcefulness.

147

The 3.5-pound mass we call the brain consumes 30% of the body's oxygen. When we experience stress, breathing becomes shallow, and for some of the time we might actually hold our breath. For the neocortex, the site of language and reasoning, to function, the brain requires a full supply of oxygen. Stress shuttles this precious resource to the limbic system to prepare the body for physical survival. Our bodies require two deep breaths to purge carbon dioxide and reoxygenate the brain.

We are wired from birth to respond with primary emotions to certain features in our environment, such as sounds, types of motion, and physical pain. These physical factors trigger automatic emotional reactions in the limbic systems of our brains that release chemicals that alter cognition in response to the stimulus (Damasio, 1994).

Our brains and bodies also respond to the content of our thoughts, triggering secondary emotions. Both primary and secondary emotions create surges of electrochemical response throughout the body. Each type of emotional response uses the same neural pathways. In other words, perception is reality.

To manage your emotions, try the following:

1. Recognize and label your feelings as you are having them.

2. Listen for "makes me" language in yourself and others. Replace "makes me" with "I am choosing," or "I have." Instead of "He made me angry," say, "When he does that, I feel anger." Instead of "They upset me," say, "I feel upset when they do that."

3. Take two deep breaths to restore oxygen to your brain.

4. Adopt a body posture of calmness and centeredness.

5. Walk or vigorously exercise to burn off excess adrenaline.

6. Learn your body's responses. Respect its physiological functions. Walk away from a conflict when you are too tired, too hungry, or too provoked to be flexible and resourceful.

How to Double Your CQ (Conflict Quotient)

When you are presented with conflict, you bring your entire personal history to the stage. You also bring consciousness, the human capacity to overcome conditioning and to work effectively with your physiological responses to fear, anger, disagreement, discomfort, and discord. When you notice that your response to conflict and your strategies for dealing with it change according to whom you are in conflict with, it is a reminder that conflict begins inside you.

We've experienced tremendous value by freeing ourselves from energy traps. Groups can easily learn to apply these ideas in order to learn from discord. By honoring deeper principles they will double their capacity to live and work more gracefully with conflict.

Principles are important because maximum success in any enterprise is guaranteed by clear outcomes and by applying principles—not rules—to achieve them. Rules are principles in chains. Rules restrict; they are useful some of the time but disastrous at other times. To start and end meetings on time is a rule. To honor a group's time and energy is a principle. Sometimes you must break the rule to maintain the principle. At a community meeting in a western state, for instance, a parent raised an important concern, about the district's effort to set student learning standards, 10 minutes before the announced closing time for the meeting. The superintendent wisely asked the group's permission to stay and engage this topic for the next 45 minutes. By doing so, she averted 3 months of potential community upset and untold hours of communication and conflict-resolution efforts.

Both the literature and our own experiences provide several important principles for using conflict as a resource within groups. Betty Achinstein (2002), building on the work of Louis and Kruse (1995), reminds us of the importance for leaders to do the following:

1. Develop forums for teachers to explore their differences.

2. Reinforce community values to set the frame for what to talk about and how to talk about issues and differences.

3. Demonstrate a willingness to live with ambiguity and reinforce the idea that all problems don't have neat solutions.

4. Model critical self-exploration and vulnerability.

5. Foster openness to different perspectives.

6. Don't become the final authority; support teachers in resolving conflicts themselves.

7. Provide structures, resources, professional development, and practice in the skills of inquiry and shared decision making.

The ultimate principle for seeing and using conflict as a resource is to listen well to yourself and others. By calming down and calming others, we develop empathy for both ourselves and them. Then we can maintain our own resourcefulness and develop shared capacities for graceful fighting about the important issues that are at the heart of true community in schools.

action items to use conflict as a resource

listen (calmness)

Chapter 10 Capacities for School Change

The essential notion of adaptivity (see chapter 1) frames the work of developing the underlying capacities for school change. To be adaptive, schools and school personnel must continually clarify their identities and not be attached to form. Earlier chapters examined fundamental strategies for carrying out this work. In this chapter we expand on the *what* of adaptivity—the 12 capacities for school change. The first six capacities are organizational, and the last six are professional. They are as follows:

1. Vision, values, and goal focus
2. Systems thinking
3. Initiating and managing adaptation
4. Interpreting and using data
5. Developing and maintaining collaborative cultures
6. Gathering and focusing resources
7. Collegial interaction
8. Cognitive processes of instruction
9. Knowledge of the structure of the discipline
10. Self-knowledge, values, beliefs, and standards
11. A repertoire of teaching skills
12. Knowledge of students and how they learn

The 12 capacities for school change interact with one another and cannot be addressed in isolation if schools and professionals are to become increasingly adaptive in response to the changing needs of the students they serve. These capacities are living examples of the dynamical principle that everything influences everything else.

The six organizational capacities and the six professional capacities form a synergistic whole that must be continually addressed. It is never a case of either-or but always a case of both-and. We are persuaded that all the staff development in the world, and all the knowledge and skill building that we provide to individuals, will have only minimal impact if districts and schools do not also put energy and resources into altering the deep structure of the organization.

At the beginning of this book we introduced three focusing questions: Who are we? Why are we doing this? Why are we doing this way? The answers to these questions are the short response to the *how* of adaptivity in schools. The 12 capacities make up the long answer.

Steven Covey (1989) reminds us of the need to balance production and production capacities. His retelling of the fable of the farmer who killed the goose that laid the golden egg points to the ongoing need to develop the *capabilities* to do important work as much as the need to do the work itself. If we are not careful, the "goose" of school improvement will die from a lack of food and water.

This is a perennial problem in schools that

are starved for time: to do the important work for students and to support continual adult and organizational learning. We will make the case here that time is just one element in the puzzle. Many factors organize time choices; the clock and the calendar are only two of the elements at work.

Schools are living organisms, and like all healthy living organisms they are characterized by continual flow and changes in their metabolism that involve thousands of biochemical reactions. Stable systems are dying systems (Capra, 1996). In scientific terms, chemical and thermal equilibrium leads to death. Vital schools, like all living organisms, continually maintain themselves in a state far from equilibrium. This is the state of life. Stability emerges through the average, over time, of the ebb and flow of energy through the system. Attention to the six organizational capacities for adaptivity and the six professional capacities for adaptivity helps this energy flow.

As you read this chapter, please have in mind some of the persistent problems you see in the schools around you. As with the languishing high school profiled earlier (see chapter 2), you may notice particular capacities that are underdeveloped. We hope that you also notice specific capacities that are well-developed in your settings. The essential question, then, is: Where should leaders now focus the system's attention to make a difference in the situation?

The Organizational Capacities for Adaptivity

Schools do not develop organizational capacities as abstractions. They do so by addressing meaningful problems. Skilled leaders use problems as opportunities for learning. This approach meets both production and production capacity needs. Working alongside leaders who understand this informs our learning as well.

Recently we spent time with a school that addressed the six organizational capacities (Figure 10-1) in the manner described below.

A school that we will call Sea View Elementary tackled the issue of low scores on a statewide fourth-grade writing assessment. The test was new to both this school and others in the state. It emphasized narrative and expository writing. Although the fourth-grade teachers were not happy about the scores, they were not terribly surprised. When they first saw the test, they realized that the school's writing program had some gaps, given the expectations embedded in the examination. As a clearer picture of student writing performance began to emerge, the principal organized a series of meetings. We were fortunate enough to participate in some of them. Appendixes I and J offer some practical approaches to engage others in collecting and reporting data and to structure conversations about data.

The first two organizational capacities—vision, values, and goal focus and systems thinking—forge the context for the other four.

Vision, Values, and Goal Focus

When we learned about the writing problems at Sea View, our first question was "In what way is this issue about raising test scores, and in what way is it about long-term improvements in student writing and in the writing program?" The principal assured us that the change effort was aimed at long-term systemic improvements in the teaching of writing. In fact, she was willing to take some political heat from parents and central office administrators, if necessary, to keep the focus long-term and not just fix what was showing.

Several other values contributed to the project's success, such as a belief in the power of cumulative effects for learners. As we describe in the systems thinking section, collec-

Figure 10-1. The Six Organizational Capacities

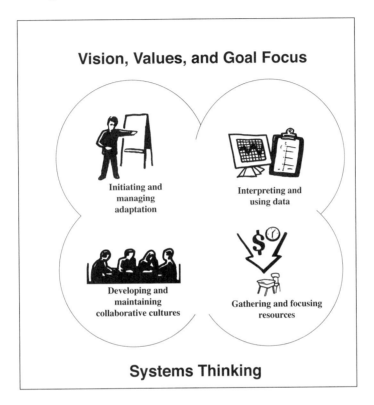

tive efforts matter. September of the fourth grade is much too late to start a concentrated writing program. The assessment of the system at that point was viewed by the school as an assessment of the whole, not that specific part.

The other operating value and vision was an image of continual improvement for all students. The emerging writing-skills matrix was seen as a developmental road map, not as a curriculum to be covered by each grade level in turn. If a third grader had difficulty crafting simple sentences, that is where the teacher started. Paragraphs could wait until foundational skills were in place.

Systems Thinking

The writing problem at Sea View was soon seen by the teachers as a systems problem. A fledging sense of collective responsibility for student learning motivated the work of vertical teams. K–3 staff members were openly supportive of their fourth- and fifth-grade colleagues and agreed to work collaboratively on an improvement plan and effort.

One of the vertical teams produced a draft-skills matrix for the teaching of both narrative and expository writing. This systems view was developed through rotating 2-hour planning sessions, with each new team adding to and filling in the gaps in the work of previous teams. Several teachers even came back during their lunch breaks to participate with colleagues on other teams.

One by-product of this work was increased confidence on the part of the lower-grade teachers that their efforts in developing fundamental writing skills would be appreciated by their upper-grade colleagues. When they could see the system of which they were a part displayed in matrix form on the wall of the meeting room, they could see where their efforts led and view with ease their part in the whole.

Upper-grade teachers also benefited when they spotted the gaps in the writing instruction on the grid. One glaring example was the lack of emphasis on expository forms. The state assessment first pointed this out, and the skills matrix reinforced it. This also inspired changes in another part of the system, because the district writing rubric did not provide guidance or standards in this area. Several Sea View teachers volunteered to be on the revision committee to tackle the rubric. With their draft-skills matrix in hand, they greatly influenced the process. In the course of this work, they shared their efforts informally with several other schools and engineered a resource swap with teachers in other buildings who were working on different parts of the writing and literacy-development puzzle.

Systems thinking is a critical skill in a world of messy problems. In this emerging field, practitioners model systems using mathematics, complex diagrams, and rigorous analysis of variables. Ultimately, such work leads to leverage points in the system that can be modified or perturbed enough to positively influence systems change. One challenge here is that both thing and energy models apply to the same system. Finding and modifying systems requires both ways of seeing and acting.

Initiating and Managing Adaptation

The principal at Sea View intuitively knew that shared dissatisfaction is the first step in initiating change. This, along with shared vision and knowledge of practical tools and strategies, must be strong enough to outweigh the cost of any change.

The following simple formula (adapted from Beckard & Harris, 1987) captures these factors:

$$\text{Change} = (A \times B \times C) > X$$

X = the cost of change

A = shared dissatisfaction

B = shared vision

C = knowledge of practical tools and strategies

Without shared dissatisfaction, all the vision and strategies in the world do not promote a desire to change. Too much dissatisfaction without practical tools will shut down the system. Vision that is neither shared nor connected to the other two resources sputters out into inspirational vagueness. All change has a cost for both individuals and organizations. The left side of the change formula must overcome the right side.

The work of William Bridges (1991) mentioned in chapter 9 is a useful guide in this area. He points out that *change* in organizations is not the problem; it is *transitions* that are bewildering. Transitions are the psychological readjustments to change. They have three phases: (a) endings, (b) a neutral zone, and (c) new beginnings. Each phase has special characteristics and special requirements for it to be navigated successfully.

Endings must be marked concretely and symbolically. Many change processes stall because the people in the organization have not let go of the old. Curriculum changes in schools often meet this difficulty. Teachers cling to the tried-and-true, and in some cases they hope to leap to the new like a trapeze artist high above the crowd. They are often unwilling to let go and hang suspended in midair with one hand on each trapeze.

At Sea View, the writing meetings that were initiated marked a transition from old ways of working to new ones. They were symbols of a new order and at the same time marked the ending of isolation and scapegoating. The principal did not have to name this. Freeing teachers for these meetings with substitutes symbolically and practically conveyed this message.

During an ending, a group needs to ask, "Who is losing what in this change?" and "Who needs what support to work through the transition?" At Sea View this took the form of a change in curriculum materials for the language arts. Although it was widely recognized that the textbooks were outdated and falling apart, some teachers still needed an opportunity to express their concerns about the new materials and the need for greater planning and lesson preparation time. Early meetings provided the opportunity for these conversations and the emotional support that was needed by these staff members.

The neutral zone is a time of anxiety and discomfort for many participants, but it is also a time of great creativity. At Sea View, dialogue, reflection, and the sharing of practical materials and tools organized this phase. The principal was always supportive and nonjudgmental, allowing teachers to express their feelings and concerns about increased accountability and their work in progress.

Bridges (1991) reminds us that new beginnings require an acknowledgment of the problem, not a solution. At Sea View, the writing issue was owned by the staff. In fact, as the teachers began this project, they knew much more about the shortfalls in student writing performance than they did about the solutions.

Bridges (1991) also admonishes readers to remember the marathon effect. Thousands of runners compete in the Boston Marathon each year. The world-class runners, with their faster qualifying times, line up at the start of the pack. By the time the runners in the rear cross the starting line, these leaders are several miles up the course.

In school-change processes, early adapters must remember and pay attention to those who follow. To produce cumulative effect in schools, these people must pace themselves and support the learning of their slower colleagues. The race is not fully under way until everyone crosses the starting line. Appendix K describes five stages of change and maps a process for productive action.

Interpreting and Using Data

The assessment results from the state had merely confirmed the fourth-grade teachers' expectations of low performance by their students. Thus, rather than discounting the results or questioning the validity of the test, these teachers began an informal dialogue with the principal and the other teachers. Part of this dialogue explored comparisons between the state assessment and writing samples collected from the fifth-grade students. This in turn led to conversations with the third-grade teachers and an examination of writing samples from their students.

As this example illustrates, data can be both quantitative and qualitative. The number of Sea View students in each performance quartile carried some meaning for the teachers. Actual samples of student writing carried other meaning. In these ways, teachers with a variety of mindsets had the opportunity to engage with the problem in the manner that was best suited to their preferences. Numbers spoke to some people, whereas artifacts of learning spoke to others. See Appendixes I and J for tips about structuring conversations about data and engaging others in collecting and reporting data.

Developing and Maintaining Collaborative Cultures

A sense of collaboration governed this project from the beginning. A leadership team composed of a cross-section of teachers and the principal organized the project and monitored its progress. This team steeped itself in the norms of collaboration (see chapter 3). They kept communication open among grade levels and provided a bird's-eye view of the school and the project.

Vertical teams attended the meetings. In this way, each group had information about K–5 writing approaches and access to knowledgeable practitioners from every grade level.

At one point it became obvious that all the teachers in the school were not teaching and using the same proofreading marks. Group members said, "You know, we all don't need to talk about this." So we asked them to name three people in the school whom they all respected and who had the technical knowledge to handle this task. They quickly named three people, who agreed to develop a simple set of grade-level appropriate proofing marks for faculty approval at the next whole-group meeting.

Gathering and Focusing Resources

This project demonstrates the power of the capacity to gather and focus resources. Our contract with the district and the school emphasized the development of collaborative skills and process tools. Schools need an engaging vehicle to carry this work. At Sea View, the principal and leadership team used the writing issue as their mode of transport.

Time and money were budgeted for meetings, for some staff members to attend in-depth training in expository writing, and for new curriculum materials. Other issues in the school that could be set aside were done so. A bulletin board in the hallway near the office proudly displayed an ever-changing sampling of student work in this area. The parent newsletter provided updates and progress reports.

One of the innovations that most contributed to project success was the use of substitute teachers and a careful scheduling of the vertical-team meetings to best align with teacher preparation periods. In this way the teachers were free, while school was still in session, to participate in 2-hour sessions for planning and problem-solving purposes. On most project days this required the services of six to eight substitutes.

The district staff-development director understood the nature of this work and readily agreed to cover the cost of substitutes. District staff-development practices are moving beyond the notion of course-based training as the only means of professional development. Time with peers in focused work sessions contributes to learning for all participating adults and simultaneously supports direct payoffs for student learning.

The Professional Capacities for Adaptivity

The professional capacities for adaptivity (Figure 10-2) work in tandem with the organizational capacities. In the example from Sea View Elementary School, improvements in the writing program arose from attention to both areas. Within this arena, individual teachers and teams of teachers set out to become smart about both writing and the teaching of writing.

Collegial Interaction

Who teachers are to one another matters. In a sometimes lonely profession, isolation in the individual cells of an "egg-crate" school does not promote personal or professional growth. Parallel play might socialize youngsters in

Figure 10-2. The Six Professional Capacities

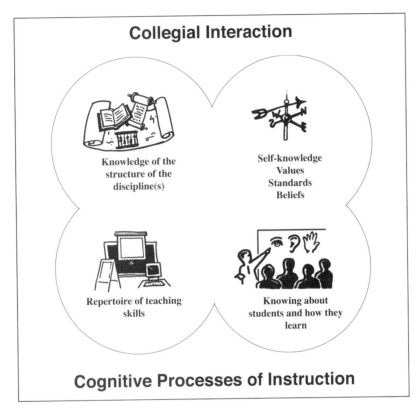

sandboxes, but it limits learning for adults.

To be a colleague requires sharing one's knowing and not knowing. It means sharing and creating materials together. It means teaching one another about the craft of teaching. We are still somewhat surprised when we find out how many teachers in a given school have never seen another teacher teach. Their experiences of the other teachers consist mostly of passing in the hallways, with or without students in tow.

Study after study (e.g., Little & McLaughlin, 1993) stresses the importance of collegial interaction for growth in teaching and growth in student achievement. Adult learning, like all learning, is both an individual and a collective act. Where collegiality is strong, communities of practice bloom (Brown, 1994). These communities support distributed cognition, which means that people become smart together.

At Sea View Elementary School, it was safe not to know everything there was to know about teaching writing. Several teachers immersed themselves in learning to teach expository writing. As they tried out these ideas in their classrooms, they shared their successes and shortfalls with other teachers and encouraged them to adopt the techniques that seemed to be working.

A new kindergarten teacher brought a wealth of experience in language development for early childhood programs. The first- and second-grade teachers opened up a dialogue with her as they eagerly awaited the next school year(s) and the arrival of these youngsters in their classrooms.

The hallway bulletin board, with its rotating display of student work, became a focal point for conversations about student writing and teaching students to write. These conversations led to lesson swapping and more conversations.

Collegiality is different from conviviality. The teachers at Sea View had both, but they didn't confuse lunch-table chatting with professional dialogue. Mindfully talking about one aspect of the instructional program allowed the school as a community to focus its energy and use talk as a vehicle for learning and productive change.

Cognitive Processes of Instruction

Teaching is a cognitively demanding profession. Decisions made in quiet moments and decisions made on the fly influence success and failure in the classroom. Many variables add to the complexity of the thinking tasks that confront teachers every day. Planning and reflecting skills energize and organize good teaching.

In planning, teachers consider the following (Borko, Livingston & Shavelson, 1990):

1. Information about students—who they are, what they know and can do

2. The nature of the instructional task—subject matter, activities, materials

3. The context of the school—class size, scheduling, grouping

4. Their own beliefs—their conception of learning, of teaching, and of the particular subject or topic

In reflecting, skilled teachers consider three areas: the technical, the practical, and the critical (Calderhead, 1996). Technical reflection focuses on whether the objectives were met, based on specified criteria for success. Practical reflection focuses on the effectiveness of the actions and the ends to which those actions led. Critical reflection focuses on the purposes of education and the assumptions that underlie practice.

The "bookends" of planning and reflecting frame lesson execution. It is here that additional cognitive resolving power pays off for students and teachers as learning comes into focus. A teacher's "with-it-ness" supplies the necessary cognitive and emotional flexibility for maintaining concentration on the big picture while modifying and adjusting along the way. One of the early and ongoing challenges for the Sea View writing project was to not get hung up on a lesson plan during the actual lesson. Learning to write is a messy business. Following the students and their needs is much more important than following the plan.

Sea View teachers are still hard at work learning to plan, teach, reflect on, and apply new understanding from their writing skills matrix. Becoming better teachers of writing calls on all their cognitive processes of instruction.

Knowledge of the Structure of the Discipline

What teachers know and can do greatly influences student learning. A teacher's knowledge of the structure of a given discipline translates directly into daily instructional decisions, curriculum choices, and lesson designs. Individual teachers teach different subjects differently (Shulman, 1987). An elementary teacher's math lesson will be structured and conducted in a manner different from the same teacher's literature circle.

Expert teaching calls for an understanding of the subject matter that is thorough enough to organize the topics so that the students can create meaningful cognitive maps (Darling-Hammond, 1997). Teachers with such a level of knowledge can use it flexibly to address ideas as they come up in the course of teaching. Real learning is messy. Students do not always stay within or even fit within the boundaries of a lesson plan. Teachers' knowledge of content topics and of fields of learning must therefore always be wider and deeper than that of their students. This enables fluid movement within subject matter and enables responsiveness to student questions and perceived student needs.

Shulman (1987) breaks down knowledge of the structure of disciplines into several important subsets. One is content knowledge itself. If the teacher does not know a subject, the students will not come to know it. Another area is knowing the structure of the subject matter—the organizing principles and concepts.

A second grader sorted out an important idea in mathematics one day when he observed with excitement, "Numbers are made up of other numbers—you can take them apart!" Many second graders never reach this conclusion on their own. It is more likely to happen if their teachers understand this big idea themselves.

It is also important to know the habits of mind in a given field. The principles of inquiry are different in literature than they are in the physical sciences. How are ideas developed in social studies? Who is a valid source in literary criticism? How do mathematicians solve problems? These are all examples of this idea applied to different content areas. This supports students in understanding how new ideas are added to a field and how deficient ones are dropped by those who produce knowledge in a domain.

Students too have habits of mind. Each content area is a minefield of misconceptions and error patterns. Knowing these allows the expert teacher to anticipate, carefully structure lessons and units, and respond appropriately to the fragile half constructions of their novice learners. Shulman (1987) calls these adaptations pedagogical content knowledge. This blending of content knowledge, learner knowledge, and teaching knowledge binds the subject matter to specific learning devices. Expert teachers draw from a rich menu of analogies, models, and explanatory devices that support them and their students in representing ideas and understanding in a variety of ways.

The writing project at Sea View struggled with all these issues. The teachers' knowledge of writing and writing processes grew alongside that of their students. A practical developmental continuum for the stages of student writing began to emerge, and the teachers forged important connections between student writing and other areas of literacy, such as student reading difficulties. This triggered an inquiry into the structure of the reading program as the teachers wondered aloud about the most appropriate balance of fiction and nonfiction books to use with students at all grade levels. They are still exploring the connections between exposing students to quality nonfiction through guided reading experiences and translating that into writing lessons.

Self-Knowledge, Values, Standards, and Beliefs

Little children playing school vividly demonstrate beliefs about teaching that shape the rules of this play and the power relationships among the players. When some of these children grow up and become real teachers, their beliefs, values, and personal standards will implicitly and explicitly guide their decisions about what and how to teach.

Values and beliefs influence the perceptions

and judgments that carry teachers through their days. They are not always consciously understood or named by individuals, but their presence simmers beneath the surface of a teacher's practice. Values shape the standards that teachers hold for their own work and for that of their students. Values are filters for what elements of the vast subject matter are emphasized and reinforced. Ultimately, they are each teacher's true curriculum and true lasting lessons.

One of the central issues at Sea View was—and is—what is good writing. This standards issue is an interactive construction forged by individual teachers and their collaborative colleagues. The ebb and flow of changes in their students' writing focuses this clarification process while challenging their beliefs about teaching and learning. This clarification process is the deepest level of inquiry at Sea View. Teaching writing is a vehicle for exploring the ways and means of learning about learning, both for students and for adults.

Repertoire of Teaching Skills

Teaching is a craft skill built on action—knowledge honed by trial and error. It begins with the teacher's own understanding of what is to be learned by students and how this learning is most appropriately orchestrated for the population that is being served. Understanding teaching is a lifetime journey. There is always something new to learn about oneself, one's students, the content, the process, and the dynamic interactions of these elements.

Master teachers, like concert artists, consciously expand their performance repertoires. They develop and assemble microroutines that can be combined and reconstituted to fit a variety of settings. These experts automatize many routines to free cognitive space for more complex perceiving and more sophisticated instructional problem solving. This unconscious

competence is the hallmark of an expert in the classroom.

One of the tensions and energy drains for the novice writing teachers at Sea View was this very lack of automaticity. Daily writing tasks demanded that conscious attention be placed on seemingly mundane lesson details. When everything is important, sensory overload sets in. Peripheral vision, both literal and metaphorical, was not a sufficient resource for managing the physical, emotional, and cognitive demands of high-quality writing instruction at this stage of teacher learning.

Knowledge of Students and How They Learn

Learners and teachers need each other. Each is incomplete without the other. Who they are in this relationship forms a delicate balance of minds, hearts, and souls. The desire for smaller class sizes and smaller schools is a response to the need to know each other. In an increasingly diverse world, direct and personal knowledge is even more necessary as old assumptions and operating rules lose their guiding power.

All the teaching repertoire in the world is wasted if it is not well matched to the needs of learners (Saphier, Haley-Speca, & Gower, 2008). The exploding knowledge about learning styles, multiple intelligences, developmental differences, and cultural variation supports Shulman's (1987) notion of the need for pedagogical learner knowledge on the part of all teachers.

Developmental differences do not end in the third grade. Grade by grade, the span, in Piagetian terms, widens. Many learners in middle school and high school operate at a solidly concrete operational level. They often stumble when they bump head-on into a curriculum organized by abstraction and taught through symbol systems. When flexible teachers start with the concrete and scaffold learning to the abstract, these same students grasp complex ideas and perform at high levels.

Developing culturally respectful teaching approaches is an increasing need in many schools. Methods and materials that work with one population might confuse or offend another. Language differences play an important role here. One often unnoticed variable is the difference between students' social discourse and their knowledge of the structure and norms of academic discourse. Lee and Fradd (1998) refer to this sophisticated matching as instructional congruence. This means that teachers mediate the nature of academic content with students' language and cultural experiences. This makes content accessible, meaningful, and relevant.

Learning about student writers at Sea View energized and at times terrorized the teachers. The more they looked, the more differences they spotted. This led to dialogue and discussions about the best ways to intervene with individuals—when and how do you coach young writers, and when and how do you consult with them in a more directive manner? Other conversations explored alternative ways to group students for instruction. One direction this took was to experiment with cross-grade groupings for targeted minilessons.

A World of Both-And

Neither the organizational nor the professional capacities for adaptivity would have sufficed on their own to make a difference at Sea View. In this world of both-and, the twin goals reinforced one another. Developing each capacity within a spirit of collegiality and inquiry led to a natural flow within and among the areas.

These 12 capacities frame the windows through which we can look at schools and districts. Current project successes can usually be located here. Current logjams in the system also have their roots in these areas. This, then, is a diagnostic tool and a curriculum for organizational and professional development.

Chapter 11 Community Doesn't Just Happen

And thou shalt have the grace of great things.
—*Rainer Maria Rilke*

Community doesn't just happen in schools. It is simultaneously a fragile resource and a state of being. "Community is an outward and visible sign of an inward and invisible grace, the flowing of personal identity and integrity into the world of relationships" (Palmer, 1998, p. 90). These networks of relationships bind people to one another and to important ideas and work.

The modern sense of schools as communities is relatively new. Not long ago, the individual teacher was the center of most attempts to improve the quality of teaching and learning in schools. Today, new promise is held in the growing recognition of the power of school-based professional communities to support teacher development and improve student learning. Louis and colleagues (1996) found that professional communities in schools are characterized by a shared sense of purpose, a collective focus on student learning, collaborative activity, deprivatized practice, and reflective dialogue. Such communities develop collective responsibility for student learning, producing school-wide gains in student achievement.

Rosenholtz (1991) found that a major difference between stuck schools and moving schools is teacher talk and teacher efficacy. Studying secondary schools, Little and McLaughlin (1993) found that teacher membership in a learning community is strongly related to student learning in specific subject areas and

at entire schools, significantly exceeding the learning of control groups. However, Elmore (1995) cautions that efforts at school restructuring do not necessarily result in student learning. In fact, he finds only a weak relationship between the two. Reorganizing the school by modifying schedules, grouping patterns, and teaching arrangements does not automatically ensure a collaborative climate.

True collaboration arises from beliefs and skills. In this dynamic, teachers are reinventing instruction and co-creating responses to educational dilemmas. We have stressed that for professional community to exist, teachers must talk. Equally important, however, is what they talk about. We have identified the sources for professional conversations that lead to improved student learning. It seems that when teachers talk about real students, real student work, and ways to reinvent instruction to support greater student learning, achievement soars.

Developing school communities is even more complex, because all group members belong to other groups as well. The site-based decision-making team has members who think of themselves as primary teachers, special education teachers, parents, administrators, taxpayers, and many other roles. To be a member of a given group, each individual must sort out and resolve conflicting loyalty and identity issues. This is a central "Who am I?" question that each group member must clarify.

The Principles of Community

Creating communities requires vision, values, perseverance, hard work, and time. Community doesn't just happen. Sergiovanni (1994) notes that schools are more like a functional family than a fast-food chain. Like any healthy family, a community requires work to develop it and keep it together. We offer the following seven principles in this important journey:

1. Community doesn't just happen.
2. Community is the other face of conflict.
3. Diversity enriches community.
4. Both things and energy matter.
5. We cannot not be connected.
6. Community lives within.
7. Community doesn't last forever.

Community Doesn't Just Happen

If values are the heart of a community, communication is the pulse, bones, and physiology. Most teaching groups, isolated from peers for so many years, need to learn ways of talking together. The task is complicated because it requires at least four languages. First is the language of emotion and passion, providing speech for what moves us. After nearly 2,000 years in Western civilization, the role of emotion in professional life and its necessity for sound decision making is finally being legitimized by Goleman (1995), Damasio (1994), and others.

Second is the language of logic and analysis, to apply a variety of perspectives in reasoned reflection and planning. Third is the language of dialogue, to develop shared understanding, and fourth is the language of discussion, to make decisions that stay made. Dialogue and discussion are ways of talking that are fundamental to the success of any community (see chapter 4).

Developing community also requires paying attention to the environmental level of the nested levels of learning (see chapter 8). Teachers need space and time to collaborate. Darling-Hammond (1997) describes how "push-in" efforts in a number of restructuring elementary and high schools allow more time for collaboration, involve staying with the same students for 2 or more years, and provide teaching teams with distributed expertise. These schools are eliminating "pull-out" services to students, and special staff members are reassigned to reduce teacher-pupil classroom ratios. She describes an elementary school in Chicago in which the teachers teach 4 full days of academic classes each week and spend the fifth day planning in multigrade teams as the students rotate to resource classes in music, fine arts, computer lab, physical education, library science, and science lab.

At an elementary school in South Carolina, the teachers have 80 minutes per day for planning. In Cincinnati, an elementary staff reorganized the schedule to free up $5^{1}/_{2}$ hours per week for planning time and reduced the pupil-teacher ratio to 15 to 1 by using push-in strategies. We've even heard of a school in the central valley of California where an impenetrable fog sometimes delays the start of school. Buses are delayed until visibility is safe. School leaders realized that if fog could keep the kids home, so could the teachers' need for collaborative work time. Once a week, now, the schools in the district have a "teachers' fog day."

Only 32% of instructional-staff time in

traditional high schools is spent teaching, compared to 60%–85% of staff time in elementary schools, intermediate schools, and alternative high schools, according to Cooper, Sarrel, and Tetenbaum (1990). Yet high schools too are creating more time for the school's major purpose: teaching. The same study finds that nonteaching time in traditional high schools is not spent on collaborative planning and curriculum work, which is the case in other countries. Changing this is not easy, yet restructuring high schools are modifying these realities, most often at a great cost in terms of the psychological effects of change.

Darling-Hammond (1997) describes International High School, in which the principal, the assistant principals, and all the other staff work with students in advisory councils. Guidance counselors are attached to teaching teams. The librarian is a teacher with classes. Full-time teachers constitute 67% of the staff. At Central Park East Secondary School, virtually everyone works with students, and full-time teachers constitute 73% of the staff. Darling-Hammond observes the following:

> Shared time for planning, professional development, and governance is much more extensive in the restructured schools. In International High School, cluster teachers share 70 minutes of planning time daily and a half day each week for staff development and collective work while students are in clubs. (p. 185)

To accomplish the structural changes described above requires more than communication skills. Communities must keep their values clear and continue developing the resources to see themselves and their students through rough times. Not the least of these resources are the five energy sources for high performance that we have discussed: efficacy, flexibility, craftsmanship, consciousness, and interdependence.

Community Is the Other Face of Conflict

Community and conflict are intertwined. Conflict is a manifestation of interdependence; without people's need for one another, there would be no conflict. Conflict is necessary in order to have community. Conflict forges new life forms. Canyons, beaches, and mountains are created from conflicting energies. Because human conflict is uncomfortable, groups often seek to avoid it. When they do so, they live in a state of community building that Scott Peck (1987) calls pseudocommunity. This is a stage of extensive politeness. Being comfortable is the goal. Members of pseudocommunities ignore or make light of problems, withholding their true feelings. They ignore individual differences and avoid people or issues that make them uncomfortable.

Groups move from this stage by asking transition questions: "Who are we?" "Why are we doing this?" "What is our purpose?" Challenging nominalizations and generalizations will also move the group to the next stage of development: chaos.

Peck's use of the term *chaos* is different from, but not totally unlike, the meaning of the term in quantum physics: a dynamical system in which many variables are constantly interacting—each affecting another, which affects another, and so on. In Peck's model, chaos is a time of fighting and struggling. Differences move into the open. Most often the fighting at this stage is neither respectful nor skillful. Members try to convert others to their views. They demonstrate fix-it behaviors and try to heal. Others resist the attempts to change. They look for someone to blame and develop cliques and alliances.

Groups have two choices at this point: toward community or away from it. Many groups and leaders attempt to achieve peace by overregulating potential problems. Organizations attempt to resolve differences by developing policies, structuring committees, and establishing chains of command, but these treat only the surface manifestations of conflicts.

The way toward community at this point is through engaging conflict and embracing it with special tools. Peck calls this stage emptiness. Members empty themselves of the need to convert or fix others. They empty themselves of the need to control, of the sense that there is one right way, of ideologies, and of prejudices against other people. Members empty themselves of barriers to communication and work to make a transition from rigid individualism to an acceptance of interdependence. Individualism is valued, but so is collegiality. Ways are sought to achieve the best of both worlds. Silence is an asset. Also prominent in the tool kit are the metacognitive strategies of suspension and the balcony view (see chapter 4). Concepts about and tools for conflict (see chapter 9) are also helpful.

At Peck's next stage, groups realize true community. Here people are open, lucid, vulnerable, and creative. They bond together across their differences for common purposes.

Diversity Enriches Community

Healthy biological cultures are diverse. Monocultures are at greatest risk for disease and trauma. If only one type of pine tree grows in the forest, then one species of insect, fungus, or other parasite can destroy all the trees. Botanists cross-pollinate, splice genes, and graft stems to different root stocks to increase the resistance to pestilence and disease. On the edges of ecosystems, at points of transition between habitats, life forms are the most profuse and evolving.

As long as the group and its subgroups know that they are a system, diversity of cog-

nitive style, educational beliefs, ethnicity, culture, gender, role, and age increases the quality of group decisions and offerings to students. In fact, there are some indications that a staff that is too heavily weighted with males will have greater difficulty working collaboratively than a group that has more gender balance (Louis & Kruss 1995).

Diverse ideas help groups to form rich responses to educational perplexities. Disagreements that focus on substantive, issue-related differences of opinion actually improve team cohesiveness, commitment, and effectiveness. Disagreements that become expressed as personal attacks or judgments about others, however, insert a destructive energy flow into group work. What groups need to know and be able to do in order to engage in cognitive conflict without affective conflict includes the collaborative norms (see chapter 3), dialogue and discussion (see chapter 4), and using conflict as a resource (see chapter 9).

Both Things and Energy Matter

Throughout this book we have advocated building the energy resources of schools; yet energy is not enough. Prairie Ridge High School in the Crystal Lake District in Illinois was designed as an adaptive facility, capable of supporting independent and interdependent activities within the building (Saban et. al., 1998). Constructed to operate as an 1,800-student high school, the building can also be transformed to work as two 900-student schools or four 450-student schools. The thoughtful placement of special spaces, such as science labs, and the flexibility of interior walls that are not weight bearing make this so. Prairie Ridge was designed to serve the relationships among the mind (classroom and academic areas), the body (physical education and athletic areas), and the spirit (the theater and art area).

Each of these areas is zoned to be able to act independently from the others, yet in the course of a normal school day the three areas interdependently form a total learning community. In addition, each area contains design elements to support the staff and the students in developing the five energy sources of high performance: efficacy, flexibility, craftsmanship, consciousness, and interdependence. A prime example of this is the lack of separate offices for each academic department. Teachers share a well-provisioned common preparation area.

Although this example is exceptional in its scope and execution, things do matter in achieving educational aims. The "surround," as David Perkins (1992) terms it, is tantamount to being a thinking member of the human community, interacting in countless ways to influence human learning.

One of the authors is reminded of his first year as a fully credentialed teacher. The principal met him outside the building on the first day of school and asked, "Are your desks in rows?" Trembling with anger and anxiety, the young teacher asked if the conversation could be continued in the principal's office. Once there, he asserted that he understood his role to be the responsibility for learning in that class, and if that was the case, he would decide the furniture arrangement that would best suit that purpose.

Values matter. Values have life as energy. Statements of mission and beliefs are things that are printed, framed, and hung on the wall. Things without energy are not enough; the things must support the energy. To focus group energy we offer the following tips—based on our work over the last decade with many seminar participants and group leaders in a variety of settings—for setting and maintaining goal focus:

1. Adopt the meeting standards (see chapter 5).

2. Rotate the facilitator and recorder roles (see chapter 5).

3. Select one or two of the collaborative norms to develop (see chapter 3).

4. Decide what is nonnegotiable.

5. Teach the essentials of group development (see chapter 8).

6. Provide space, tools, and time.

7. Lighten up: Laugh a lot, learn from experience, and locate power within the group.

We Cannot Not Be Connected

If there is no other, there will be no self. If there is no self, there will be none to make distinctions.
— Chuang Tzu, Chinese philosopher

Wherever we look, we find only ourselves. This appears to be true at every level of organization of which we can conceive.

Physicist Fritjof Capra (1982), writing about quantum theory, explains that subatomic particles are not isolated grains of matter. Rather, they "are probability patterns, interconnections in an inseparable cosmic web that includes the human observer and her consciousness" (pp. 91–92).

Albert Einstein disclosed that even space and time are products of our five senses. We see and touch things and experience events in sequential order.

Depak Chopra (1993) advises that the atoms of hydrogen, oxygen, carbon, and nitrogen that you exhale were, just a moment ago, locked up in solid matter. "Your stomach, liver, heart, lungs and brain are vanishing into thin air, being replaced as quickly and endlessly as they are being broken down" (p. 9).

Scientists and sages seek to understand a universal connectedness in which individual entities exist but have no separation. About the process of self-creation, Wheatley and Kellner-Rogers (1996) say the following:

Differentness comes into the world, a desire to be something separate. From a unified field, individual notions of self arise. This process, like all those that describe self, is enticingly paradoxical. First, something appears for which there is no known antecedent. Where does the self that is organizing originate? Or why does it attempt to separate itself from the unified fields? Why does this movement toward differentiation even start? (p. 51)

Aikido master Thomas Crum (1998) recommends that personal boundaries do not determine our identity. Boundaries are misperceived if we interpret them as separations from others. If the self does not remember its connectedness, it will expire. Each act of ours creates the conditions for other lives.

Fritjof Capra (1996) reminds us that to understand our essential interdependence is to understand our relationship to other people and other things. "It requires the shifts in perception that are characteristic of systems thinking—from parts to the whole, from objects to relationships, from contents to patterns" (p. 298).

Community Lives Within

As a friend of ours used to say, "This one is an inside job." Being in community involves a tension, nearly always present, between self-assertion and integration. It requires an acceptance of the self as both whole and part, a dichotomy described by Arthur Koestler (1972) as holonomy. The word *holonomy* comes from the Greek *holos*, meaning "whole," and *on*, meaning "part." This conveys a combination of opposites, functioning autonomously while working interdependently. Although all five energy sources contribute to consciously holonomous living, interdependence makes the most direct contribution.

Ultimately, the success of individuals depends on the success of the community as a whole, and the success of the community depends on the growth and development of each member.

There seems to be no objective reality; perception combined with intention creates reality. As you see a thing, that is what you will have. As you describe a thing, that is what you will see.

Community Doesn't Last Forever

Of one thing we are certain: Things change. Experiences accumulate; learning occurs at different rates in different areas for different people. Life stages bring new developmental challenges to the young adult, the middle-age professional, and the person near retirement. Although community is robust and can prevail for long periods, it is also fragile and subject to changing conditions. Groups that lose their capacity to work effectively with conflict plunge back into chaos. They can recover, move back toward organizing conflict away, or move into pseudocommunity. Wheatley and Kellner-Rogers (1996) ask the following questions:

As we act together in the world, our organization's identity grows and evolves. It helps periodically to question what we have become. Do we still love this organization? Do we each organize our work from the same shared sense of what is significant? We return to the place where our community took form, where we first became inspired by what we could be in the world. From remembering that place, together we can decide what we want to be now. (p. 62)

Widening Our View

We've been talking about collaboration and being in true community as the cutting edge of our work, the leading edge of professional learning. Yet it might be the oldest story of all human stories. Our ancestors on the plains of

Africa lived in collaborative communities: the hunters and the gatherers, the fishers and the cooks, the weavers and the spinners, all working together and sharing a life.

What are the organizers for community? For West African cultures, it is the drum. It is from these cultures that drumming music has become an essential element in the music of much of the world: In South America, Central America, and North America, the beat is present. The Afro-Cuban rhythms sound through salsa, blues, jazz, rock, and country music. The essential difference in the music of the villages of West Africa is that the beat is polyrhythmic—twos, threes, and fours, interacting, intertwining, setting the rhythms for the dance. As West African women pound corn, the children don't mimic the beat, they clap and pat counter rhythms, seeking their voice within the village.

To be a drummer in this culture is to be a person of distinction. For the drummer not only keeps the rhythm but also knows the history of the people. The drummer calls people to the dance by naming their ancestors: Bring all of who you are to the center and dance. The tradespeople are called to the dance with their own signature rhythm—the carpenter, the potter, the weaver, the shepherd. The dancers, too, play off the beat, adding their own rhythm to the mix. The African dancer picks up and respond to the rhythms of one or more drums, depending on his or her skill. In the best dancing, the dancer, like the drummer, adds another rhythm, one that is not already there. The dancer's ear is tuned to hidden beats, responding to gaps in the music (Chernoff, 1981).

You don't have to dance on the beat to be part of the village, but you are expected to honor the beat and blend your movement with the movements of others. In fact, to dance with disregard for the beat is considered to be mentally disturbed, because this represents a breakdown of communication, awareness, and community.

The goal is to find the beat, honor the beat, add your voice, and dance. Welcome to the dance!

Appendix A Strategies: A Process Tool Kit for Facilitators and Teams

How to Use This Appendix

The strategies can be located alphabetically in this appendix. They also appear in alphabetical order under the following subheadings:

- Decisions
- Facilitator Moves
- Inclusion
- Information Processing
  - (a) Activating and Engaging
  - (b) Exploring and Discovering
  - (c) Organizing and Integrating

Clear intentions, the ability to read groups, and flexibility are the keys to selecting processes to facilitate groups. This compilation of more than 150 ideas is a resource for varied and flexible approaches to situations encountered by groups: bonding, information processing, marking transitions, giving directions, dialoguing about data, converting negative energy, making decisions, exposing assumptions, problem solving, starting sessions, and many more. An ultimate goal for facilitators is to invent their own strategies, and familiarity with the application of processes in this collection should help to build this capacity.

Strategies provide structures for conversations that might otherwise meander and be less productive. Effective strategies provide three functions: focus, efficiency, and psychological safety. Participants need a sense of safety to risk putting their ideas on the table, to acknowledge what they do not know, and to participate. Safety is different from comfort. Group members should occasionally be uncomfortable in work conversations; if they are not, they are probably not talking about the right issues. Discomfort is

the expression of the disequilibrium that is experienced when current knowledge and conceptions give way to new perceptions and solutions. It is a doorway to learning. Yet conversations must be safe enough to foster learning. To cognitively engage with others, especially in hierarchical groups, requires psychological safety. For some this means an opportunity to talk and not be overridden by others. It means having the sense that one's contributions are recognized. It means being free of losing face, of embarrassment, and of feelings of inequality. Very important, it also means freedom from having to be certain. To speak only with certainty is one of the greatest barriers to deeply understanding situations and generating informed theories of causation and solution.

Two considerations are important in selecting strategies. First is the degree of tightness or looseness. Facilitators develop a repertoire of tight to loose structures. When hard-to-talk-about topics are on the table, the facilitator tightens the degree of structure to provide greater emotional safety and more focused thought. Cognitive complexity, high emotion, or new content might call for tight structures. First Turn/Last Turn is an example of a strategy with a tight structure. It gives shape to the conversation by providing a focus for talking, naming the processes to be used, indicating the cognitive skills that are required, and setting boundaries for behavior and topic.

When the topic is easier to discuss, less restrictive strategies are used. "Tell the person next to you one of your experiences with this idea." This is a very loose structure, in which the only musts are the topic and with whom to talk.

Group size also influences safety. In general, pairs are safer than trios, which are safer than quartets, and so on. The least safe is the full-group conversation.

A second consideration is the degree of focus on task, relationship, or process. Wellman and Lipton (2004) offer a metaphor of a street entertainer spinning plates. In selecting processes, facilitators may choose to give more support to one of three "plates": task, process, or relationship. As in a vaudeville act, all plates do not require constant attention. The facilitator notices which one is wobbling and gives that one a little more spin, noting the spin by saying something like "This interaction has been structured so that you can appreciate the views of others at your table. Notice how others at the table give you ideas you did not have on your own."

Facilitators make a number of subtle "moves," perhaps not noticeable unless one is looking for them, that increase or deflect group energy, direct attention, affect information flow, promote memory, communicate respect, and create psychological safety. These are largely nonverbal. We classify them as moves in contrast to a strategy when they are unplanned, are executed spontaneously, and have no more than one or two parts to them. Choose Voice, Visual Paragraph, Finger Minutes, and Most Impor-

tant Point (MIP) are examples. These, and the majority of nonverbal ideas in this collection, emanate from the work of our friend and mentor Michael Grinder (2007).

Group members will have dispositions of either task people or process people. Task-oriented people become uncomfortable with what they regard as too much process, and process people don't have a lot of tolerance for conversations that exclude process. Good facilitators will make these tensions public and encourage tolerance for alterative styles.

All highly evolved processes recur in simpler, repeating processes. It is better to know a few processes well than to attempt many poorly.

List of Strategies With Classification

A B Each Teach
Information Processing: Exploring and Discovering

Adjournment Directions
Facilitator Moves

Airplane Stacking
Facilitator Moves

Analogy Prompts
Information Processing: Activating and Engaging

Applause
Facilitator Moves

Around the Room and Back Again
Information Processing: Activating and Engaging

Ask for Sabotage Ideas
Facilitator Moves

Assumptions Challenge
Information Processing: Exploring and
Discovering

Assumptions Inquiry
Information Processing: Exploring and
Discovering

Assumptions Wall
Information Processing: Exploring and
Discovering

Attention First
Facilitator Moves

Banned Words
Inclusion

Brainstorm Modalities
Information Processing: Activating and
Engaging

Brainstorm Questions
Information Processing: Activating and
Engaging

Break and Breathe
Facilitator Moves

Caping
Facilitator Moves

Card Games
Facilitator Moves

Card Stack and Shuffle
Information Processing: Exploring and Discovering, Activating and Engaging

Carousel Brainstorming
Information Processing: Activating and
Engaging

Carousel Interview
Information Processing: Exploring and
Discovering

Catalogue
Information Processing: Organizing and
Integrating

Causal Loop Diagram
Information Processing: Exploring and
Discovering

Check In
Inclusion

Choose Voice
Facilitator Moves

Choreograph an Opening
Inclusion

Clarify Conflicting Mental Models
Information Processing: Exploring and Discovering, Activating and Engaging

Clearing
Inclusion

Close the Discussion
Decisions

Closing the Window
Facilitator Moves

Combine Opposites
Decisions

Conflict Conversation Template
Information Processing: Exploring and Discovering

Content Check
Information Processing: Organizing and Integrating

Corners
Information Processing: Organizing and Integrating

Criteria Matrix
Information Processing: Exploring and Discovering

Decision Options
Decisions

Decontaminate Problem Space
Facilitator Moves

Delve and Dialogue
Information Processing: Exploring and Discovering

Disagreement Grid
Facilitator Moves

Diversity Rounds
Information Processing: Exploring and Discovering

Done/Yet-to-Do Questions
Information Processing: Organizing and Integrating

Eliminate the Negative
Decisions

Energy Sources Team Survey
Information Processing: Exploring and Discovering

Existing State–Desired State Map
Decisions

Finger Minutes
Facilitator Moves

First Job
Inclusion

First Turn/Last Turn
Information Processing: Exploring and Discovering

Fishbone Diagram
Information Processing: Exploring and Discovering

5-3-1
Information Processing: Organizing and Integrating

Focused Reading
Information Processing: Exploring and Discovering

Focusing Four
Decisions

Force-Field Analysis
Information Processing: Exploring and Discovering

Forced-Choice Stickers I
Decisions

Forced-Choice Stickers II
Decisions

Foreshadow
Facilitator Moves

Four-Box Synectics
Information Processing: Activating and
Engaging

Freeing Stuck Groups
Decisions

Freeze Body
Facilitator Moves

Freeze Gesture
Facilitator Moves

Futures Wheel
Information Processing: Exploring and
Discovering

Gatekeeping
Information Processing: Exploring and
Discovering

Give One to Get One
Inclusion

Gots and Wants
Information Processing: Organizing and
Integrating

Greeting Circle
Inclusion

Grounding
Inclusion

Group Groan
Inclusion

Here's What, So What, Now What
Information Processing: Exploring and
Discovering

High Fives
Facilitator Moves

Histomap
Information Processing: Organizing and Integrating, Exploring and Discovering

Hopes and Fears
Information Processing: Activating and
Engaging

Inner-Outer Circle
Information Processing: Exploring and Discovering, Activating and Engaging

Inventories: Meeting
Information Processing: Organizing and Integrating, Exploring and Discovering

Inventories: Norms I
Information Processing: Organizing and Integrating, Exploring and Discovering

Inventories: Norms II
Information Processing: Organizing and Integrating, Exploring and Discovering

Inventories: Norms III
Information Processing: Organizing and Integrating, Exploring and Discovering

Inventories: Norms IV
Information Processing: Organizing and Integrating, Exploring and Discovering

Inventories: Other
Information Processing: Organizing and Integrating, Exploring and Discovering

Is/Is Not
Decisions

Issues Agenda
Information Processing: Activating and
Engaging

175

Jigsaw Carousel
Information Processing: Exploring and
    Discovering

Jigsaw to Learn Information
Information Processing: Exploring and
    Discovering

Journal
Information Processing: Organizing and Inte-
    grating, Activating and Engaging

Key Concepts/Key Ideas
Information Processing: Exploring and
    Discovering

Key Words
Information Processing: Organizing and
    Integrating

Knots
Facilitator Moves

Know, Think You Know, Want to Know
Information Processing: Activating and
    Engaging

Lasso
Information Processing: Exploring and
    Discovering

Learning Partners
Facilitator Moves

Left-Hand Column
Information Processing: Exploring and
    Discovering

Like Me
Inclusion

Lineups
Facilitator Moves

Matchbook Definitions
Information Processing: Organizing and
    Integrating

Mix-Freeze Pair
Facilitator Moves

Modified Jigsaw
Information Processing: Exploring and
    Discovering

Most Important Point (MIP)
Information Processing: Organizing and
    Integrating

My Bonnie Lies Over the Ocean
Inclusion

Naive Question
Information Processing: Exploring and
    Discovering

Not A or B but C
Decisions

100% Consensus
Decisions

1-2-6
Decisions

One-Word Summary
Information Processing: Organizing and
    Integrating

Outcome Mapping
Information Processing: Organizing and Inte-
    grating, Exploring and Discovering

**PAG/PAU (Process as Given, Process as
    Understood)**
Facilitator Moves

Paired Squares
Facilitator Moves

Paired Verbal Fluency
Information Processing: Activating and Engaging, Organizing and Integrating

Paired Weighting
Decisions

Paraphrase Passport
Information Processing: Exploring and Discovering

Partners Report
Information Processing: Organizing and Integrating

People, Place, Thing Cards
Information Processing: Activating and Engaging

People Search
Information Processing: Activating and Engaging, Organizing and Integrating

Pluses and Wishes
Information Processing: Organizing and Integrating

Polarity Mapping
Information Processing: Exploring and Discovering

Process Check
Facilitator Moves

Pyramid
Information Processing: Exploring and Discovering

Quartet Facilitation
Information Processing: Exploring and Discovering

Ranking
Decisions

Read and Example
Information Processing: Exploring and Discovering

Recipe
Information Processing: Organizing and Integrating

Reenergize
Facilitator Moves

Relevancy Challenge
Facilitator Moves

Responsibility Charting
Decisions

Role Clarification
Facilitator Moves

Role Hunt
Information Processing: Activating and Engaging

Round-Robin Reflection
Information Processing: Organizing and Integrating

Rule of One-Third
Decisions

Satisfy, Satisfy, Delay
Facilitator Moves

Say Something
Information Processing: Exploring and Discovering

Scrambled Sentences
Information Processing: Organizing and Integrating, Activating and Engaging

Sensing Interviews
Information Processing: Exploring and Discovering

Set and Test Writing Arrangements
Decisions

7-11 Conversation
Information Processing: Organizing and Integrating

Show, Don't Say
Facilitator Moves

Signal Role Change
Facilitator Moves

Six-Position Straw Poll
Decisions

Slip Method
Decisions

Song Writing
Facilitator Moves

Songs
Information Processing: Activating and Engaging

Sort Cards
Information Processing: Organizing and Integrating, Activating and Engaging

Sound and Motion Symphony
Information Processing: Organizing and Integrating

Spend a Buck
Decisions

Spot Analysis
Information Processing: Exploring and Discovering

Stack and Pack
Facilitator Moves

Stem Completion
Information Processing: Exploring and Discovering, Activating and Engaging

Stir the Classroom
Information Processing: Organizing and Integrating

Stop and Redirect
Facilitator Moves

Stoplight
Information Processing: Organizing and Integrating

Strategy Harvest
Information Processing: Organizing and Integrating

Structure Conversations About Data
Information Processing: Exploring and Discovering

Success Analysis
Information Processing: Exploring and Discovering

Sufficient Consensus
Decisions

Swap Meet
Inclusion

Table Regrouping
Facilitator Moves

TAG/TAU (Topic as Given/Topic as Understood)
Facilitator Moves

Text Rendering
Information Processing: Exploring and Discovering

Third Point
Facilitator Moves

Three Balloons
Information Processing: Organizing and Integrating

3-2-1 Plus 1
Information Processing: Organizing and Integrating

Thumbs Up
Decisions

Triad Inquiry
Information Processing: Exploring and Discovering

Trios PPPI (Pause, Paraphrase, Pause, Inquire)
Information Processing: Exploring and Discovering

Triple Track
Information Processing: Organizing and Integrating

Value Voting
Facilitator Moves

Visual Paragraph
Facilitator Moves

Vocabulary Review
Information Processing: Organizing and Integrating

Volunteer Stand
Facilitator Moves

Walk About
Information Processing: Organizing and Integrating, Activating and Engaging

Wicked Problems Map
Information Processing: Exploring and Discovering

Working Agreements
Inclusion

Yellow Light
Facilitator Moves

List of Strategies by Category

Decisions

- Close the Discussion
- Combine Opposites
- Decision Options
- Eliminate the Negative
- Existing State–Desired State Map
- Focusing Four
- Forced-Choice Stickers I
- Forced-Choice Stickers II
- Freeing Stuck Groups
- Is/Is Not
- Not A or B but C
- 1-2-6
- Paired Weighting
- Ranking
- Responsibility Charting
- Rule of One-Third
- Six-Position Straw Poll
- Slip Method
- Spend a Buck
- Sufficient Consensus
- Thumbs Up
- 100% Consensus

Facilitator Moves
- Adjournment Directions
- Airplane Stacking
- Applause
- Ask for Sabotage Ideas
- Attention First
- Break and Breathe
- Caping
- Card Games
- Choose Voice
- Closing the Window
- Decontaminate Problem Space
- Disagreement Grid
- Finger Minutes
- Foreshadow

- Freeze Body
- Freeze Gesture
- High Fives
- Learning Partners
- Lineups
- Mix-Freeze Pair
- PAG/PAU
- Paired Squares
- Process Check
- Relevancy Challenge
- Role Clarification
- Satisfy, Satisfy, Delay
- Show, Don't Say
- Signal Role Change
- Song Writing
- Stack and Pack
- Stop and Redirect
- Table Regrouping
- TAG/TAU
- Third Point
- Value Voting
- Visual Paragraph
- Volunteer Stand
- Yellow Light

Inclusion
- Banned Words
- Check In
- Choreograph an Opening
- Clearing
- First Job
- Give One to Get One
- Greeting Circle
- Grounding
- Group Groan
- Like Me
- My Bonnie Lies Over the Ocean
- Swap Meet
- Working Agreements

Information Processing

	Activating & Engaging	Exploring & Discovering	Organizing & Integrating
A B Each Teach		X	
Analogy Prompts	X		
Around the Room and Back Again	X		
Assumptions Challenge		X	
Assumptions Inquiry		X	
Assumption Wall		X	
Brainstorm Modalities	X		
Brainstorm Questions	X		
Card Stack and Shuffle	X	X	
Carousel Interview		X	
Carousel Brainstorming	X		
Catalogue			X
Causal Loop Diagram		X	
Clarify Conflicting Mental Models	X	X	
Conflict Conversation Template		X	
Content Check			X
Corners		X	
Criteria Matrix		X	
Delve and Dialogue		X	
Diversity Rounds		X	
Done/Yet-to-Do Questions			X
Energy Sources Team Survey		X	
First Turn/Last Turn		X	
Fishbone Diagram		X	
5-3-1			X
Focused Reading		X	
Force-Field Analysis		X	
Four-Box Synectics	X		
Futures Wheel		X	

	A & E	E & D	O & I
Gatekeeping		X	
Gots and Wants			X
Here's What, So What, Now What		X	
Histomap		X	X
Hopes and Fears	X		
Inner-Outer Circle	X	X	
Inventories: Meeting		X	X
Inventories: Norms I		X	X
Inventories: Norms II		X	X
Inventories: Norms III		X	X
Inventories: Norms IV		X	X
Inventories: Other		X	X
Issues Agenda	X		
Jigsaw Carousel		X	
Jigsaw to Learn Information		X	
Journal	X		X
Key Concepts/Key Ideas		X	
Key Words			X
Know, Think You Know, Want to Know	X		
Lasso		X	
Left-Hand Column		X	
Matchbook Definitions			X
Modified Jigsaw		X	
Most Important Point (MIP)			X
Naive Question		X	
One-Word Summary			X
Outcome Mapping		X	X
Paired Verbal Fluency	X		X
Paraphrase Passport		X	
Partners Report			X
People, Place, Thing Cards			X
People Search	X		X

	A & E	E & D	O & I
Polarity Mapping		X	
Pyramid		X	
Quartet Facilitation		X	
Read and Example		X	
Recipe			X
Role Hunt	X		
Round-Robin Reflection			X
Say Something		X	
Scrambled Sentences	X		X
Sensing Interviews		X	
7-11 Conversation			X
Songs	X		
Sort Cards	X		X
Sound and Motion Symphony			X
Spot Analysis		X	
Stem Completion	X	X	
Stir the Classroom			X
Stoplight			X
Strategy Harvest			X
Structure Conversations About Data		X	
Success Analysis		X	
Text Rendering		X	
Three Balloons			X
3-2-1 Plus 1			X
Traffic Light	X		
Triad Inquiry		X	
Trios PPPI		X	
Triple Track			X
Vocabulary Review			X
Walk About	X		X
Wicked Problems Map		X	

The Strategies

Personalize this collection by printing from the accompanying CD-ROM and adding your own notes.

A B Each Teach

Information Processing: Exploring and Discovering

PROCESS
- Pairs designate one partner as A and one as B.
- Person A reads one section of text.
- Person B reads another section of text.
- When both are ready, they teach their section to their partner.

ALTERNATIVES
- Pairs conclude by developing a summary of the text essence.
- Pairs join another pair and develop a summary.

TIPS
- If energy is needed, create pairs through use of partners, or any device that will get people to move about the room.
- First, give instructions on the structure of the task, then name the partner with whom they will be working.
- Participants need to stack, pack, and move their possessions.

Adjournment Directions

Facilitator Moves

PROCESS
Facilitator says, "To close the day, four things. Listen, then do. When I am done talking, you will do several things":
1. One of the teammates will put "gots" and "wants" (see strategy in this appendix) in the appropriate place.
2. Another team member will put the equipment back in the equipment bag.

3. Recycling—another team member will put all the pop cans on the side table and trash into trash barrels.
4. Another team member will push the chairs in neatly.

ALTERNATIVE
- Vary according to your environment.

TIP
- Purse packing, paper filing, and watch checking are normal activities at the end of a session. Be sure to get full attention before giving directions.

Airplane Stacking

Facilitator Moves

PROCESS
- Explain metaphor related to control tower at airport directing the order in which planes are to land.
- Assign numbers to those with raised hands. Advise them to remember their number.
- Call on number 1, then number 2, and so on.
- Do not comment on participant responses. If a question is posed, list on a flip chart for later attention.
- When more hands are raised, add these to this list or start another list.

ALTERNATIVES
- None

TIPS
- Since participants know when they will be called, they will be less anxious and listen more effectively to others.
- Participants will hear many ideas in a short amount of time without intervening (and lengthy) facilitator comments.

Analogy Prompts

Information Processing: Activating and Engaging

PROCESS

- Pose prompts as analogies, such as:
  - o How do runners manage to have a speed-up kick left for the finish?
  - o How did the stagecoaches of the American West manage to race across great distances in just a few days?
  - o How do the answers to the above relate to a challenge faced by the group?

ALTERNATIVE

- Dialogue or brainstorm.

TIP

- Look for connections, such as the realization that stagecoaches changed horses frequently; this can lead to rotating and delegating school improvement tasks.

Applause

Facilitator Moves

PROCESS

- At the close of small-group work, ask participants to give themselves a hand.
- Model by clapping your hands.

ALTERNATIVES

- None

TIPS

- Whole-group applause reunites subgroups and restores a sense of group community.
- Collective applause generates electrochemical energy in the brain, which contributes to a resourceful state for learning.

Around the Room and Back Again

Information Processing: Activating and Engaging

PROCESS
- Write one response to a prompt.
- Next, without taking notes, move about the room and share your response, mentally cataloguing the responses of others.
- When your head is full, or when you are signaled, return to your seat and list the responses you heard from others.
- Table groups pool responses.

ALTERNATIVE
- Brainstorm a list of items.

TIP
- Connect the prompt to something being studied (e.g., things that go wrong in meetings) and refer back to the pooled list during the presentation.

Ask for Sabotage Ideas

Facilitator Moves

PROCESS
- State the agreement that the group has made.
- Say, "I know that none of you would ever deliberately sabotage this agreement, but if you were to do so, under what conditions might you make that choice?"

ALTERNATIVE
- Ask pairs or small groups to talk about this question.

TIPS
- Elicits hidden reservations or unconsciously held conditions under which members would not keep an agreement
- Provides an opportunity to clarify misunderstandings, develop ideas to overcome perceived obstacles, or reshape the decision

Assumptions Challenge

Information Processing: Exploring and Discovering

PROCESS

- Participants set aside two to four good ideas from a generated list.
- Each idea is explored for conditions in which the idea would be productive and conditions in which it would be counterproductive.
- Discuss how good ideas are rarely rules, but instead represent principles.

ALTERNATIVE

- Use the process above to select ideas that address the needs of the group.

TIP

- Especially when the group has generated the ideal list, stress that this is not a right or wrong conversation.

Assumptions Inquiry

Information Processing: Exploring and Discovering

PROCESS

- Invite members to list their assumptions related to a challenge or an initiative. Assumptions related to professional development, for example, might include that there is limited time for professional development, that professional development must take place in seminar settings, or that some teachers are resistant.
- Invite the group to inquire about these assumptions. What data inform them? What might be alternative interpretations to the same data? In which aspects are the assumptions generalizable, and in which aspects are they situational?

ALTERNATIVE

- See Card Stack and Shuffle in this appendix.

TIP

- Review and encourage pausing, paraphrasing, and inquiring.

Assumptions Wall

Information Processing: Exploring and Discovering

PROCESS
- Individuals list assumptions about a topic.
- Have participants choose one that most informs their behavior.
- Participants write their choice on sentence strip in 8–12 words.
- Post assumptions on the wall.
- Facilitator models inquiry (approachable voice, plurals, invitational stems, and positive presuppositions) and inquiry categories (importance, under what conditions, source, data, beliefs, values). Example: "I'm curious about that assumption. Whose is it? Help me to understand what are some reasons you value that highly."
- Individuals inquire about posted assumptions in round-robin fashion.

ALTERNATIVE
- The group lists assumptions related to a topic. One to three assumptions are selected. The group makes inquiries about these assumptions. The group then identifies implications of the selected assumptions.

TIPS
- Use groups of 4–12.
- Caution the group not to "beat to death" the first assumption explored.
- Model approachable voice.
- Intervene and correct whenever the inquiry begins to sound like interrogation and disbelief.

Attention First

Facilitator Moves

PROCESS
- With a credible voice, call for attention. Example: "Look in this direction, please."
- Maintain a frozen body and frozen gesture (see strategies below).
- When the group is attentive and still, breaks eye contact, breathe, and step into another space (see Break and Breathe, described below).
- With an approachable voice, give the next direction.

ALTERNATIVE

- With a credible voice, say, "Thank you" when the majority of the group is attentive.

TIP

- As groups tire, they become less responsive to verbal directions. The visual nature of this strategy gets attention from visual-processing people, whose silence alerts auditory processers to attend.

Banned Words

Inclusion

PROCESS

- Table groups identify a few words they would like banned from this session.
- One or two words are heard from each group and charted.
- The group agrees to collectively groan whenever one of these words is heard.
- The group practices the groan.

ALTERNATIVES

- None

TIPS

- Explain that sometimes words are overworked in organizations. This will give participants an opportunity to be free from them during this session.
- Periodically use one of the banned words to playfully stimulate a response.

Brainstorm Modalities

Information Processing: Activating and Engaging

PROCESS

- Define the subject.
- Give everyone a minute or two to think.
- Invite members to call out ideas.
- A member records ideas on flip chart.

- Code the first 10 ideas as visual, auditory, or kinesthetic.
- Compute a ratio for each modality.
- Brainstorm again, focusing on the least-represented modality.

ALTERNATIVES
- Use paired conversations for think time.
- Have pairs or small groups brainstorm, code, and brainstorm again instead of working as a full group.

TIP
- Explain that considering the topic from the least-used perspective will bring fresh ideas to the surface.

Brainstorm Questions
Information Processing: Activating and Engaging

PROCESS
- Define the subject.
- Give everyone a minute or two to think.
- Invite members to call out questions.
- A member records questions on a flip chart.
- Categorize the questions and determine what information is necessary and how it might be gathered.

ALTERNATIVES
- Use paired conversations for think time.
- Have the work done in pairs or small groups.
- Precede the activity with dialogue.

TIP
- Explain that generating questions can illuminate the group's work.

Break and Breathe
Facilitator Moves

PROCESS
- Pause, drop all nonverbal gestures, move to a different spot, and then bring up a different voice pattern from the one used in the previous location.

ALTERNATIVES
- Most often used to transition between getting attention and presenting information.
- Also useful when the facilitator wants to recover from a mistake or shift thinking in the room.

TIP
- Drop eye contact and do not speak while moving to a different spot.

Caping
Facilitator Moves

PROCESS
- The facilitator records a participant's idea on a chart and says, "That's an important idea. Let's come back to it when we can give it full attention."

ALTERNATIVES
- The facilitator directs the recorder to record.
- Some might know this strategy by the name Parking Lot.
- Encourage self-directed recording.

TIP
- It is important to return to this item in some way. Options include the following: at the end of the meeting, in a subgroup after the meeting, or on the next agenda.

Card Games

Facilitator Moves

PROCESS

- Distribute a playing card to each individual (Jack = 11, Queen = 12, King = 13, Ace = 1)
- Ask people to stand, find others with cards appropriate to the patterns below, gather their materials, and sit together.

ALTERNATIVES

- Pairs — same number, same color
- Pairs — same number, different color
- Pairs — same number, different color, different suit from last time
- Pairs — cards add up to 14 (same color)
- Pairs — cards add up to 14 (different color)
- Three — cards add up to 21 (same suit, different suit)
- Four — four of a kind
- Five — best poker hands (can do a number of times)
- Any number— form into runs: same suits, same color, different color
- Four groups — by suit
- Other combinations limited only by your imagination

TIP

- Shuffle or consciously arrange cards to break up cliques or table groups.

Card Stack and Shuffle

Information Processing: Exploring and Discovering,
Activating and Engaging

PROCESS

- Participants complete two stems, such as "Good student writers . . . " and "Good teachers of writing . . . "
- Each response is written on a separate 3 × 5 card.
- Table groups, stack cards, and shuffle them. Pass them to the table on your right.
- Person A selects a card and reads it to the group.

- Members identify possible assumptions related to the response on the card.
- Group members then explore the implications of those assumptions.
- Repeat the pattern, with people B, C, and D drawing cards in turn.

ALTERNATIVES

- Use only one stem.
- Preface this activity with instruction about assumptions and implications.

TIPS

- Demonstrate drawing a card and eliciting assumptions.
- Demonstrate exploring implications of one of those assumptions.
- Encourage paraphrasing and inquiring.
- This can be a scaffold for dialogue.

Carousel Brainstorming

Information Processing: Activating and Engaging

PROCESS

- Members call out ideas while a recorder charts them.

ALTERNATIVES

- Post topics or questions on charts.
- Cluster members into groups of three to five and have each group stand before a chart with a marker color that is different from that of other groups.
- Each group calls out ideas, which are recorded on the charts.
- Each group moves clockwise to the next chart, reviews what the previous group has written, and adds ideas with the colored pen with which they first recorded.
- Members take a gallery walk to read all posted ideas.

TIP

- Stress that brainstorming means that there is no talking about the items, but rather the groups are just to list items. Even mature groups tend to forget this.

Carousel Interview

Information Process: Exploring and Discovering

PROCESS

- Prepare interview-recording sheets, one for each question.
- Form groups of six, each person with one question.
- Round 1: Write a response to your own question in the top space.
- Round 2: 1 and 2 interview each other; 3 and 4 interview each other; 5 and 6 interview each other.
- Round 3: 1 and 3; 2 and 5; 4 and 6.
- Round 4: 1 and 4; 2 and 6; 3 and 5.
- Round 5: 1 and 5; 2 and 4; 3 and 6.
- Round 6: 1 and 6; 2 and 3; 4 and 5.
- Join others with the same question.
- Share the responses and create a synthesizing statement.
- Be prepared to share your statement with the large group.

ALTERNATIVES

- Form groups of four, each person with one question.
- Have groups create a graphic, rather than a statement, to share with the large group.

TIPS

- Provide a recording page for each question, six spaces on each page.
- Make sure the questions are open-ended and varied.

Causal Loop Diagram

Information processing: Exploring and Discovering

PROCESS

- Advise members of the following:
  - o In single-loop learning, groups modify their actions according to the difference between expected and obtained outcomes.
  - o In double-loop learning, groups question the values, assumptions, and policies

that led to the actions in the first place.
- Identify and list the intended and unintended results of an action.
- Identify and list the mismatches between intentions and outcome
- Through dialogue, question the ways in which the framing of the problem, assumptions, values, and policies might have affected the outcome.

ALTERNATIVES
- None

TIPS
- Emphasize that this conversation is not about winning.
- Challenge attributions without examples.
- Invite the public testing of assumptions and ideas.
- Explain that the reasoning processes normally used by members in organizations inhibit the exchange of relevant information necessary for double-loop learning to occur. This includes making inferences without checking validity or advocating one's ideas as abstractions without illustrating or explaining one's reasoning.

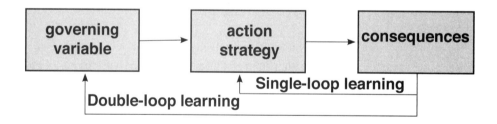

Catalogue

Information Process: Organizing and Integrating

PROCESS
- Return charts from the previous session to the meeting room.
- Fix chart papers on the wall, one on top of the next, with the heading of each visible.
- Review charts for data on prior conversations as useful.

ALTERNATIVE
- Post in left-to-right sequence on the wall.

TIPS
- Number each chart when recording group deliberations.
- Alert participants to the presence of the charts.

Check In

Inclusion

PROCESS
- Explain that this is a transition from outside the meeting to inside the meeting. For many people, sharing a little personal data helps them to make the transition. Members go around the circle, briefly naming their mood and anything that might detract them from fully participating.
- Ask a volunteer to go first. Ask the volunteer to indicate when he or she is finished by saying,"I'm finished" or another appropriate phrase.
- Stress that there is no side talk.
- At the end, make a summary paraphrase.

ALTERNATIVE
- Be the first speaker to model brevity.

TIP
- Stop anyone who interrupts a speaker.

Choose Voice

Facilitator Moves

PROCESS
- Credible voice is used for sending information. The rhythm is flat, with a narrow modulation of voice, and tends to drop at the end of sentences.
- Approachable voice is used for receiving information. The approachable voice is

rhythmic; one hears a relative rise and fall in pitch within a sentence or string of sentences. The voice tends to rise at the end of sentences.

ALTERNATIVE

- The range of voice modulation is unique for every person and varies from culture to culture.

TIPS

- The visual recognition of a flat voice rhythm includes a still head and often a dropping of the chin as a sentence comes to an end. This voice is often associated with giving procedural instructions, direct management, and making important content points.
- The visual recognition of a rhythmic voice pattern includes moving the head while speaking.
- Use the visual recognition patterns to assess the probability that work groups are on task (credible) or engaged in social talk (approachable).

Choreograph an Opening

Inclusion

PROCESS

- "Thank you for coming." Make high eye contact with the group. Use a credible and approachable voice. Open your hands palms up.
- "On the agenda are four topics." Use a credible voice, look at the agenda, pause after reading each topic. Turn to the group, freeze body, and count internally 3, 2, 1.
- "Before we start." Walk a few feet from the flip chart (presentation space).
- "I imagine some of you would rather be in classrooms today, and for good reason. Rooms must be set up, final touches done for opening day, and materials have to be organized." Gesture outside, toward classrooms. Pause periodically. Use credible voice, pause, and internally count 3, 2, 1. Then move halfway back to the flip chart.
- "At the same time, given your passion for serving students in the most complete ways possible, you might be wondering what can happen here that can make this worth your while." Use an approachable voice. Turn palms up, gesturing to group. Use inclusive language.
- "The first topic today is _____." Walk back toward the flip chart. Look at and point to the flip chart. Use a credible voice.

ALTERNATIVE

- Language choices: *some of you*, *all of you*, *a few of you*, *many of you*.

TIP

- Language for the reasons for being in classrooms and about passion for students should be artfully vague. If it is too specific, you will lose some listeners; they will say to themselves, "That is not me."

Clarify Conflicting Mental Models

Information Processing: Activating and Engaging, Exploring and Discovering

PROCESS

See the following strategies in this appendix: Assumptions Inquiry, Assumptions Wall, Card Stack and Shuffle, Delve and Dialogue, and Round-Robin Reflection.

Clearing

Inclusion

PROCESS

- Begin a meeting by inviting members to clear any thoughts that are on their minds.
- Nothing is irrelevant.
- Allow members to speak only twice.

ALERNATIVE

- Use a round-robin approach or invite members to speak whenever they wish.

TIP

- Silence is okay.

Close the Discussion

Decisions

PROCESS

- The person in charge displays decision options.
  - o Participants can vote on whether to keep the discussion going or not.
  - o The person in charge decides whether to end the discussion or extend it.
  - o Everyone has one more chance to make a point.
  - o Continue the discussion but limit it to a specific topic.
  - o Close the discussion if someone calls for closure and two others agree.
  - o Delegate the decision making to a subgroup.
  - o Talk until a predetermined time limit has been reached. The person in charge makes an executive decision if the group hasn't decided by then.
- The members explore the advantages and drawbacks of each option.
- The group selects an option to use on a regular basis.

ALTERNATIVE

- The group selects a few options for consideration when approaching a decision.

TIP

- The goal is efficiency, consistency, clarity, and flexibility.

Closing the Window

Facilitator Moves

PROCESS

- The facilitator says, "You have this much time left on this topic" while moving his or her hands closer together, starting at shoulder-width apart.

ALTERNATIVES

- None

TIPS

- Move hands slowly together while scanning the group for any signals that someone wants to speak.

- This strategy can stimulate contributions from people who have been sitting on an idea but have not yet said it.

Combine Opposites
Decisions

PROCESS
- Use when the group is stuck. Ask if two sets of people with divergent views would be willing to step outside and bring a recommendation back to the group.
- Ask the group if this idea is agreeable.
- Determine a time for the subgroup to converse. Their choices are now, outside the meeting room, or later, at a break. The only limitation is that the recommendation must be made today.
- Clarify the subgroup's decision-making authority with the full group. Determine whether the subgroup will be making a decision to which the group will abide or bring a recommendation for group consideration.

ALTERNATIVES
- None

TIPS
- Request or suggest that certain members serve on the committee. Asking the most impassioned voice to serve increases the likelihood of group acceptance.
- Set a time limit for the subgroup.

Conflict Conversation Template
Information Processing: Exploring and Discovering

PROCESS
- The facilitator poses the following questions, providing time and processes for related conversations.
    1. What is your relationship to this conflict?
    2. How do you feel about it?
    3. What are your expectations?

4. What are the worst possible outcomes of addressing this conflict?
5. What are the worst possible outcomes of not addressing this conflict?
6. What are the best possible outcomes of addressing this conflict?
7. What do you imagine the other person (or group) thinks are the worst and best outcomes?
8. What are you willing to do to achieve the best possible outcomes?
9. What would you like the other person (or group) to do to achieve the best possible outcome?

ALTERNATIVES

- Divide the questions into sections, summarizing at the end of each section. Example: 1, 2, 3; 4, 5, 6; 7, 8, 9.
- Have members summarize or make facilitator observations.
- Use this process with both parties when a conflict exists between pairs or small groups of people.
- Use this to help a group think through its perceptions about a conflict with another group.

TIP

- The term *relationship* in question 1 is deliberately vague, so that members can speak from whatever viewpoint is safest or for which they have energy.

Content Check

Information Processing: Organizing and Integrating

PROCESS

- Randomly distribute cards numbered 1 through 4.
- Display a chart with the following ideas:
  1. Walk out knowing what to do.
  2. Why are we doing it?
  3. What are we expecting to see?
  4. What are our next steps?

The numbers members receive determine which meeting summary statement they make.

ALTERNATIVES
- Members draw a playing card.
- Numbered cards are thrown on the table, and members scramble for their questions of choice.
- Add other summary checks for groups larger than four. Some examples might be as follows:
  o Who needs to know what happened in this meeting?
  o By when are the next steps due?
  o What should be highlighted in the minutes of the meeting?

TIP
- Make the process routine for greatest results or alternate with Process Check in this appendix.

Corners
Information Processing: Organizing and Integrating

PROCESS
- Post labels in corners of room.
- Participants move to the corner of greatest interest.
- Form clusters of two or three. Ask participants to explore and share their reasoning for selecting this topic.

ALTERNATIVES
- Use three corners instead of four.
- After a period of time, instruct people to move to the corner of their second choice and repeat the sharing in clusters of two or three.
- Ask people to stand in the corner that represents their position on an issue.

TIPS
- It is sometimes helpful to remind participants to form small groups by moving to corners where people have not yet clustered.
- Learning is enhanced when participants identify interests within a topic.
- On the second day, ask the participants to return to their corners of choice and, in small clusters, talk about what connections they are making to their topic of interest.

Criteria Matrix

Information Processing: Exploring and Discovering

PROCESS

- Identify a decision you wish to make and the alternatives you are considering.
- Identify the criteria you consider important.
- Assign each criterion an importance score.
- Determine the extent to which each alternative posseses each criterion.
- Express as high, medium, or low.
- Assign number values such as high = 3, medium = 2, and low = 1.
- Record on a criteria matrix and analyze the scores to see which alternative has the highest total points.
- Based on your reaction to the selected alternative, determine the next steps.

ALTERNATIVE

- Assign a point value to each criterion if some are more important than others.

TIPS

- Group needs only rough agreement on high, medium, and low ratings.
- Should two alternatives appear to be equally desirable, dialogue or add other criteria.

Criterion	A	B	C
Available resources	H	H	H
Could serve as stimulus to another desired change	H	M	M
Staff readiness	M	L	L
Congruence with another program	M	L	M
Numerical values	10	7	8

Decision Options
Decisions

PROCESS
- Executive Decision
  - o Clarify whether the group's function is to inform or to recommend.
  - o Announce when a decision will be made and the manner in which it will be communicated to the group.
- Fallback position
  - o Limit group decision-making time.
  - o Define a decision process if the group cannot decide within the allotted time.
- Subgroup decision
  - o Clarify whether the subgroup will be bringing back a decision or a recommendation.
  - o Provide decision parameters.

ALTERNATIVE
- Specify the decision-making strategy to be used. (See Close the Discussion above, and other strategies listed as "Decisions" in this appendix.)

TIP
- Select an option before discussion begins.

Decontaminate Problem Space
Facilitator Moves

PROCESS
- Locations evoke memory. When a negative or counterproductive statement has been made, the location from which it was made evokes emotional recall.
- Step away from any location in which a statement distressing to the group was made.

ALTERNATIVES
- If the person introducing you is disliked by the group or says something that causes distress, begin your work in any space other than the space occupied by the introducer.
- If you say something clumsy or offensive, step out of the space in which it was said,

point back to the space, and say, "Did I say that?" Or "That was stupid, I apologize for that."

- Rooms also evoke memories. If you are required to work in a room in which the participants have negative reactions, redesign the work space and change the furniture arrangement.

TIP

- The stronger the emotional message, the greater the decontamination effort. Move to the back of the room to decontaminate the effect of intense negative messages.

Delve and Dialogue

Information Processing: Exploring and Discovering

PROCESS

- Read a selection of text and make connections to some aspect of your work.
- In groups, share some of your connections.
- Honor the spirit of inquiry with pausing, paraphrasing, and inquiring.

ALTERNATIVE

- Assign this to trios instead of a group.

TIPS

- Review the principles of dialogue prior to starting this process.
- Because not listening is a common default pattern, you might want to periodically stop the action and ask people to notice what is happening in the conversation or engage them in the Round-Robin Reflection described in this appendix.

Disagreement Grid

Facilitator Moves

PROCESS

- Ask participants to participate in the next activity as a warm-up to conversations in which diverse opinions are held.

- Draw a 4 × 4 grid on a chart. Ask the participants to assume that each square is equal in dimension to the other squares.
- Ask the participants how many squares they see.
- As each number is offered, write it on the chart margin without comment.
- After several numbers are recorded, stop. Ask, "Who saw [one of the higher numbers of squares]? Would you please explain to the group where you see these squares?"
- Mark on the grid as a member explains what he or she sees.
- Ask "Was the person who said 16 wrong? 17? 24?"
- Addressing the whole group, say, "As we move into the conversation that follows, let me suggest that when you have a difference of opinion, you can say, 'I see it a different way.'"

ALTERNATIVE

- Prepare a slide with the grid.

TIP

- This can be an appropriate time to talk about other language forms that can be used when disagreement occurs. Suggest that participants use the word *and*, which implies addition, instead of *but*, which implies that the first speaker is wrong.

Diversity Rounds

Information Processing: Exploring and Discovering

PROCESS

- Indicate that the directions will be purposively vague so members can decide which subgroup they will report to.
- The facilitator chooses categories that fit the group's purpose, going from lesser to greater levels of sensitivity. Examples: birth order, decade of birth, sex, cognitive style, time in the organization, ethnicity.
- As each category is named, stand and search for three or four people who fit the criteria.
  - o How has this identity criteria shaped or influenced you as a professional?
  - o Talk in subgroups for 8-10 minutes.

- Hear reports from group.
- The facilitator names a new category, and the pattern is repeated 3 or 4 times.
- Members write responses to prompts, such as the following: What I am noticing about myself, the group, and the effect of being in various subgroups? How do I feel about the various subgroups that I selected? What might we do to maximize the unique contributions of the various subgroups?
- Responses are shared in heterogeneous groups.
- Each group develops a summary paraphrase of its findings and recommendations.

ALTERNATIVE
- Instead of journal entries, small groups might converse about their responses to the prompts.

TIP
- This is best for a group of at least 20 people. If a group becomes too large, divide into smaller subgroups.

Done/Yet-to-Do Questions
Information Processing: Organizing and Integrating

PROCESS
- Regarding a group project, individual members record a list of tasks that are done, tasks that are yet to be done, and questions about getting the work done.
- In table groups, share the information.
- Get agreement on the next most important things to be done.

ALTERNATIVES
- Identify tasks that should be discarded even if not done.
- Run the process as a facilitated full-group activity.

TIP
- Members are often so deep in the complexity of work that it hard to see where they are and generate focus and energy for the next tasks.

Eliminate the Negative

Decisions

PROCESS

- Assuming that members have clarified items on a list, ask, "Are there any items you would be okay removing?"
- When a member names an item, ask if anyone objects. If not, remove the item.
- If there is an objection, do not remove the item. No discussion is required.
- When this process is complete, move to the next step in the decision-making process.

ALTERNATIVES

- None

TIP

- Explain that this process saves the group the time of talking about items in which the group has limited interest.

Energy Sources Team Survey

Information Processing: Exploring and Discovering

PROCESS

- Aquire a survey from *www.adaptiveschools.com*.
- Team members individually respond to questions about their team.
- Tabulate scores for each energy source for each person.
- Use the data to dialogue about its meaning.

ALTERNATIVES

- Use either an electronic version or a paper version.
- It might be useful to calculate a mean, median, and mode.
- Use the instrument in a prescriptive manner to determine what actions might be taken to increase certain energy sources in the group.

TIPS
- Emphasize that the data is nonevaluative and serves as baseline impressions.
- Use the data to dialogue about its meaning.
- Consider the strengths of the group as well as discrepancies.
- It is particularly useful to do item analysis.
- When items are considered, they become sources of understanding for goal setting.
- Copies and scoring can be purchased at www.adaptiveschools.com.

Existing State–Desired State Map
Decisions

PROCESS
- Display a desired-state map, as shown below.
- Explain that defining the desired state establishes a goal and is more important than exploring why the problem exists.
- The group names a desired state in broad terms.
- Develop a behavioral description. What would one see and hear when the desired state is achieved?
- Identify the resources required to achieve the desired state. Consider skills, knowledge, and behavior.
- Select the most catalytic of resources and develop a plan for creating them.

ALTERNATIVE
- Generate a description of the existing state, and then describe the desired state as a direct contrast to existing state elements.

TIPS
- The facilitator should preview the stages and sequence of thinking required in this approach.
- When members do not have the same information about an issue, it is useful to describe the existing state from the various perspectives. Otherwise, public display of the existing state is rarely of great value.

DESIRED STATE MAP

| Existing State | Resources → | Desired State |

Finger Minutes
Facilitator Moves

PROCESS
- During an activity, ask the group to pause.
- Participants in a group are to decide how many minutes they need to finish and designate one person to raise his or her hand to indicate how many minutes the group needs to finish the activity. Set a limit by indicating a fist (0) to the maximum number of minutes (with fingers) you want to allow (0, 1, 2, 3, 4, or 5).
- Name the finger numbers you see so the large group is aware of variations.
- Compute a rough average (what you believe to be a number that will allow most groups to be satisfied with the additional time and limit the frustration of groups that are already finished).
- Share the allotted time with the group.

ALTERNATIVE
- Without giving a range of times, ask the groups how much more time they need.

TIP
- Another value of this strategy is that it helps the groups to recognize that their group is a subset of the whole and that the facilitator is attending to the needs of the entire assembly.

First Job

Inclusion

PROCESS

- In round-robin style, each person reveals his or her first paid job. Responses might include jobs like babysitting, shucking corn, and picking fruit.

ALTERNATIVE

- Explore the possible relationships between the first paid job and current work.

TIP

- Comment on how we are all the same in terms of the universality of some experiences.

First Turn/Last Turn

Information Processing: Exploring and Discovering

PROCESS

- Form groups of four to eight.
- Silently and simultaneously, members read a section of text and highlight three or four items that have particular meaning for them.
- The facilitator names a person to start in each group.
- In turn, members share one of their items but do not comment on it. They simply name it.
- In round-robin fashion, group members comment about the identified item with no cross-talk.
- The initial person who named the item now shares his or her thinking about the item and therefore gets the last turn.
- Repeat the pattern around the table.

ALTERNATIVES

- When possible, have members read the text before coming to the meeting. When they have read prior to the meeting, allow 3–4 minutes for them to review what they marked. This can save face for those who forgot to read.

- Reading sources can include journal articles, policy statements, mission statements, a sample of student work, or original writing by members on a common topic.

TIPS

- Select the first speaker geographically (e.g., the person sitting with his or her back most directly against the wall). Selection that is both structured and random can interrupt problematic patterns that occur in group dynamics (e.g., having one person always be the first responder).
- Stress that there is no cross-talk. Explain that when cross-talk occurs, it takes the focus off the speaker, changes the topic, diminishes the speaker's influence, and interferes with listening.
- Explain that structured dialogue allows members to develop the necessary emotional skills and values for high-quality dialogue. This experiential learning will serve as a scaffold as participants learn to dialogue.
- Monitor and intervene when cross-talk occurs as groups begin.
- Groups of six are ideal.

Fishbone Diagram

Information Processing: Exploring and Discovering

PROCESS

- Draw a fishbone diagram on chart paper, as shown below.
- Code sections of the chart that are related to an existing condition of an issue. For example, for tardiness, you might list getting to school, school responses to tardiness, and school staff.
- Brainstorm factors that might be affecting the existing condition and record on the diagram.
- Explore pros and cons of various combinations of solution approaches.

ALTERNATIVES

- Have subgroups brainstorm each of the categories and record them on a separate chart.
- Report and explore the various charts. Allow additions.

TIP
- Protect the group from delving into too much minutiae.

Discovers cause-and-effect reasons for
existing program results. Determins focus
of improvement effort.

5-3-1

Information Processing: Organizing and Integrating

PROCESSES
- Members identify five words that represent today's learning.
- Share the ideas, one at a time, in round-robin fashion. Explore the ideas as they emerge.
- Select three central ideas.
- If these three ideas were to go into a container with a label, what would that label be?

ALTERNATIVE
- Use this strategy for what you want to remember from today's meeting or accomplishments.

TIP
- Foreshadow that there will be several steps, but do not tell the name of the strategy.

Focused Reading

Information Processing: Exploring and Discovering

PROCESS
- Members read and mark text for purposes, such as:
  - o √ Affirms prior knowledge
  - o ! Surprises you
  - o ? You wish to know more about this
- Within small groups and in round-robin fashion, members explore the items they marked. Each member shares only one item at a time.
- Explore only items marked as ! or ?.

ALTERNATIVE
- Change the prompts to fit the purpose of the task. Other prompts might include the following: what concerns you, what excites you, what neither concerns nor excites you.

TIP
- Use for text that the members are to read before a session.

Focusing Four

Decisions

PROCESS
- Explain task, topic, and process.
- Check for understanding.
- Brainstorm ideas and record on chart paper.
- Push for between 12 and 18 ideas.
- Members ask questions of clarification. The "author" responds.
- Members advocate items.

- By using the Rule of One-Third strategy in this appendix, determine which items are of greatest interest to the group. Use a hand count.
- Conclude by determining a process to narrow the choices down to one or two if necessary. See Close the Discussion in this appendix.

ALTERNATIVE

- Occasionally have partners confer before a new step in the process begins.

TIPS

- Each step in the process must be kept separate.
- Statements of advocacy must be stated in the positive, such as "I advocate this because . . . ," and never "I don't like this because . . . "
- Tell group members they will be guided, not bound, by the numbers. For example, in a group of 15 members, item A gets 9 counts and item B gets 11; that might not be a sufficient enough difference to select B. In cases like this, the facilitator will ask the group how it wants to handle the situation.
- View video available at www.adaptiveschools.com

Force-Field Analysis

Information Processing: Exploring and Discovering

PROCESS

- Post a T-chart with a topic or goal at the top. On the left side, write "forces for" and on the right side, write "forces against."
- Members list forces that fall into either category.
- Members may paraphrase or question for clarity.
- Limit each list to about six items. Once the list is deemed complete, mark the three strongest forces on either side.
- Explore how the forces against might be made weaker and the forces for might be strengthened. This phase may take the form of dialogue.
- Rate the forces and how feasible it would be to modify them.
- Select one or more on which to work.

ALTERNATIVES

- Assign the first three tasks above to small work groups, then chart and post group results.

- As a full group, entertain questions of clarification.
- Continue with the process as a full group.

TIPS

- Some forces may legitimately appear on either side of the chart.
- It is usually easier to weaken the forces restraining change than it is to strengthen the helping forces.
- Topics such as to decrease dropout rates, to increase attendance, or to increase student motivation to write might prove challenging, because their complexity exceeds this simple analysis.

Forced-Choice Stickers I

Decisions

PROCESS

- List options on a flip chart.
- Distribute an equal number of stickers to each member.
- Instruct members to spend all their stickers.
- Members place stickers near preferred options.
- The stickers represent a vote and are binding.

ALTERNATIVE

- Distribute stickers based on a Rule of One Third formula.

TIP

- Clarify options before members spend stickers.

Forced-Choice Stickers II

Decisions

PROCESS

- Chart and post various options from which to select.
- Invite members to stand by the chart of their first choice. Ask the members to talk

about why they value this option. Have each group select a spokesperson.
- Each spokesperson gives a brief advocacy statement.
- Entertain questions of clarification.
- Provide each member with an equal number of stickers.
- Stickers are spent.

ALTERNATIVES
- The group examines sticker distribution and decides which few options should receive further consideration and conversation.
- Post options on several flip charts. Subgroups should stand by the options that represent their choices and tell the group the rationale for their choices.
- After advocating and inquiring about each member's choices, fresh stickers are distributed and spent.

TIPS
- Some members will want to know if they can spend all their stickers on one option. Discourage this.
- It is acceptable to place more than one of one's stickers on an item.
- Prior dialogue is valuable.

Foreshadow

Facilitator Moves

PROCESS
- Before a break, name the next topic or activity to occur.

ALTERNATIVE
- Build suspense by not naming the topic but suggesting that the information will be surprising.

TIP
- Anticipation serves the function of an advance organizer.

Four-Box Synectics
Information Processing: Activating and Engaging

PROCESS
- On chart paper, draw a 2 × 2 box. Post.
- A recorder at each table draws a similar box to collect the group's thinking.
- Elicit recommendations for an object or a concept to place in each of the boxes. Suggest each time that the next recommendation be as different as possible from the previous recommendation (examples: lamppost, sailboat, hammer, daisy).
- Instruct table groups to brainstorm three or four responses for each box to the prompt you provide. (Example: Professional communities are like a lamppost because _____. Professional communities are like a sailboat because _____.)
- Give groups 2 minutes to select their best items and a spokesperson.
- Elicit responses from the groups using a full statement such as "A professional community is like a lamppost because _____."

ALTERNATIVES
- People synectics. Provide each table group with three to five postcards that have images of famous people on them. Ensure that the postcards represent diversity.
- Direct the groups to talk about what they know about each person on the cards.
- Have the groups select one card and complete the phrase: [Name the person] is like [the topic you are working on] because_____
- Complete the phrase: [Name the person] is not like [the topic you are working on] because_____.

TIPS
- Explain that *synectics* is derived from two Greek roots: *syn* (bringing together) and *ectics* (diverse elements). This activity draws from the metaphoric brain, which hold information holistically.
- There is a whole-model of teaching on synectics developed by the Cambridge Synectics Group.
- Select topics that relate to your work, the environment, or the group.

Freeing Stuck Groups

Decisions

PROCESS

- The facilitator asks, "What's stopping us from making a decision?" or "Who would be willing to meet with ___ and ___ and develop a proposal for the next meeting?" or "Are you willing to give the subcommittee the authority to make that decision?" or "Would it be agreeable to the group if we asked ___ to bring us more information before we proceed?" or " I think this is a decision for ___. Shall we ask her to make it?"

ALTERNATIVES

- Group members can also pose these questions.
- See Naive Questions in this appendix.
- See Close the Discussion in this appendix.

TIP

- Identify, when possible, the time available in the meeting to reach closure.

Freeze Body

Facilitator Moves

PROCESS

- Stand. Say "Please look [insert a pause] this direction [pause]. Thank you." Maintain eye contact with the group and keep your body still.

ALTERNATIVE

- Add a frozen gesture. A frozen gesture is held in space for an extended amount of time, with little or no significant movement. Break from your frozen body, frozen gesture, and silence at the same time.

TIPS

- Kinesthetically oriented learners often do not process the information they hear; thus, the frozen body indicates to them, in a respectful way, "Be quiet and pay attention."
- When groups are tired, the first modality to weaken is the auditory.

Freeze Gesture
Facilitator Moves

PROCESS
- Hold a gesture in space for an observable amount of time with little or no significant movement. This occupies the listener unconsciously.

ALTERNATIVES
- Working with a group, combine with frozen body to focus attention.
- Working with an individual, combine the gesture with averted eyes to hold silence from the other until you are ready to speak.

TIP
- Explore various gestures in order to develop a few with which you are comfortable.

Futures Wheel
Information Processing: Exploring and Discovering

PROCESS
- Draw a wheel on a chart.
- Write the name of the innovation or idea that the group will be working with in the center of the wheel.
- Work outward from the center to the first layer of circles.
- Identify two positive consequences and two negative consequences. Have the positive and negative be as different as possible.
- Continue in this manner to the second layer, then the third and fourth.
- Dialogue about the findings. How might this information influence the perceptions and decisions of a planning team?

ALTERNATIVES
- Through this process, a need for more information might surface. Determine what is needed and how to gather it.
- Two small groups could work on the same decision, then share results to gain greater perspective.

TIPS
- These are not predictions. They are possible consequences.
- An analysis of the data may lead a group to abandon the idea.
- An analysis of the data can inform a group of ways of implementing the idea that would avoid some negatives.
- Use the information to learn what must be communicated to whom and in what ways.

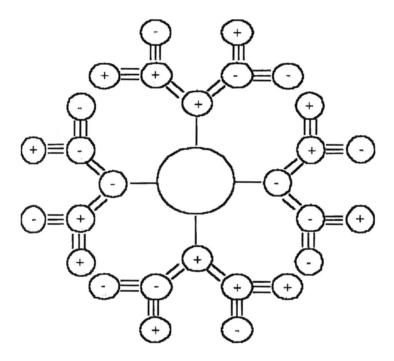

Gatekeeping

Information Processing: Exploring and Discovering

PROCESS
- A member notices that a colleague has not talked.
- The member says, "[Name], I'm aware you have not talked for a while. Is there anything you would like to add?"

ALTERNATIVES

- "[Name], I know you served on a committee addressing this. Do you have anything you'd like to say?"
- "[Name], from where I'm sitting, your eyebrows look furrowed. Any comments you'd like to make?"

TIP

- Phrase the questions so that the colleague can gracefully decline to speak.

Give One to Get One
Inclusion

PROCESS

- Individuals write data on a 3 × 5 card. Example: name, role, agency, time I spend doing _____, a trick of the trade about _____, a technique that works for me.
- Members move about the room and share the information on their card with another person. Members paraphrase and inquire so they can, in a moment, share their partner's card and the information with another person.
- At a signal, members trade cards.
- Members then locate a new partner and share the new card and information they just acquired with their new partner.
- At a signal, return to table groups. Share what you learned.
- As a group, identify what patterns or themes you detected.

ALTERNATIVES

- Do a third round.
- Provide a template for the sharing of patterns. "There were three themes here: _____, _____ and _____."
- Use to activate concepts such as "A belief I have about adult learners is . . . "

TIP

- Exploring emerging patterns provides diagnostic data to both the facilitator and the group.

Gots and Wants
Information Processing: Organizing and Integrating

PROCESS
- Individuals compose "gots" on sticky notes, one idea per sticky note. A "got" might be an idea received, something learned, or a positive response to working with a colleague.
- Individuals compose "wants" on sticky notes, one idea per sticky note. A "want" might be a comment about process (go faster or slower), a request for information, or a comment about materials.
- As the group adjourns, members place their sticky notes on charts labeled "gots" and "wants."

ALTERNATIVE
- See Pluses and Wishes in this appendix.

TIPS
- After the event, categorize and label the "gots" and "wants." Use this information to adjust your practices at the next session.
- Communicate to the group your response to their needs as you open the next session.

Greeting Circle
Inclusion

PROCESS
- Form a circle.
- The facilitator (or designated person) moves inside the circle and greets the person to the left.
- Continue inside the circle, greeting each person in turn.
- Those who have been greeted follow the person who greeted them inside the circle.
- When the facilitator returns to his or her original location, those inside the circle

greet a second time.
- This time, the person inside the circle is the greeter, not the greeted. This balances the circle.
- When the greeting is complete, ask two questions: How do you feel about the activity? What did you learn from it that will make you successful?

ALTERNATIVE
- Moving right around the circle.

TIPS
- No ritual is older, says Bob Chadwicka conflict authority, and none more anxiety-ridden, than that of greeting each other. The natural tendency is to seek out those one is comfortable with, those who are like oneself.
- The greeting circle allows the anxiety and apprehension of the individuals to be encountered. It releases energy into the room as the sound of voices and laughter.
- The emotional material must be expressed first to allow learning to take place. It grounds the person in the moment and allows people to be real.
- This is useful as a grounding for sessions on conflict, hard-to-talk-about topics, or when two or more groups are brought together for difficult conversations.

Grounding
Inclusion

PROCESS
- Form groups of six to eight.
- Explain that the purpose is to set a norm for respectful listening, to get everyone's voice in the room in a manner that is not confrontational, to allow people to connect with one another, to allow for the expressions of hopes and apprehensions, to value thinking and feeling, and to elicit agendas that might not otherwise be heard.
- Explain the procedure:
  o Members take turns talking.
  o When one member talks, all others are silent.
  o Full nonverbal attention is given to the speaker.
  o After everyone has talked, the first speaker will summarize what was said.

o When the members indicate that they understand the process, the facilitator names the first speaker.
- Post on a flip chart what members are to talk about:
  o My name is . . .
  o My relationship to this topic is . . .
  o My expectations are . . .
  o How I feel about being here is . . .
- When all groups are finished, the facilitator calls on the first speaker in each group to give a summary statement to the full assembly.

ALTERNATIVE
- With 12–16 group members, the grounding can be done with the full group.

TIPS
- Since this activity's primary purpose is to provide participants with an opportunity to be heard, this activity doesn't operate on clock time.
- Use this strategy when a meeting is going to address hard-to-talk-about topics. The harder the topic is to talk about, the more valuable the full-group grounding is.
- With a group size of 40–50 people, this activity might take as long as 45 minutes.
- "My relationship to this topic" is purposefully vauge. Do not explain it.

Group Groan
Inclusion

PROCESS
- Groups list what are the best and worst things that can happen in this session.
- Hear a few and record them on a flip chart.
- Make an agreement that should any of the worst things occur, all will participate in a group groan.
- Practice the groan once.

ALTERNATIVES
- Give think time before receiving the items.
- With groups of 12 or fewer, elicit both the best and the worst from the full group. Record in two columns.

TIP
- Have each group offer at least one worst thing for you to post on the flip chart.

Here's What, So What, Now What
Information Processing: Exploring and Discovering

PROCESS
- Distribute a three-column work sheet.
- Explain the purpose of each column: "Here's What" for specific data the group is working with; "So What" for an interpretation or meaning of the data; "Now What" can be a predication, an implication, or a question for further study.
- In pairs or in small groups, members complete the Now What and So What columns.
- Conduct a full-group dialogue.

ALTERNATIVE
- Structure the task to provide skills practice in paraphrasing and inquiry.

TIPS
- Provide an example and elaborate a response for each column.
- Provide specific "Here's What" data, such as 60% of female students scored X and 40% of male students scored X, or have groups generate their own data for this column.

High Fives
Facilitator Moves

PROCESS
- Members stand.
- Participants locate two other people who are currently not at the same table and give them a high five.

- When a group of three members has been established, participants gather their belongings, find a new table, and sit and wait for instructions.

ALTERNATIVE

- Instruct members to accomplish a task when seated. Example: Review key points from a previous agenda item or activate knowledge about the item the group is about to address.

TIPS

- Use the variation above when one of your goals is to support the development of relationships within the group.
- This variation can be helpful to introverted people because it gives them something to talk about when sitting with the trio.

Histomap

Information Processing: Exploring and Discovering, Organizing and Integrating

PROCESS

- Hang chart paper on the wall for a timeline.
- Mark eras in the group's history—the year the bond issue passed, the year the new principal arrived, the loss of a federal program.
- Use icons to illustrate the different events that occurred within each of the eras.
- Groups of people add words and icons to the timeline and share their memories.

ALTERNATIVE

- Organize groups randomly or as intact working groups.

TIPS

- When people hear about the same event from different perspectives, a more complex history is understood.
- What is expressed and understood can be released and does not have to dominate the working space of the group.

Hopes and Fears

Information Processing: Activating and Engaging

PROCESS
- Briefly write your fears and hopes about this session or topic.
- Pairs share their greatest fear and greatest hope.
- Quartets (pairs squared) meet and identify themes in fears and hopes.
- Quartets report themes to full group.
- Facilitator makes comments to normalize fears and identify common hopes.

ALTERNATIVES
- Pairs report all fears and hopes.
- Conduct process as full group, with the facilitator eliciting and charting.

TIP
- With either alternative, start with private reflection.

Inner-Outer Circle

Information Processing: Activating and Engaging, Exploring and Discovering

PROCESS
- Form an inner circle facing outward and an outer circle facing inward, with one-to-one correspondence.
- Inner-circle people respond to first prompt. Example: "As a student, my favorite teacher . . ." or " Students in grade 6 should . . ."
- Outer-circle people paraphrase the inner-circle people. Because paraphrasing evokes another response, allow the conversation to continue a few minutes with the outer-circle person only paraphrasing.
- Outer-circle people rotate clockwise three or four places.
- Outer-circle people respond to the same prompt while the inner circle paraphrases.
- Repeat the pattern with another prompt, if desired.

ALTERNATIVES
- If space does not permit one large set of circles, run activity in more than one circle.
- Use this to review or refine other skills, such as pausing or probing for specificity.

- Use this to explore concepts.
- Use this as a preface to dialogue.

TIPS
- Demonstrate the double-circle configuration with eight participants.
- Use this as an activator before instruction.

Inventories: Meeting

Information Processing: Exploring and Discovering, Organizing and Integrating
See Appendix L or www.adaptiveschools.com

PROCESS
- At the end of a meeting, individuals complete a meeting inventory.
- The meeting inventory data is then presented at the start of the next meeting.
- Subgroups study data and make recommendations about which standards to work on in the current meeting.

ALTERNATIVE
- Conduct the study and recommendations as a full group when group size is 12 or fewer.

TIPS
- Meeting effectiveness and efficiency will improve when the use of this tool becomes habituated.
- Download a sample meeting inventory from www.adaptiveschools.com. Modify as necessary.

Inventories: Norms I

Information Processing: Exploring and Discovering, Organizing and Integrating
See Appendix B or www.adaptiveschools.com

PROCESS
- Administer the norms inventory.

- Members mark the frequency with which they usually use these norms in meetings.
- Share with a partner.
- Explore what would have to happen for individuals to increase the frequency of some of the norms.
- As a group, identify one or two norms to which the group will rededicate its energy.
- Commit to periodically monitoring the group's use of the norms.

ALTERNATIVE
- Conduct the study and recommendations as a full group when group size is 12 or fewer. When the full assembly is much larger than 12, conduct the study and recommendations in groups of about 6.

TIPS
- These norms are behaviorally descriptive and therefore different from the "setting norms" process that groups sometimes use. These norms are viewed as working agreements.
- If individuals resist because they think the norms are a way of controlling behavior, help members to reframe that perception by stating that the norms of collaboration are about respect, courtesy, and contribution.
- Download full instructions and inventories from www.adaptiveschools.com.

Inventories: Norms II

Information Processing: Exploring and Discovering, Organizing and Integrating
See Appendix C or www.adaptiveschools.com

PROCESS
- Select a facilitator.
- In the current meeting, trios or individuals assess how the full group is adhering to the seven norms of collaboration and their subsets.
- Individuals average their data on each of the norms and mark the average.
- Individuals select a pen color different from the others and plot their data on a master scale.
- Facilitators lead a conversation in which group members share their perceptions and personal goals.
- As a group, identify one or two norms to which the group will rededicate its energy.
- Commit to periodically monitoring the group's use of the norms.

ALTERNATIVE
- Conduct the study and recommendations as a full group when group size is 12 or fewer. When the full assembly is much larger than 12, conduct the study and recommendations in groups of about 6.

TIPS
- These norms are behaviorally descriptive and therefore different from the setting-norms process that groups sometimes use. These norms are viewed as working agreements.
- If individuals resist because they think the norms are a way of controlling behavior, help members to reframe that perception by stating that the norms of collaboration are about respect, courtesy, and contribution.
- Download full instructions and inventories from www.adaptiveschools.com.

Inventories: Norms III

Information Processing: Exploring and Discovering, Organizing and Integrating
See Appendix C or www.adaptiveschools.com

PROCESS
- Select a facilitator.
- Have trios use the norms inventory to assess how the full group typically adheres to the seven norms of collaboration.
- Trios average their data for each norm and plot their averages on a master chart.
- The facilitator leads a conversation in which the members learn what the other trios were paying attention to that led them to mark certain norms the way they did.
- As a group, select one or two norms to which the group will rededicate its energy.

ALTERNATIVES
- Conduct the study and recommendations as a full group when group size is 12 or fewer.
- This process can also be used to introduce the norms.

TIPS
- Groups must "own" data in order to act on it. In this process the group arrives at a common description of the existing state (a state in which various perceptions exist

and are known).
- The nonjudgmental exploration of perceptual differences is essential to a collective understanding of group perception and dynamics.
- Download full instructions and inventories from www.adaptiveschools.com.

Inventories: Norms IV

Information Processing: Exploring and Discovering, Organizing and Integrating
See Appendix E

PROCESS
- In the current meeting, trios or individuals assess how the full group is adhering to the seven norms of collaboration using an abbreviated scale. Members mark their responses on transparency film.
- Stack the transparencies and place on an overhead projector. This allows all members to see the distribution of responses.
- The group seeks to understand what led to different perceptions.
- As a group, identify one or two norms to which the group will rededicate its energy. Explore ways to do that.

Inventories: Other

Information Processing: Exploring and Discovering, Organizing and Integrating

PROCESS
- Provide the rationale and possible applications for administering an inventory.
- Administer the inventory, score, and make the data public.

ALTERNATIVE
- Groups collectively assess themselves using an inventory.

TIPS
- Responses on inventories are not good or bad. Inventories provide information that carries whatever meaning the group assigns to it.
- Many inventories can assist a group in learning about itself, either as individuals within the group or collectively.
- Some examples of individual inventories include cognitive style, educational belief

systems, modality preferences, people search, and five states of mind.
- Some examples of collective inventories include the six domains of group development, the concerns-based adoption model, and the five energy sources.

Is/Is Not
Decisions

PROCESS
- In one column write the facts that are known about a problem, where it is, what its effects are, when it occurs, and so on. For example, the boys scored higher than the girls in four of the five test batteries.
- In a second column, write the facts that are known to not be part of the problem. For example, boys and girls are doing equally well in daily assignments.

ALTERNATIVES
- Small groups generate "is" and "is nots." Report and agree on the most significant examples.
- Follow this with data gathering based on the is/is not analysis.

TIPS
- Provide categories for "is": Where, when, to what extent, and with whom does the problem occur?
- Provide categories for "is not": Where, when, to what extent, and with whom does this not occur? Therefore, what might explain the pattern of occurrence and nonoccurrence?

Issues Agenda
Information Processing: Activating and Engaging

PROCESS
- Brainstorm issues related to a project.
- Dialogue on degrees of importance, desirable attention sequences, and connections.
- Develop and agree to a timeline.

ALTERNATIVES
- After brainstorming, develop a criteria matrix (see strategy in this appendix) to analyze importance and attention sequences.
- An issues agenda can be conducted informally, focused only on topics to be addressed during the current meeting.

TIP
- Remind members of brainstorming rules. Even experienced groups can forget these without a reminder.

Jigsaw Carousel

Information Processing: Exploring and Discovering

PROCESS
- Form groups, one for each concept. (Example: If working with four concepts, you will need four groups.)
- Each group describes a concept in its own words.
- Give behavioral examples. (Example: What would they see and hear as indicators of this concept?)
- Have groups identify and describe situations in school, life, or work in which it would be important to draw on this concept.
- Pose questions intended to help others become aware of this concept in their life or work.
- Have groups create a logo or a simile as a reminder of this concept.
- Complete the simile: This concept is like a _____ because_____.
- Compose a brief statement or slogan that summarizes the concept.
- Report work to full assembly.

ALTERNATIVES
- None

TIPS
- Provide an advance organizer for the entire process.
- Have each member be responsible for learning one concept and then teaching it to others.

Jigsaw to Learn Information

Information Processing: Exploring and Discovering

PROCESS

- Cluster members into groups of five (if five topics are to be studied) and count off 1 to 5. Each number is assigned a reading.
- Have all the number 1s, 2s, 3s, and so on move into expert groups of like numbers.
- In the expert groups, members read the material, then converse about its meaning.
- Members determine what ideas they will share and how they will share the ideas in their home groups.
- Return to the home groups and share what has been learned in the expert groups.

ALTERNATIVE

- Expert groups develop an image or perform a skit to convey information.

TIPS

- While there is value in member choice, assigning topics takes less time than allowing members to choose their own topics.
- Provide prompts for expert-group conversations.

Journal

Information Processing: Activating and Engaging ,Organizing and Integrating

PROCESS

- Give the reason for a prompt and tell how it will be used in the session.
- Provide the prompt. Clarify terms.
- Set a time limit.

ALTERNATIVE

- Journal writing can be used for stimulating thinking prior to dialogue, reflecting time in a think-pair-share activity, leveling the playing field when various roles or cognitive styles are present, or capturing ideas in a fast-write format after being presented with information.

TIP
- Write the prompt using attributes of mediational questions: plurals, tentative language, syntactical substitutions, and positive presuppositions. For example: "As learners in this territory [positive presupposition], what things [plural] might [tentative language] you be doing [another positive presupposition] to be resourceful, receptive, and generative?" See Putting Inquiry First in chapter 3.

Key Concepts/Key Ideas
Information Processing: Exploring and Discovering

PROCESS
- Organize members into pairs.
- Assign a reading.
- Individuals read text, marking key concepts and ideas.
- When both have finished reading, they take turns sharing and exploring the concepts and ideas marked by each partner.

ALTERNATIVE
- Assign the reading in sections. After each section, share concepts and ideas.

TIP
- As with all text-based learning, remind members that a key value of this strategy is the different experiences and perspectives that each member brings to the topic.

Key Words
Information Processing: Organizing and Integrating

PROCESS
- In round-robin fashion, each member shares a key word that captures some important aspect of his or her learning that day.

ALTERNATIVES
- The facilitator offers a summary paraphrase at the end of the process.
- Table groups identify a keyword.

TIPS
- Participants tell why the word is important.
- Many can have the same word but for different purposes.

Knots
Facilitator Moves

PROCESS
- Form groups of eight into circles.
- Everyone places one's left hand in the circle and grasps the hand of one other person whose hand is in the circle.
- Now place right hands in the circle and grasp the hand of one other person whose hand is in the circle.
- Everyone now should be holding the hands of two other persons.
- Without letting go of the grips, untangle the human knot.

ALTERNATIVE
- Place the right hand in first.

TIP
- A group of six to eight is ideal. Ten is possible. Twelve is too many.

Know, Think You Know, Want to Know
Information Processing: Activating and Engaging

PROCESS
- Label chart paper with three columns: Know, Think You Know, Want to Know.
- Give a topic to the groups and have them complete the charts.
- Post the charts and have the group look for patterns and themes.

ALTERNATIVE
- The facilitator responds to the "Want to Know" column by providing responses to

the large group.

TIP

- If groups disagree on the "Know" column, encourage them to place content in the "Think You Know" column.

Lasso

Information Processing: Exploring and Discovering

PROCESS

- Circle or lasso words on a flip chart that lack specificity.
- Invite members to define the words within the context of the group's work.
- Example: "How to solve drug use at schools." Ask what you mean by drugs, which ones, which schools, what age levels, and even what you mean by "solve"—reduce, eliminate entirely, prevent?

ALTERNATIVES

- Ask pairs or small groups to define the words and report for group reinforcement or adoption.
- Record the definitions on chart paper.

TIPS

- Classes of language most useful to clarify: vague nouns or pronouns, vague verbs or action words, universal quantifiers, modal operators, and comparators. See chapter 3.
- As a general rule, clarify vague nouns and pronouns first.
- Make sure you are not trying to solve two problems at once.

Learning Partners

Facilitator Moves

PROCESS

- Distribute a page on which spaces are provided to sign up four partners.
- Explain that learning partners will be used for standing conversations or sometimes

to regroup and sit with a partner at a new location.

- Demonstrate asking a member to be your partner, writing the member's name on your page, and the member writing your name on the member's page.
- Members will sit when they have all four partners.
- Give an expectation for the amount of time this will take, perhaps 90 seconds.
- When most are seated, get the group's attention.
- Ask if anyone is missing a partner for the number 1 choice. If two raise their hands, make them partners. If only one raises a hand, indicate that he or she should go to the front of the room when that partner choice is called, signaling that he or she is available if another person cannot locate a partner at that time. If no one appears, he or she should join the "brightest" pair.

ALTERNATIVES

- Develop your own partner symbols (e.g. hats, sports teams) to reflect the culture or location of the group.
- Other partner systems: Call for eye contact partners (someone sitting at a table different from yours with whom you make eye contact), shoes partner (different shoes from yours), or color partner (matching clothing color)

TIP

- When announcing a partner search, remind members to come to the front of the room if they are not able to find one's partner.

Left-Hand Column

Information Processing: Exploring and Discovering

PROCESS

- During dialogue, members maintain a split-sheet format for recording items in either a right- or left-hand column.
- Record in the right-hand column data or ideas one wants to remember.
- Record in the left-hand column what one notices about self-talk and reactions to the conversation.
- Examples include: what I need to set aside in my listening in order to stay present; my intentions; my judgments; my feeling in the moment, and is the feeling evoked by a correct interpretation of the interaction, or am I responding to "noise in my

head" or personal history in some way? What are my assumptions and what can I learn about me from my reactions?

ALTERNATIVE
- Provide members with two-column recording sheets, with prompts in the left-hand column like assumptions, feelings, judgments, and supportive data.

TIP
- Invite members to talk together on what they learned about themselves and dialogue.

Like Me
Inclusion

PROCESS
- Participants move chairs back from tables so it will be easy to stand if appropriate.
- Name categories like "My work is done at the elementary level" or "I have been in this district 5 or more years" or "I am a principal" or "I am typically up before 6 a.m."
- As people stand, remind them to look around and see who else is also in that group.
- Finally, make the category "other" for roles. (In other words, if your role has not been called, please stand.) The facilitator asks standing members to state their roles.

ALTERNATIVE
- For parent groups, change the prompts (My first child in this school, I attended this school, I speak a language other than English).

TIPS
- Because this strategy is done as an inclusion activity when you do not yet have a relationship with the group, it is important to state the multiple purposes of inclusion activities like this one. They include setting norms of participation, focusing mental energy inside the room, answering the question "who am I in relation to others in the room" and beginning the journey from an aggregate of individuals to a group.
- The category "other" is essential. People feel left out if their role is not acknowledged.

- Do not ask participants to say "Like me" when they stand. Perhaps this is appropriate for elementary children, but it is embarrassing for adults.

Lineups
Facilitator Moves

PROCESS
- Announce that the purpose is to regroup and energize.
- Designate a space in the room for members with low responses to stand and for members with high responses to stand. Others will form a line representing their response in relationship to those two points.
- Provide a topic (e.g., how hot do people like their salsa, birth dates) by anther desired profession, if not in education (alphabetically).
- Sample responses from different parts of the lineup.
- Cluster people into working groups by counting off or by moving along the line by threes, fours, or whatever group size is desired.

ALTERNATIVE
- Have half the line step forward. These people will walk toward the other half, forming a double line, with people facing each other. Facing members become partners for the next activity.

TIPS
- Structure lineups around the perimeter of the room for the best use of space.
- Choose a topic based on group members' knowledge of one another; intact groups might be more interested in alternative professions than groups whose members do not know one another.
- Choose a topic based on the amount of time available; some lineups require more reporting (e.g., years in the district), whereas others do not (e.g., how hot you like your salsa).

Matchbook Definitions

Information Processing: Organizing and Integrating

PROCESS
- Following the introduction of a topic, groups craft a "matchbook" definition.
- As on a matchbook cover, very few words can be used (8–12).
- Groups have 5 minutes to craft and post the definition.

ALTERNATIVE
- Use this strategy to check understanding by summarizing conclusions from a discussion or dialogue.

TIPS
- Keep the definitions posted for later reference.
- Use half sheets of chart paper to encourage short definitions.

Mix-Freeze-Pair

Facilitator Moves

PROCESS
- Mill around the room.
- At a signal, freeze and pair with the nearest person.
- Explore the designated topic.

ALTERNATIVES
- Use this strategy as an activator, to organize and integrate information, to check understanding on an action agreement, or to understand a concept.
- Use music to move to, and when the music stops, freeze and pair.
- Be seated with the first partner. See Stack and Pack in this appendix.
- Add music while members are milling around.

TIPS
- Working with different partners stimulates new perceptions and combinations of thought.
- Provide think time before members start this activity.

Modified Jigsaw

Information Processing: Exploring and Discovering

PROCESS

- Form groups of 4, number off 1 through 4.
- Assign numbers to topics in text.
- Each read all pages and take notes.
- Pass notes to designated "expert".
- "Experts" study notes and make a summary statement about the topic.

ALTERNATIVE

- See Jigsaw in this appendix.

TIP

- Learning and reporting are enriched in this variation of the classic jigsaw activity.

Most Important Point (MIP)

Information Processing: Organizing and Integrating

PROCESS

- Invite the group to reflect on something learned or a conversation held.
- Stand, locate a partner. and share your most important point.

ALTERNATIVES

- Add Partners Report (in this appendix) to this activity. Members will report to the full assembly the most important point of their partners. The reporting does not have to be reciprocal, and reporting is best done while members are still standing.
- Instead of locating another partner, share MIPs at tables and agree on a table MIP.

TIPS

- Learning partners, eye-contact partners, or any configuration of partnerships can be used. See Learning Partners in this appendix.
- When partners report, the same people who usually talk might talk, but because they are reporting their partners' ideas, they will be briefer.

My Bonnie Lies Over the Ocean

Facilitator Moves

PROCESS

- Describe that the purpose of this activity is to promote energy for the next portion of the meeting.
- Lead the group in singing "My Bonnie Lies Over the Ocean." When the letter *B* is used in the song, stand if you have been seated, and sit if you have been standing.

ALTERNATIVES

- None

TIP

- Advise members to take care of any physical needs during the activity. Protect your knees and back.

Naive Question

Information Processing: Exploring and Discovering

PROCESS

- A group member asks a naive question, to which the group responds. Examples: Who is making this decision? How much detail do we need to move this item? What parts of this issue exist in our area of responsibility? Who will do what by when? Is there something we are not talking about?

ALTERNATIVE

- The facilitator asks a question: "Given what you know about meeting standards, what seems to be going on right now?"

TIP

- A naive question is one asked with innocence, a desire to know, and in a melodic, approachable voice. This is a powerful way for group members to offer corrections to group work.

Not A or B but C

Decisions

PROCESS

- The group is polarized on two options.
- Ask if anyone can suggest a third option (C) that might contain what seems to be attractive about the first two (A and B).

ALTERNATIVES

- List the desirable features of A.
- List the desirable features of B.
- Have small groups generate options that contain the positive aspects of A and B while minimizing the negative aspects of each.

TIP

- If the group remains stuck, use Criteria Matrix (in this appendix).

100% Consensus

Information Processing: Organizing and Integrating

PROCESS

- In a group of six or fewer, invite someone to volunteer to be a facilitator and someone to be a scribe.
- Define the facilitator's role as calling on people and keeping the process intact. The scribe's role is to chart exactly what each person says, then make the exact corrections requested by subsequent group members.
- The facilitator poses a question such as what should be the role of the project leader or how shall we define completion.
- In round-robin fashion, members are called on to contribute one sentence, which is recorded word for word by the scribe.
- Before the process is complete, both the facilitator and scribe can have someone briefly take their roles while they contribute a sentence.
- When all sentences are charted, the facilitator asks, "Is there anyone who cannot live with the first sentence?"
- Members may raise their hand and offer different wording for parts of the sentence.

Without consultation, the scribe scratches out the original and adds the new.
- The facilitator asks again, "Is there anyone who cannot live with the first sentence?" The process continues until no more changes are suggested for the first sentence.
- The facilitator repeats the process for the second sentence.
- The process is repeated for all the remaining sentences.

ALTERNATIVE
- For larger groups, have subgroups work on the same task. Report results to the full group, then have the scribes draft a statement containing all the words of the several versions.

TIPS
- Schedule a couple of hours for this strategy.
- Don't wordsmith. Request corrections only if the corrections refine the meaning.
- Do not go along with something you are uncomfortable with.
- This will go slowly at first. About midway through it will pick up speed.

1-2-6
Decisions

PROCESS:
- Give a written task to individuals, such as naming one area to work on this year. (2 minutes)
- Pairs meet, share, and agree to one statement. (6 minutes)
- Each pair meets with two other pairs, shares, and agrees to one statement. (12 minutes)
- Each group of six records its one idea on a sentence strip (8–12 words) and posts it in the front of the room.
- The facilitator leads an inquiry session in which members ask questions of clarification. The authors of the item being questioned respond.
- The facilitator leads an advocacy session in which members advocate the items they think are most important.
- Rank ideas by using the Rule of One-Third (in this appendix) to determine a few items of the greatest interest of the group.
- Name a subcommittee to gather data on these items and bring back information or recommendations that should be perused.

ALTERNATIVE
- Have pairs converse before either inquiry or advocacy.

TIPS:
- Individuals, not groups, should inquire, advocate, and rank.
- Use with large groups up to 120 members.

One-Word Summary

Information processing: Organizing and Integrating

PROCESS
- Write one word that summarizes the central idea from this conversation.
- Share with a neighbor or a group.

ALTERNATIVE
- See Scrambled Sentences in this appendix.

TIP
- Allow open text, in which members might review notes or text before arriving at a one-word summary.

Outcome Mapping

Information Processing: Exploring and Discovering, Organizing and Integrating

PROCESS
- Reveal the purpose and process to the group.
- Display six columns with these headings:
  - o Presenting problem
  - o Tentative outcome
  - o Desired behavior of selected others
  - o Internal resources required to achieve desired behaviors
  - o Change-agent strategies to build resources
  - o Internal resources required for change agent to perform strategies

- Elicit responses from group; paraphrase and record responses.
- If there is disagreement on what the group members say, dialogue may be scheduled for another meeting.

ALTERNATIVES
- Facilitate the use of this map with a change agent from another group or individual.
- Use as a group facilitation tool.
- Direct the focus to others or to self as a group.
- Use to explore potential strategies to promote growth for an individual.

Change Agent(s)

6	5
Change agent's Internal	Change agents Strategies

Focus of Change

4	3	2	1
Others Internal Resources	Others Desired Behaviros	Tentative Outcome	Presenting Problem

TIPS
- This is task-analysis work and must be followed in sequence. Intuitive leaps and leaps to a solution should be set aside. Don't prescribe solutions until the exact behaviors and required resources are known.
- *Presenting problem.* Doesn't need specific descriptors. Example: Doesn't function as a team.
- *Tentative outcome.* Doesn't need specific descriptors. Example: Uses team work.
- *Desired behavior.* State behaviorally: what, by when, how much.
  o Behaviors must be specific, measurable, achievable, relevant to the larger outcome, and tactical. Tactical means the positive by-product of the existing state can be maintained.
  o Select a few behaviors that are the most amenable to change in the near future for the analysis that follows.
- *Internal resources.* Answers the question "What knowledge, skills, attitudes, or states of mind would be necessary to perform these behaviors?" The assumption is

that if they were present, the behaviors would be present.

- *Change-agent strategies.* Answers the question "What strategies might the change agent perform in order to have the group access the required resources?"
- *Internal resources for the change agent.* Answers the question "What knowledge, skills, attitudes or states of mind would the change agent need to have to perform identified strategies?"

PAG/PAU (Process as Given, Process as Understood)
Facilitator Moves

PROCESS
- With a credible voice, the facilitator gives directions for the next activity.
- The facilitator pauses, breaks eye contact, silently moves to a new space, and in an approachable voice says, "Just to be sure that I stated that clearly, what are you about to do?"

ALTERNATIVES
- Ask specific questions, such as what will you do first, next, and so on.
- Invite pairs or table groups to clarify the directions.

TIPS
- This strategy respectfully places any failure of communication on the facilitator.
- The effectiveness of the two messages are enhanced because they are communicated in space, voice, and language.

Paired Squared
Facilitator Moves

PROCESS
- Each member locates a partner.
- Each pair locates another pair, gathers materials, and sits together.

ALTERNATIVES
- Use the same principle with 3 sets of pairs to form groups of 6.
- See Learning Partners in this appendix.

TIP
- Provide a simple task to do as soon as the new groups form. This helps to bypass moments of discomfort, particularly for introverted members, and serves as an inclusion activity for the group. Examples: Share your concerns, ideas, and experiences relating to the next topic. Recall the most useful ideas from the last topic.

Paired Verbal Fluency

Information Processing: Organizing and Integrating, Activating and Engaging,

PROCESS
- Form pairs.
- Describe the process:
  - A and B will take turns responding to a prompt.
  - At a signal, one will speak and one will listen.
  - At a signal after a number of seconds, the other will speak while the first speaker listens.
  - Each time, no one is allowed to repeat anything that was said by the other.
  - Check for clarification.
- Repeat the cycle 2 or 3 times. For activating prior knowledge:
  - First round 20 seconds each
  - Second round 40 seconds each
  - Third round 60 seconds each
- For organizing and integrating:
  - First round 60 seconds each
  - Second round 40 seconds each
  - Third round 20 seconds each

ALTERNATIVE
- Gauge the time allotted for the second and third rounds by the level of participant engagement. The purpose of the declining amounts of time is to focus thinking. The purpose of the increasing amounts of time is to broaden thinking.

TIP
- Announce the time allotted for rounds only after the exercise is completed so participants can apply this strategy elsewhere without knowing the structure until experiencing it.

Paired Weighting
Decisions

PROCESS
- Individuals compare each item with every other item according to importance. Example: Which is more important, A or B? A or C? A or D? and so on.
- Participants go through the items, comparing each pair, circling their preferences. They count up all the As, Bs. and so on.
- When counting up their responses, participants count across the A line. From then on, they count down and then across, starting with B in the top line and then down (counting only the circled letters); then C down and across, D down and across, and so on.

ALTERNATIVE
- You can also compare the items in reference to performance: How are we performing? Which are we performing better? A or B? A or C? A or D? and so on.

TIPS
- These processes are complicated and require a lot of time.
- The recording page for participants looks something like the following:

A A A A A A A = _____
B C D E F G

B B B B B B = _____
C D E F G

C C C C C = _____
D E F G

D D D D = _____
E F G

Paraphrase Passport

Information Processing: Exploring and Discovering

PROCESS

- Provide a prompt for a conversation.
- Groups explore a topic:
  - o Person A makes an initiating statement.
  - o The group pauses for 5 seconds.
  - o The next group member (anyone) paraphrases the previous statement before inquiring or adding related ideas.
- Repeat the pattern as time permits.
- To close the talk, the group constructs a summarizing and organizing paraphrase of the full conversation.

ALTERNATIVES

- The person designated to paraphrase could be sitting next to A, and other players round-robin from there.
- After a speaker has been paraphrased, any member may inquire or add ideas.

TIPS

- This process would typically serve two purposes: (a) to deepen paraphrasing skills and norms, and (b) to increase understanding of each other and a specific topic. Forecast these multiple purposes at the beginning of the activity.
- Have the group reflect on the benefits they realized from listening and being listened to and the metacognitive disciplines they used.

Partners Report

Information Processing: Organizing and Integrating

PROCESS

- Partners engage in conversation knowing they might be asked to report their partner's ideas.
- Provide 2 minutes for each person to paraphrase his or her partner.
- Ask for a volunteer to share.
- Repeat the pattern as time permits.

ALTERNATIVE

- To increase energy, partner people from different locations and have them stand throughout this exercise.

TIPS

- It is not necessary for both partners to share. One speaker does not obligate the other.
- When possible, sequentially call on people from different quarters of the room, because this causes listeners to adjust body positions to hear, thus maintaining energy.

People, Place, Thing Cards
Information Processing: Activating and Engaging

PROCESS

- Place cards on each table. These may be postcards of famous people, pictures of places, or pictures cut out from magazines.
- Ask groups to engage in a question regarding the cards. (See alternatives below.)
- Share with large group.

ALTERNATIVES

- Put enough place cards on a table so that each person can choose one. Ask a processing question (e.g., "Which picture best describes where you are in your journey right now?"). Ask each person to share his or her response with the group.
- Put one person card on each table and ask the group to fill in the blanks with a stem (e.g., _____ is like a facilitator because _____ ; _____ is not like a facilitator because _____). Each table shares with the large group.

TIPS

- Be sure people cards represent diversity.
- Scaffold the activity by having people say what they know about the person, place, or thing before responding to the prompt.

People Search

Information Processing: Organizing and Integrating, Activating and Engaging

PROCESS
- Construct a handout that lists the content information being learned (e.g., the seven norms of collaboration), the ways in which the participants might have applied the content (e.g., using a norm in a meeting), or interesting information about participants (e.g., drives a sports car). Provide a space by each item for a name to be recorded.
- Ask participants to stand and find one person who can respond positively to an item on the page. The participant places the person's name beside the item, thanks the person, and then finds another person who can respond to another item.
- Continue until time is called, filling blanks with different names.

ALTERNATIVE
- Provide a prompt with each item so that participants engage in a brief conversation about the effect of that item.

TIPS
- Be sure the participants understand that they must ask each other questions; they cannot just hand their sheet to a person and ask them to sign one of the lines.
- Use information about the participants to help people get to know each other.
- Use content information to connect people to their learning.

Pluses and Wishes

Information Processing: Organizing and Integrating

PROCESS
- Inform the group that you will be requesting members to name pluses (things they appreciated or things that supported their learning) and wishes (things they wish the group had done more of, less of, or differently).
- Use two to four flip charts, depending on the size of the group. Each chart is dis-

played as a T-chart, with pluses at the top left and wishes at the top right.

- Recruit recorders.
- Members orally report pluses—what they valued about content or processes—while a recorder charts the ideas.
- Next, report wishes—what they wish had been done more, less, or differently, or wishes for the next session.

ALTERNATIVES

- With a small group, up to 10 or so people, you can serve as both facilitator and recorder.
- Use multiple recorders to speed the charting process.
- Gots and Wants is another strategy in this appendix that serves this purpose.

TIPS

- After initial contributions, always ask "What else?" rather than "Is there anything else?" to elicit further comments.
- State as "What are some plusses . . . ," not "Are there any pluses"?
- After the session, organize each category into subtopics and report to the group at the next session how its ideas will inform this session.
- Keep your facial and verbal responses neutral.

Polarity Mapping

Information Processing: Exploring and Discovering

PROCESS

- Identify an ongoing chronic issue.
- Identify a key polarity.
- Agree on value-neutral names for each of the poles.
- Draw the map below on chart paper.
- Write the pole names on the map.
- Brainstorm content for each quadrant.
- Agree on a name for the highest purpose and deepest fear.
- Facilitate a conversation so members can view and explore the dilemma as a whole and various perspectives.
- Develop strategies for realizing the upsides of both poles while avoiding the downside of each pole.

ALTERNATIVES
- See an expanded description of Polarity Mapping at www.adaptiveschools.com, or appendix L.
- See the polarity Web site, www.politymanagement.com.

TIPS
- Naming purpose and fear integrates oppositional views and provides a reason to manage the tension between the two views.
- Some examples of polarities are work and home; individual and team; stability and change; independence and interdependence; responding to global warming or not responding.
- Empathetically paraphrase the participants, for all need to know that they are being understood for the process to proceed.

A Polarity Map

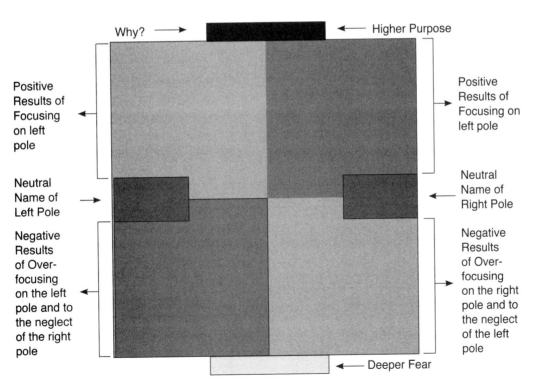

Process Check

Facilitator Moves

PROCESS

- At the end of the meeting the group reflects about its processes, guided by posted questions.
- Display the following questions on a chart:
  - o Was this meeting successful? Why or why not?
  - o Did we achieve our objective in this meeting?
  - o In what norm has our group shown progress?
  - o On what norm does our group still need to work?

ALTERNATIVES

- Randomly select a person to initiate the conversation and converse about the topics in a round-robin fashion, each member adding a new idea.
- Draw cards to indicate who will speak to which question.

TIP

- Make the process routine for the greatest results.

Pyramid

Information Processing: Exploring and Discovering

PROCESS

- Give a written task to the individuals.
- The individuals meet in pairs and share common elements.
- Quartets meet and share common elements from pairs.
- Octets meet and share common elements with the large group.
- The work of the octets can be charted for large-group processing.

ALTERNATIVE

- Use trios to sextets.

TIP
- It is difficult for groups larger than eight to find common elements. If there is lack of consensus when charts are shared with the large group, time for dialogue should be scheduled.

Quartet Facilitation
Information Processing: Exploring and Discovering

PROCESS
- Seat one person, the facilitator, across from the other three with no table between them.
- Give a task to the group and ask the one person to facilitate the conversation with the group. The facilitator listens to what will probably be egocentric comments and paraphrases at summary-organize and shifting logical levels.
- End of round 1: processing. To facilitators: What were you paying attention to internally and externally that was guiding your decisions as a facilitator? Silence. Facilitators report so the whole group hears them.
- Change facilitators for round 2: same topic. End of round 2: no processing.
- Change facilitators for round 3: same topic. End of round 3: reflection questions for group members. "What decisions did you make about your participation in the dialogue? What effect did your decisions have on you and other group members?" Silent reflection only.
- Change facilitators and topic for round 4: "What insights and big ideas are you taking from here about facilitation?"

Ranking
Decisions

PROCESS
- Distribute 10 option slips to each member.
- Each member labels options A, B, C, and so on.
- Each member ranks options according to personal preference: 10 = high, 1 = low.
- Gather all the slips and separate according to letter.
- Add up the numerical values for each letter.
- Post the result on a flip chart.

ALTERNATIVE
- Ask subgroups to tally the papers.

TIPS
- This is time-consuming but very useful when groups have limited trust in the facilitator, themselves, or the process.
- This can be used for groups as large as 50.
- This provides a more exact ranking than the Rule of One-Third.

Read and Example

Information Processing: Exploring and Discovering

PROCESS
- Letter people as A and B.
- Each partner reads the first paragraph.
- Pairs generate examples of this idea in action.
- A summarizes.
- Repeat the pattern, alternating the summarizing role.

ALTERNATIVE
- Structure as a trio, with each person reading the paragraph, A and B giving examples, and C paraphrasing and summarizing. Rotate roles.

TIP
- Producing examples can be challenging for some individuals, so always have at least a pair generating examples.

Recipe

Information Processing: Organizing and Integrating

PROCESS
- Provide format: "Recipe for_____; Name of Dish____; From the Kitchen of____; Serves____; Ingredients____"

- Groups develop and post recipes on chart paper.
- Spokesperson from each table makes a brief presentation to the group.

ALTERNATIVES
- Provide ingredients with which the dish will be made.
- Share the recipes.

TIP
- Give a time estimate, usually about 15 minutes.

Reenergize
Facilitator Moves

PROCESS
- Notice if the group seems tired or unfocused.
- Ask each person to respond to this question on a sticky note: "What would it take to get you reenergized?"
- Members place their notes on a flip chart or the wall.
- Members organize the notes into categories and label them.
- Explore ways to respond to the ideas.

ALTERNATIVE
- Small groups respond to the question and report one idea to be charted and discussed by the group.

TIPS
- The simple act of recognizing fatigue reenergizes people.
- This process itself will usually provide all the reenergizing that is necessary.

Relevancy Challenge

Facilitator Moves

PROCESS
- A group member says something unrelated to the group's topic.
- The facilitator, with an approachable voice, says, "[Name], help us to understand how your comment relates to the topic being explored."
- Speakers will either explain the relevance, in which case the conversation proceeds, or take it off the table.

ALTERNATIVES
- The facilitator records the item on chart paper, announcing that the group will return to it at an appropriate time.
- See Caping in this appendix.

TIP
- A topic delayed must be returned to at some time. Options include have a subgroup after the meeting, add to this or the next meeting agenda, have one or two people draft a statement to consider the topic for the group's consideration at the next meeting or in some other venue.

Responsibility Charting

Decisions

PROCESS
- List all major responsibilities on the left side of a chart. List the names of team members and other people related to the responsibilities along the top.
- Review all responsibilities and code R to mean responsible for the task, A to indicate who must authorize decisions, S to indicate members providing support, and I for those who must stay informed.

ALTERNATIVE
- Do this work with a subcommittee to reduce full-group meeting time on this task.

TIP
- This can become cumbersome to complete with a full group.

Role Clarification

Facilitator Moves

PROCESS
- The facilitator introduces him- or herself to the group and indicates that his or her job is to support the group in getting its work done.
- A facilitator providing basic facilitation (see the alternatives below) will specify that his or her services are to do the following:
  o Monitor time and guide processes.
  o Intervene when processes are interfering with the group achieving its goals.
  o Monitor and guide the use of time.
  o Be neutral to content.
- A facilitator providing developmental facilitation will intervene when processes are interfering with the group achieving its goals, as above; when processes or factors hinder the long-term effectiveness of the group; or when reflecting on process will help group resilience and skills.

ALTERNATIVE
- Choose between two facilitator functions: (a) basic facilitation, in which the group uses a facilitator to temporarily improve its process to get work done; when the group has accomplished its task, its effectiveness as a group might not have increased; and (b) developmental facilitation, in which the group will accomplish a task while improving its effectiveness; after the facilitation task is completed, the group will have improved its capacity to manage its process.

TIPS
- Even when time is available, if a group is temporary and/or has changing membership, developmental facilitation might not be worth the time.
- Facilitation can be tightly or loosely structured. Ask the group how it wants you to work.

Role Hunt

Information Processing: Activating and Engaging

PROCESS

- On a 3 × 5 card, write your name, the amount of time you have spent facilitating groups, and a facilitation tool. Print so others can read your card.
- Stand and swap with a person not at your table. Paraphrase and inquire to be sure you can represent this person's idea to another.
- At a signal, find a new partner and swap again.
- At a signal, return to the groups and report.

ALTERNATIVES

- Switch for more than two rounds.
- To stimulate more complex thinking, swap abstractions, such as beliefs about facilitating adults or principles of facilitation.
- Locate persons with roles different than yours.

TIPS

- Participants must swap with people from different tables in order to collect fresh ideas for group conversation.
- Select an abstraction to swap for advanced groups only.

Round-Robin Reflection

Information Processing: Organizing and Integrating

PROCESS

- At a stopping point or at the end of the meeting, the facilitator asks, "What were some of the decisions you made about when and how to participate, and what were some of the effects of those decisions on you and the group?"
- Members reflect privately.
- In round-robin fashion, each member shares one decision and the effects of the decision.

ALTERNATIVES

- During the round-robin the facilitator paraphrases and inquires, "Did your decision produce what you intended? How did the effects of your decision compare to what you intended? How might this be a pattern for you? What are some ways you can apply this learning to future meetings?"

- Pairs share instead of the full group.
- Journal writing only.

TIPS

- Be clear that the prompt refers to decisions about participation, not the meeting content.
- Members self-direct performance improvements through this process faster and more permanently than process observers reporting participant behaviors. Teams become more accomplished.

Rule of One-Third
Decisions

PROCESS

- From a list of items on a flip chart, members select a third plus one as most important to them personally. (For example, if there are 12 items on a list, each person selects 5 items. They do not have to be in ranked order.)
- The facilitator asks to see hands for the first item on the flip chart. The recorder counts and records these in a color distinct from other colors on the chart.
- Repeat until all items have been accounted for.
- Facilitator has the group name which items were selected most often.
- The group adopts the list.

ALTERNATIVES

- The final list is given to a subcommittee for further study and recommendation.
- Selected items are subjected to another form of analysis with the full group.
- This gets the best results when it is preceded by clarifications and advocacies.

TIPS

- This is quick and does not require extensive discussion of items.
- Let members know that individuals will not make the decision, the group will. If the group agrees, an item that did not rate among the highest can be added to the list.

- An item that receives less than half the votes of the people in the group is usually not regarded as a group priority.
- This is accurate for the top and bottom third of a list.
- Members feel heard and groups feel empowered.

Satisfy, Satisfy, Delay
Facilitator Moves

PROCESS
- The facilitator notices that when one particular group member speaks, the group appears annoyed. The signals might be eye rolling, deep sighs, or facial expressions.
- The third time that this member asks to be recognized, the facilitator does *not* call on the member but calls on another or closes the conversation.
- Later, make an attempt to rehabilitate this member's status in the group by calling positive attention to a contribution.

ALTERNATIVES
- Move to another part of the room and ask if anyone from that area would like to add something.
- Direct pairs to talk on a related topic.

TIP
- The facilitator's relationship is with the group, not an individual.

Say Something
Information Processing: Exploring and Discovering

PROCESS
- Choose a partner.
- Read silently and simultaneously to designated stopping points.
- When each partner is ready, stop and "say something." The something might be a question, a brief summary, a key point, an interesting idea, or a personal connection.
- Continue the process until you have completed the selection.

ALTERNATIVE

- When feasible, assign the reading to be done before a meeting.

TIP

- Use with short reading selections—four to seven paragraphs is about as long as is useful.

Scrambled Sentences

Information Processing: Activating and Engaging, Organizing and Integrating

PROCESS

- Each person writes one word on a card or sticky note illustrative of the individual's learning.
- The group constructs a sentence that uses all the words, while adding as few new words as possible.
- Group spokespeople read the sentences to the full group.

ALTERNATIVES

- Write words for a common experience.
- After creating one sentence, the participants take their word and form another group, creating another sentence.

TIP

- Give a signal for the group work to begin.

Sensing Interviews
Information Processing: Exploring and Discovering

PROCESS
- Arrange for 30-minute confidential interviews with individuals.
- Advise that sources of information will remain confidential, but if the same idea is heard from three or more people, it will be shared with the full group.
- Ask the following: "What are you feeling good about here? What problems exist? What recommendations do you have?"
- Organize the data and publish it with the full group. Display the ideas on flip charts.
- Ask if you got the information right in order to start a conversation about the data.
- Paraphrase and inquire as members offer corrections to the data. If appropriate, change the text on the flip charts.

ALTERNATIVES
- Publish the data in the text for pairs to read and explore before a full-group conversation.
- Share the data with the leader; the leader shares the data and his or her analysis with the group.
- The facilitator might engage in public coaching with the leader.

TIPS
- Publish only those items heard from several people.
- Have small groups talk about the data if comments are not easily forthcoming. Then engage the full group in conversation.
- Use this when entering a new group as a leader or when problems exist within a group but information is not being shared about it.
- Share with the leader first, if data are sensitive or coaching the leader's public responses would be useful.

7-11 Conversation

Information Processing: Organizing and Integrating

PROCESS

- Members prepare comments they would make to a friend to summarize this meeting.
- After composing, either mentally or on paper, members mill about the room and share their comments with others.
- After a few minutes, the facilitator redirects the members to report some of their summaries to the full group.
- The facilitator and the group edit for consistency and accuracy.

ALTERNATIVES

- Summaries can be written and passed around a table for editing.

TIPS

- Frame this as a conversation in a convenience store: brief, informal, and without academic language.
- People often report different versions of what happens in meetings. This corrects this tendency.

Set and Test Working Agreements

Decisions

PROCESS

- A group member says, "I notice that our meetings are not starting on time Could we make an agreement to start on time? (Set agreement).
- The facilitator leads a conversation in which the group develops an agreement.
- In a later meeting a group member says, "I'd like to talk about the agreement we made to start our meetings on time. I notice we are not doing it. What has to happen to keep our agreement?" (Test agreement)
- The facilitator leads a conversation in which the group develops an agreement.

ALTERNATIVE

- A group member requests that this topic be placed on the agenda.

TIP

- This relates to the group-member capability of knowing when to self-assert and when to integrate.

Show, Don't Say
Facilitator Moves

PROCESS

- The facilitator, holding two fingers in the air, says, "You have this many minutes."
- Hold the posture and gesture until members have visually acknowledged the signal and have gone back to work.

ALTERNATIVES

- Stand to the side of a chart (or whatever the visual focus is to be) so that you, the chart, and the group form a triangle. Swing your shoulders and arm into a pointing gesture toward the chart. Keep your eyes on the chart. Be silent.
- Use this in a conference when you need to present hard-to-hear data (e.g, with a parent to document a student's late assignments).

TIPS

- This move interrupts pattern, jumping from the verbal to the visual, and often produces a startle effect in which members look up to get the rest of the message.
- Use the variation when you want to direct energy away from you or toward an important bit of information that the group can read by itself. Look at the data, not at the group. The group's eyes will go where yours go; you want people to be examining the data toward which you are pointing.

Signal Role Change
Facilitator Moves

PROCESS

- When you are facilitating a meeting and you want to contribute content, ask, "May I add something?" The group usually will concur.
- Move off to the side of the group. From this space, make a contribution in a credible voice.
- Without speaking, return to the facilitation space. In an approachable voice say, "Okay, let's move on" or "How does that add to your thinking?"

ALTERNATIVES

- Instead of moving off to the side of the group, ask a participant to stand in your place while you occupy that seat and make your contribution.
- If you are seated, signal the change by broad changes in posture: leaning back, removing your glasses, briefly standing.

TIPS

- Physical signals are essential. Without them, some will not realize that you are temporarily stepping out of the role and will see the process as less than honest.

Six-Position Straw Poll
Decisions

PROCESS
- Members give a poll page to a designated person who records the tallies on a wall chart.

ALTERNATIVES
- None.

TIP
- If you have a lot of 5s and 6s, you should think carefully before implementing it.

1	2	3	4	5	6
I strongly agree.	I agree.	I agree, with some reservations.	I disagree, but I'm willing to go with the majority.	I disagree, but I don't want to stop others.	I disagree strongly and will work to block it.
I really like it.	I like it.	It's okay.	I don't think it's all that great, but I'm willing to go along with the majority.	I don't like it, but am willing to go along because I don't want to stop others.	I really don't like it and will work to sabotage it.
I'll advocate it publicly and privately whether or not it's adopted.	I'll advocate it publicly and privately.	I'll support it publicly even with my reservations.	I'll support it publicly and privately when asked.	I won't object to it publicly or privately.	I'll actively object to it publicly if it's adopted.
I'll actively support its implementation.	I'll support its implementation.	I'll participate in its implementation.	I might be involved in its implementation. I will wait and see.	I won't be involved in implementing, but I won't sabotage it.	If it's implemented, I will work to sabotage it.

Slip Method
Decisions

PROCESS
- Distribute a large number of 3 × 5 cards to each member.
- State a problem in "how to" language such as "How to increase student attendance" or "How to support the lower quartile kids in mathematics."
- Members write only one idea per card.
- Collect and categorize the cards. Discard duplicate, ambiguous, or illegible items.
- Present and study categories and ideas.

ALTERNATIVES
- Use slips to prioritize items. On each slip, members record a letter for the item (A, B, C, and so on) and a number representing the priority weight they assign to it. Assuming they have 12 items, 12 would be the highest weight and 1 the lowest.
- Slips are turned in and stacked alphabetically. The numbers for each letter are tabulated and presented to the group.

TIPS
- Fifteen participants should be able to generate 150 ideas.
- Because it so mechanical and free from influence, this form of prioritizing is useful when there is low trust in the group.

Song Writing
Facilitator Moves

PROCESS
- Have individuals write the name of a song from their childhood on a sticky note.
- Next, have them write the name of a song from their high school years.
- Have them write down the name of a song they associate with celebrations.
- Using these songs as activators, direct table groups to develop a song that expresses something about the full group in which they are participating and prepare to perform it.

- Ask which group wants to go first, second, and so on. Perform and appreciate.

ALTERNATIVE

- Use this to celebrate accomplishments or transitions in the life of the group.

TIP

- Use this only when table groups have five or more members. This provides enough musical repertoire and style variance for a group to be successful.

Songs

Information Processing: Activating and Engaging

PROCESS

- Ask groups to think of song titles that represent some content that is being learned (e.g., energy sources).
- Each table names a song, and the large group identifies what content it represents.

TIP

- Give examples so that the group understands the task; name a song and ask the group what it represents (e.g., the facilitator says, "We Are the Champions of the World," and the group says, "Efficacy" or "Consciousness.")

Sort Cards

Information Processing: Activating and Engaging, Organizing and Integrating

PROCESS

- On your own, generate examples of strategies used in successful meetings. One idea per 3 × 5 card.
- Groups share, categorize, label categories, and make a display.

ALTERNATIVES

- Each group selects one person to stay at the table and answer questions.

- Others tour the displays and search for new ideas.
- Members return to home base and exchange information.
- Other topics:
  o Knowledge about any topic the group is about to address.
  o Recollections and insights about any topic the group has already addressed.
  o Considerations that should drive a decision. Identify and explore values that the considerations illuminate.
- After a tour, the groups identify and report themes in the data.

TIPS

- This levels the playing field in mixed groups.
- Stress that the rationales for the activity includes honoring member expertise, leveling the playing field, equalizing member status, and getting a lot of information in a short period of time.

Sound and Motion Symphony

Information Processing: Organizing and Integrating

PROCESS

- Groups select a collective sound and a motion to represent their learning.
- Stand and rehearse.
- When groups are ready to perform, the facilitator assumes the role of symphony conductor.
- After each section of "instruments" is rehearsed, the facilitator conducts the group, bringing different sections in and out as appropriate.

ALTERNATIVE

- The facilitator might stand on a riser or a table for greater visibility.

TIPS

- Emphasize the rationale. Explain that of the many ways humans organize and integrate knowledge, body movements bring a special opportunity for the kinesthetic learner. This activity focuses more on the affective domains of learning than the cognitive.
- Prerequisites for this activity are a safe learning environment and a trusting relationship with facilitator. Rarely would this occur on the first day of a group's work.

Spend a Buck

Decisions

PROCESS

- Members have 100 imaginary pennies they can distribute among a few options.
- Explain the options.
- Individuals decide how many pennies they will spend on each option.
- Gather and present the data to the group.

ALTERNATIVE

- Use this for individual choices rather than for a collective expression of priorities.

TIP

- Provide think time before members assign their pennies.

Spot Analysis

Information Processing: Exploring and Discovering

PROCESS

- Hang chart paper, divided into quadrants, on the wall.
- Label the four sections *strengths*, *problems*, *opportunities*, and *threats* (SPOT).
- List strengths, then problems.
- Rank the strengths and problems, if you have time.
- Brainstorm opportunities. Invite members to see potential opportunities within the problems.
- List the threats. Explore which ones could invalidate the work of the group.
- Review the chart for insights and action ideas.

ALTERNATIVES

- Next, categorize the elements of an issue to be addressed, such as curriculum, assessment, and staff development.
- List concerns or goals within each category.
- Identify connections across categories.
- Consider intervening at various starting places.

TIP
- Assign the alternative ideas to a subgroup.

Stack and Pack
Facilitator Moves

PROCESS
- Alert the group members that they are about to stack their materials, pack them up, and move to another location. Don't move yet.
- Next, reveal the location or partner to which they should move. Don't move yet.
- Finally, identify a task to address when they are seated in the new location.

ALTERNATIVES
- None

TIP
- Ask that the move be done as efficiently as possible to protect time for the topic.

Stem Completion
Information Processing: Activating and Engaging, Exploring and Discovering

PROCESS
- Members complete a thought from a prompt. For example: "I believe my culture affects my coworkers by . . ." or "In order to be more inclusive we should . . ."
- Pairs or small groups share and explore meanings from responses to the prompts.
- Small groups summarize and report.

ALTERNATIVE
- Change groups and share again.

TIP
- Select stems that would be psychologically safe for members to discuss.

Stir the Classroom

Information Processing: Organizing and Integrating

PROCESS

- Arrange group members around the perimeter of the room in groups of four.
- Number off 1 to 4 in each cluster.
- Have clusters respond to a prompt.
- At a signal, one member moves to the next cluster to bring information from the home group and learn information from the new group.
- Repeat the pattern with new prompts for the new group.

ALTERNATIVE

- Conduct the strategy with clusters seated at tables instead of standing.

TIPS

- Draw from a deck of playing cards to randomly select the next person in each group to move.
- Benefits wane after three or four rounds.

Stop and Redirect

Facilitator Moves

PROCESS

- In a credible voice say, "[Name], please hold on to that idea. We will return to it in a moment."
- Accompany the words with a slight move toward the participant, with your arms hugging yourself, as in "holding on."

ALTERNATIVES

- See Caping and Relevance Challenge in this appendix.
- Vary language and nonverbal expressions to match the culture of the group.

TIPS

- Use this when a group member has violated the one-topic-at-a-time standard.
- You have permission to use this only when the group is clear about the topic and the standard.

Stoplight

Information Processing: Organizing and Integrating

PROCESS
- Display the image of a traffic light with green, yellow, and red lights.
- Members write one thing they are going to start doing, one thing they will continue, and one thing they will stop.
- Hear a few reports.

ALTERNATIVES
- Share with a neighbor.
- Reflect and record what people will do to remind themselves to take the self-prescribed action.

TIP
- Reporting reinforces application thinking and adds ideas.

Strategy Harvest

Information Processing: Organizing and Integrating

PROCESS
- With a partner, review and clarify a list of strategies so you can explain them.
- Select two or three strategies and develop applications for your work.

ALTERNATIVE
- Assign task to an affinity group—members who work together.

TIP
- When triple-track presenting is used, strategies will be recorded on flip charts.

Structure Conversations About Data

Information Processing: Exploring and Discovering

PROCESS
- Select type of outcome and demographic or process data.
- Select the most useful organization of data.
- Determine type of analysis.

TIP
- See Appendix H, Structuring Conversations About Data.

Success Analysis

Information Processing: Exploring and Discovering

PROCESS
- In advance of the meeting, teachers develop notes describing an area in which they are finding success or making progress.
- At the meeting, the participants share their case studies of successful work.
- In round-robin fashion, members share while their colleagues take notes.
- The colleagues ask questions of clarification only, such as "When you said 'those students,' to which ones were you referring?"
- The colleagues ask questions of inquiry, such as "How did you know to move on at that point?" or "What is your sense of the most catalytic decision you made?" or "What is some learning you are taking from this situation?"
- The colleagues offer thoughts and ideas while the presenter takes notes without responding.
- The presenter initiates a conversation with the colleagues, inquiring more deeply about their thoughts.
- After the last round, the group summarizes what was learned and what can be applied from this session.

ALTERNATIVES
- Use this process for events that were not successful.
- Use this process with other role groups, such as principals or mentors.

TIPS
- A total round for one person should take about 30 minutes.
- Use small groups of three to six members.
- Expressed judgments, positive or negative, are more threatening than data or open-ended, nonjudgmental questions.

Sufficient Consensus
Decisions

PROCESS
- Determine a figure, such as 80%, that will represent consensus.
- Members clarify and advocate for items.
- Members may inquire about the reasoning of another member's choice.
- Minority-view voices must be encouraged to speak and be paraphrased to achieve sufficient consensus.
- Call for a show of hands.
- Announce the result.

ALTERNATIVES
- Determine what percentage will qualify as sufficient consensus in general.
- In any meeting, an item can be singled out for even a 10% consensus. This should be very rare.

TIPS
- No member has the right to block a group.
- Employ a guideline for members who are not budging from a position, Ask if this is a matter of principle or preference. If a principle, encourage dialogue; if a preference, after others understand the preference, set it aside.

Swap Meet

Inclusion

PROCESS

- On a 3 × 5 card write your name, the percentage of time you've spent facilitating, and a belief you have about facilitating meetings.
- Stand and swap. Paraphrase and inquire about the other person's belief. Why is this belief important to the person? Record.
- At a signal, switch to another person. Represent the person to whom you just talked. Paraphrase, inquire, record.
- At a signal, return to the groups and report.
- Given what you've heard, what inferences are you making about this group's theories on facilitation?

ALTERNATIVES

- Change the first instruction to reflect the group you are working with: presenting, coaching, leading, and so on.
- After the exercise, explore with the group the differences between espoused beliefs and acted-upon beliefs.

TIPS

- Use as an activator before instruction.
- Define *swap* for English as a Second Language groups.
- Suggest members self-monitor by reflection after performing a task.

Table Regrouping

Facilitator Moves

PROCESS

- Ask group members to number off.
- Direct all the even-numbered members to pick up their materials and move clockwise to the next table.

ALTERNATIVE

- Use different counts, like every third person.

TIPS
- As always, explain the purpose of the regrouping.
- This is a very quick way to reorganize groups.

TAG/TAU (Topic as Given/Topic as Understood)

Facilitator Moves

PROCESS
- Describe the topic to be addressed. Use a credible voice.
- Step to another space (see Visual Paragraph) and with an approachable voice ask the groups to explore what they think the topic is.
- Check for understanding by asking for different ways to state the topic.

ALTERNATIVE
- Ask the leader of the group to describe the topic before the facilitator checks for understanding.

TIPS
- Take as much time as necessary. On complex topics, groups might need as much as 30 minutes to develop clarity.
- Do not move ahead with an activity until you are certain all members understand.

Text Rendering

Information Processing: Exploring and Discovering

PROCESS
- Members review a document and highlight a sentence, a phrase, and a word that are meaningful.
- Provide strips of paper of various lengths to accommodate a sentence, a phrase, or a word.
- Each member, in round-robin fashion, posts and explains his or her strips.
- Once all the strips are posted and explained, the group agrees on one sentence, one phrase, and one word that are most meaningful.

ALTERNATIVES

- Instead of making sentence strips, have a facilitator guide a conversation as first a sentence is shared by each, then a phrase and a word. Record the phrase and the word on chart paper. The group shares insights about the document.
- In either case, use summarizing insights for the selection of a final sentence, phrase, and word.

TIP

- When working with a large group, divide into small groups of about six, allowing them to share results.

Third Point

Facilitator Moves

PROCESS

- Get the group to look at a screen or flip chart by using a frozen hand gesture pointed toward the screen and directing your own eyes at the screen.
- Walk away without making eye contact with the group. The group will continue to look at the screen.

ALTERNATIVE

- Direct attention to a section of the text for members to interact with it.

TIPS

- The group's eyes go where the facilitator's eyes are directed. When the facilitator maintains eye contact, this is two-point communication.
- Three-point communication separates the message from the messenger.
- When two-point communication is used for hard-to-talk-about data, the facilitator is considered to be connected to the problem.

Three Balloons

Information Processing: Organizing and Integrating

PROCESS
- Imagine that each member had three balloons on which there was space to write one word or phrase that captures an important idea from today's work.
- Members record their ideas.
- Members report to the full group.

ALTERNATIVE
- Do not report.

TIP
- Reporting is useful when the goal is to reinforce certain ideas, stimulate recognition of others, and contribute to a sense of *we* rather than *me*.

3-2-1 Plus 1

Information Processing: Organizing and Integrating

PROCESS
- Members draw a right-hand margin on a piece of paper. Label the margin "Plus 1."
- Individuals, in groups of three or four, write three key ideas they remember from the last meeting, two things they want to explore, and one point to ponder.
- Round-robin share one idea each. As members share, listeners may record personal notes in the right-hand margin.
- Continue the pattern through the next two categories.

ALTERNATIVES
- Start the sharing at the second item, because more value probably comes from the second two categories.
- Process the activity with the full group.
- Use as a follow-up to instruction.
- Vary the prompts.

TIP
- Assign time, perhaps 12 minutes. so the group stays focused and brief.

Thumbs Up
Decisions

PROCESS
- The facilitator or any member can call for a thumbs-up to determine the degree of agreement the group has on an item.
- Thumbs up means yes, thumbs down means no, thumbs held sideways means not sure or it doesn't matter.
- Call for a show of hands.
- Announce the result.

ALTERNATIVES
- Use as a poll to learn what direction of thinking the group is favoring prior to further conversation.
- Use as a mechanism for Sufficient Consensus.

TIPS
- Ask members with thumbs held sideways to explain their reasoning.
- Ask members with thumbs held down what would need to be modified in the proposal for them to give it thumbs up.

Triad Inquiry
Information Processing: Exploring and Discovering

PROCESS
- Trios read and highlight the first section of a text.
- Person A says, "A key point for me is____ ."
- Person B pauses and then paraphrases.
- Person C pauses and then asks, "What are some things that make that important to you?"
- Rotate roles and continue process with the remaining sections.

ALTERNATIVE
- Person C scripts the paraphrase for later analysis.

TIP

- Connect the two purposes: conversations about content and skills practice.

Trios PPPI (Pause, Paraphrase, Pause, Inquire)

Information Processing: Exploring and Discovering

PROCESS

- Letter people off as A, B, and C.
- Each reads a section of text.
- A paraphrases.
- B adds ideas.
- C pauses, paraphrases, and inquires.
- Repeat the pattern, alternating roles.

ALTERNATIVE

- A can share a key idea, B can pause and paraphrase, C can pause and inquire.

TIP

- It might be helpful to review productive areas for inquiry, such as personal meaning, values, goals, consequences, examples, counterexamples, and applications.

Triple Track

Information Processing: Organizing and Integrating

PROCESS

- Provide note-taking pages in a handout.
- Prepare a slide on which three applications of strategies you will use in this training are named:
  1. Strategies to support your learning here in this room
  2. Keeping adults engaged and tuned in at presentations or meetings
  3. Applications with students
- Chart and describe the strategies as you use them.

ALTERNATIVE
- Periodically provide time for review.

TIPS
- Describe what each strategy is, why it is useful to learners, and how to work with it to achieve the most learning.
- Participants who know why a process is being used are more likely to overcome any personal discomfort they might feel about using it.

Value Voting
Facilitator Moves

PROCESS
- Ask the group to express its response to a statement visually.
- Show five fingers for strongly agree, four for agree, three for neutral, two for disagree, one for strongly disagree.
- Phrase the statements as "I'm satisfied with the direction the group is taking" or "We should move forward on this initiative now."
- Say the number of fingers you see as you scan the group.
- Interpret what you see as "Seems to be an average of four" or "I notice responses on both ends of the scale." Share some reasons for your responses.

ALTERNATIVE
- Ask members to look around the room and compare what they see with the number of fingers they are displaying.

TIPS
- The benefit of value voting is that the responses are public, giving the group a sense of the whole.
- Use this as a straw poll only, not a final decision, unless you see a unanimous display of five fingers.

Visual Paragraph

Facilitator Moves

PROCESS

- Stand in one space and speak.
- Without speaking, break eye contact, move to a new space, pause, and speak.

ALTERNATIVE

- If seated, change your position in the chair by leaning forward, to one side, or backward.

TIP

- Use this to stress different points or to distinguish between giving directions and checking for understanding.

Vocabulary Review

Information Processing: Organizing and Integrating

PROCESS

- Ask individuals to brainstorm and list words they've learned in the training so far. The words can be new or have new meanings as a result of their learning. The more words, the better. Participants should try to think of words that others might not remember.
- After a few minutes, instruct participants to stand up, take their list and a pencil with them, and share their list with one other person.
- For every word that a person has on a list that the other person does not, a point is tallied. After sharing lists with one person, participants continue sharing with others until time is called.
- At the end of 10–15 minutes, participants sit down and tally their points.
- Share at the table and determine who at the table collected the most points. (Do not ask for a table total.)
- Survey the room by asking each table to identify the person with the most points.
- Acknowledge the highest-point person and ask him or her to identify the words on the list that received the most points.

ALTERNATIVE
- Acknowledge the highest point person and all the members the highest point person interacted with. Have them all stand for applause.

TIPS
- If more than one person in the room have close to the same number of points, acknowledge all of them.
- Be sure to emphasize that the brainstorm includes both new words and words that have new meanings.

Volunteer Stand

Facilitator Moves

PROCESS
- Announce the need for a spokesperson for each group.
- Ask a volunteer from each group to stand.
- Ask for applause for the standing members' willingness to serve.
- Instruct standing members to raise their right hand, move it in a circle above their heads, and allow the hand to drop on the shoulder of the person who will be spokesperson for the group.

ALTERNATIVE
- Add anything that will add to the suspense and light atmosphere of the instructions.

TIPS
- It is not necessary for members to remain standing.
- You might have to coax volunteers from some groups.

Walk About

Information Processing: Activating and Engaging, Organizing and Integrating

PROCESS
- Distribute the Walk About form (see below).
- Members write what they know in the left margin. (5 minutes)
- Demonstrate talking with a person from a different table. Each provides one idea to the other.
- Each records in one of the 9 cells the idea and the person's name so that others can be referred to that person for more information.
- After 10–12 minutes, have people sit down and share the data they gathered.
- Group members analyze the data they have collected, looking for themes or patterns.

ALTERNATIVES
- Reduce the number of cells from nine to four to save time.
- Select prompts, such as Know, Think You know, Want to Know.

TIP
- Ensure that people write their original barter material outside instead of inside one of the cells.

Walk About

Facilitating groups

Becoming a more skillful group member

Developing groups

Wicked Problems Map

Information Processing: Exploring and Discovering

PROCESS

- Draw a large circle on chart paper and a smaller circle in the center.
- The smaller circle describes the project the group is working on. It could, for example, be implementing rigorous content standards.
- In the outer circle, list the systems and practices that would be affected. For implementing standards, these might include curriculum alignment, parent expectations, data collection, special education, teacher evaluation, district culture, professional development, reporting practices, and so on.
- Identify complexities and factors that would have to be taken into consideration in developing an action plan.

ALTERNATIVE

- Generate a list of affected systems and practices in small-group conversations prior to developing the problem map.

TIP

- Apply this when no known solution processes are available. Often these require new mental models or are dynamical, producing emergent phenomena within systems and subsystems.

Working Agreement

Inclusions

PROCESS

- Display and describe working agreements as shown below.
- Describe Sufficient Consensus, as shown in this appendix, and its benefits.
- Ask if members can agree to these during this meeting.

ALTERNATIVES

- Eliminate sufficient consensus.
- Have the group develop working agreements.
- Once a group has agreed to these agreements, print them on each succeeding agenda.

TIPS
- When time is short and the meeting routine, this process is preferred.
- Group-developed working agreements can be useful when little trust exists but uses up valuable meeting time to develop.

Working Agreements

Demonstrate Mutual Respect (Respect people and ideas—such respect does not represent agreement.)

Employ Skillful Listening (Seek first to understand, then to be understood.)

Sufficient Consensus (Each person has an equal voice; the group works to understand all views; distinguish between dialogue and discussion; and 80% agreement of those present constitutes consensus.)

Yellow Light

Facilitator Moves

PROCESS
- Stop the group and gain attention.
- Indicate how many minutes are left in the activity.

ALTERNATIVES
- Use Show, Don't Say (in this appendix) instead of verbally announcing the remaining time.
- Indicate that if groups have not started on _____ task, they should do so now, because only _____ minutes remain.
- When groups are deep at work on lengthy tasks, move to the groups silently and hold a large sign that displays the remaining minutes.

TIP
- Use this to prepare members for transitions.

Appendix B   Norms Inventory: Rating Perceptions of Myself

Pausing to allow time for thought

1. I pause after asking questions.

Low_____/_____/_____/_____High

2. I pause after others speak to reflect before responding.

Low_____/_____/_____/_____High

3. I pause before asking questions to allow time for artful construction.

Low_____/_____/_____/_____High

Paraphrasing within a pattern of pause-paraphrase-pose questions to ensure deep listening

1. I listen and paraphrase to acknowledge and clarify.

Low_____/_____/_____/_____High

2. I listen and paraphrase to summarize and organize.

Low_____/_____/_____/_____High

3. I listen and paraphrase to shift levels of abstraction.

Low_____/_____/_____/_____High

Posing questions to reveal and extend thinking

1. I pose questions to explore perceptions, assumptions and interpretations.

Low_____/_____/_____/_____High

2. I inquire before putting ideas on the table and before I advocate.

Low_____/_____/_____/_____High

3. I seek specificity of data, assumptions, generalizations and the meaning of words.

Low_____/_____/_____/_____High

Putting ideas on the table and pulling them off

1. I state the intentions of my communications.

Low_____/_____/_____/_____High

2. I provide relevant facts, ideas, opinions and inferences.

Low_____/_____/_____/_____High

3. I remove or announce modification of ideas, opinions and points of view.

Low_____/_____/_____/_____High

Providing data to structure conversations

1. I present specific, measurable, observable information.

Low_____/_____/_____/_____High

2. I present data without judgments, opinions or inferences.

Low_____/_____/_____/_____High

3. I offer multiple types of data to broaden understanding.
Low_____/_____/_____/_____High

Paying attention to self and others to monitor our ways of working

1. I balance participation and open opportunities for others to contribute and respond.

Low_____/_____/_____/_____High

2. I restrain my impulses to react, respond or rebut at inappropriate times or in ineffective ways.

Low_____/_____/_____/_____High

3. I maintain awareness of the group's task, processes and development.

Low_____/_____/_____/_____High

Presuming positive intentions to support a nonjudgmental atmosphere

1. I communicate respectfully whether I agree or disagree.

Low_____/_____/_____/_____High

2. I embed positive presuppositions in my paraphrases, summaries and comments.

Low_____/_____/_____/_____High

3. I embed positive presuppositions when I pose questions.

Low_____/_____/_____/_____High

Appendix C   Norms Inventory: Rating Our Perceptions of Our Group

Pausing to allow time for thought

1. We pause after asking questions.

Low_____/_____/_____/_____High

2. We pause after others speak to reflect before responding.

Low_____/_____/_____/_____High

3. We pause before asking questions to allow time for artful construction.

Low_____/_____/_____/_____High

Paraphrasing within a pattern of pause-paraphrase-pose questions to ensure deep listening

1. We listen and paraphrase to acknowledge and clarify.

Low_____/_____/_____/_____High

2. We listen and paraphrase to summarize and organize.

Low_____/_____/_____/_____High

3. We listen and paraphrase to shift levels of abstraction.

Low_____/_____/_____/_____High

Posing questions to reveal and extend thinking

1. We pose questions to explore perceptions, assumptions and interpretations.

Low_____/_____/_____/_____High

2. We inquire before putting ideas on the table and before we advocate.

Low_____/_____/_____/_____High

3. We seek specificity of data, assumptions, generalizations and the meaning of words.

Low_____/_____/_____/_____High

Putting ideas on the table and pulling them off

1. We state the intentions of our communications.

Low_____/_____/_____/_____High

2. We provide relevant facts, ideas, opinions and inferences.

Low_____/_____/_____/_____High

3. We remove or announce modification of ideas, opinions and points of view.

Low_____/_____/_____/_____High

Providing data to structure conversations

1. We present specific, measurable, observable information.

Low_____/_____/_____/_____High

2. We present data without judgments, opinions or inferences.

Low_____/_____/_____/_____High

3. We offer multiple types of data to broaden understanding.

Low_____/_____/_____/_____High

Paying attention to self and others to monitor our ways of working

1. We balance participation and open opportunities for each other to contribute and respond.

Low_____/_____/_____/_____High

2. We restrain our impulses to react, respond or rebut at inappropriate times or in ineffective ways.

Low_____/_____/_____/_____High

3. We maintain awareness of the group's task, processes and development.

Low_____/_____/_____/_____High

Presuming positive intentions to support a nonjudgmental atmosphere

1. We communicate respectfully whether we agree or disagree.

Low_____/_____/_____/_____High

2. We embed positive presuppositions in our paraphrases, summaries and comments.

Low_____/_____/_____/_____High

3. We embed positive presuppositions when we pose questions.

Low_____/_____/_____/_____High

Appendix D   Personal Seven Norms Assessment

Pausing to allow time for thought

Low_____/_____/_____/_____High

Paraphrasing within a pattern of pause-paraphrase-pose questions to ensure deep listening

Low_____/_____/_____/_____High

Posing questions to reveal and extend thinking

Low_____/_____/_____/_____High

Putting ideas on the table and pulling them off

Low_____/_____/_____/_____High

Providing data to structure conversations

Low_____/_____/_____/_____High

Paying attention to self and others to monitor our ways of working

Low_____/_____/_____/_____High

Presuming positive intentions to support a nonjudgmental atmosphere

Low_____/_____/_____/_____High

Appendix E Group Seven Norms Assessment

Pausing to allow time for thought

Low_____/_____/_____/_____High

Paraphrasing within a pattern of pause-paraphrase-pose questions to ensure deep listening

Low_____/_____/_____/_____High

Posing questions to reveal and extend thinking

Low_____/_____/_____/_____High

Putting ideas on the table and pulling them off

Low_____/_____/_____/_____High

Providing data to structure conversations

Low_____/_____/_____/_____High

Paying attention to self and others to monitor our ways of working

Low_____/_____/_____/_____High

Presuming positive intentions to support a nonjudgmental atmosphere

Low_____/_____/_____/_____High

Appendix F The Responsibilities Dilemma of the Teacher-Facilitator Person

Teachers in school-based leadership positions whose responsibilities include facilitating school improvement efforts, and whose roles have been determined in part by special funding sources or district policy, often face the dilemma of having to sort out their working relationship with the school principal or other administrator to whom they normally report.

This is complex, for two reasons. First, any employee-supervisor relationship is governed by multiple factors: district policy, negotiated agreements with employee organizations, the management and leadership style of the principal, the work culture in the school, the style characteristics of the employee, and the interpersonal relationship of the principal and the teacher-leader.

Because informal personalized factors have a greater influence on working procedures than do the hypothetical relationships described in program descriptions, the actual relationship is negotiated between the two people.

However, becoming clear about the working relationship is further complicated, because knowing who is to be served in a support role is complex for even the most practiced consultant or facilitator.

Because one cannot serve two masters, an early task for a consultant or facilitator is to learn who the primary and ultimate clients are. It is these parties whom the resource person is committed to serve. Thus, besides the question of the teacher-principal working relationship, there are several other questions that the teacher-leader and the principal must address:

1. Because of the potential for having role requirements given to the teacher-leader from sources beyond the principal, who exactly is the teacher-leader's primary and ultimate client, and what is the teacher-leader's responsibilities to those clients?

2. Under what conditions can the principal be a primary client?

3. Under what conditions can a working committee of the entire faculty be a primary client?

4. What are the core values that will guide this work?

5. Who is the client?

A contact client is a person who makes the initial contact with the teacher-leader. This establishes an expectation for serving a principal or a school according to the goals and descriptions of the funding program. Sometimes the contact comes from the following:

- A personnel office
- A staff development office
- An administrator in charge of special programs

An intermediate client is involved in the early contracting arrangements between the teacher-leader and the school. This person is often responsible for administrating the districtwide program under which each teacher-leader has been assigned. The intermediate client will communicate program goals, procedures to follow, and job descriptions for the teacher-leader. These guidelines set the parameters within which the principal and teacher-leader are to work.

The primary client is the group with which the facilitator will work. Because specific goals and working procedures can be developed only with the primary client, the teacher-leader must be clear about who this is. Three prerequisites for being successful as a primary client are as follows:

- The primary client has made a free and informed choice to ask the facilitator for services.

- The primary client has accepted responsibility for the problem being worked on.

- The primary client has or can access the information necessary to develop solutions.

The ultimate clients are the stakeholders, whose interests should be protected even if they are not in direct contact with the meeting processes. These would include the organization as a whole, students, parents, and community members.

The larger the school system, the greater the chance that communications between the support-role person and the contact, intermediate, and primary clients will be incomplete, contradictory, or confusing. Large school systems, even with the best of intentions, have communication problems. This is a systems problem, not a people problem. The most effective level for aligning incongruent understandings about role and function is with the two people closest to the action, the teacher-leader and the principal. If necessary, the district resource teacher or the administrator who leads the program can help.

In some situations, the primary client might also be the contact and intermediate client. For example, a department chairperson asks you to facilitate a meeting to develop faculty consensus on a set of educational values. The chairperson then works with you to develop agreements on mutual responsibilities as well as the goals and agenda for this meeting. During the meeting that you facilitate, the chairperson is also a member of the group that is receiving your services.

A principal can be the primary client when he or she will receive, or be a member of the group that receives, direct services from the facilitator. The principal will be an effective primary client when he or she has met the three prerequisites listed above for being successful as a primary client.

A working committee of the entire faculty can be the primary client when it represents the full range of opinions of the faculty and when the same three conditions for success as a primary client have been met.

The ideas below are recommended as generic core values to guide all facilitation work.

What is the presenting problem, diagnosis, and plan? Facilitators should not assume that the client has accurately or inaccurately defined and diagnosed the problem. The confident client has already defined the problem, its causes, and a method for solving it, and asks, "Can you help me accomplish this?" The searching client has identified the problem but is not clear about its causes or the methods to solve it, and asks, "How can you help us with this problem?" The puzzled client has not yet identified the problem, and asks, "Can you help us to figure out what is going on and what to do about it?" The reluctant client talks with a facilitator because job expectations require it; this person asks, "What does the project want you to do?"

What are the resources and motivation for change? Two often overlooked resources for change are the group's strengths and the critical voices of selected group members. Just because a group seeks help does not mean that it is interested in changing its behavior. Groups require resources to change. These include time, information, skills, knowledge, and motivation. Motivation to change can result from the following forms of discomfort:

- An internal dissatisfaction with the status quo

- Organizational pressure to improve

- An unachieved vision

- A drive toward craftsmanship and continual improvement

What type of facilitation services are being requested? In basic facilitation, the group seeks only to solve a substantive problem. The group engages a facilitator to temporarily improve its processes in order to work on the problem. When the problem is resolved, the group's process knowledge and skills are relatively unchanged. The basic facilitator is like a mechanic who fixes the group's car well enough to get it to a destination. Facilitation and agenda development tend to be done by one or two individuals, and the group expects the facilitator to use whatever processes he or she considers effective.

In developmental facilitation, the group seeks to permanently improve its processes while solving a substantive problem. When the problem is resolved, the group will also be more knowledgeable and skilled at solving future problems. The developmental facilitator is like a staff developer who leads the group in learning how to monitor, repair, and redesign its own car so it can use the vehicle to reach any destination it seeks. Facilitation and agenda development are shared, and the group periodically reflects to learn from its experience.

Appendix G   Contracting for Facilitation Services

ENTER and develop the RELATIONSHIP

Goals

- Establish trust
- Develop a relationship
- Establish mutual learning and empowerment as goals
- Determine mutual expectations

Questions

- Are the people here who need to be here?
- Whose voices are we not hearing?
- Who are the contact and intermediate clients?
- Who is the primary client?
- Who is the ultimate client?
- How does the person I'm talking to fit within the system?
- What are the client's expectations?
- What should be the nature of the consulting services?

ELICIT and process INFORMATION

Goals

- Distinguish between the presenting problem and the underlying problem
- Collaboratively determine the desired state
- Determine specific facilitator goals, plans, working procedures, and assessment design
- Understand the systems in which facilitation is to occur

Questions

- Who will be involved in defining the problem?
- Who will be involved in determining the desired state?
- How will you know if you and the client are successful?
- What lenses are represented by the primary client and the systems in which the client works?
- What data is relevant?
- What data-gathering and reporting mechanisms will be used?
- What values and principles will guide decision making?
- What feedback loops should be established?
- Who will assume which responsibilities for this endeavor?

EXECUTE and monitor a PLAN

Goals

- Appropriate interventions provided by the facilitator
- Consultant and primary client action
- Learning from doing
- Desired state achievement
- Client empowerment

Questions

- What will you do to keep the relationship a priority?

- How will you keep your communications descriptive and nonjudgmental?
- What will you do to maintain personal authenticity?
- How will you keep your eye on the ball in a chaotic situation?
- How will you know that the interventions are working and that the client is learning?
- How will you know if revising goals or strategies is called for?
- How will you know that you are finished?

EXIT and complete the RELATIONSHIP

Goals

- A decision to extend the facilitation relationship, recycle with a new problem, or end the relationship
- Client clarity and commitment to personal next steps
- Client empowerment to act independently
- Client feedback to the facilitator on the facilitator's services

Questions

- How will we know if the relationship should be extended, recycled, or ended?
- How do I know if the client has the resources to successfully pursue the next steps?
- How can I clarify and transfer my own learning from this relationship?

In the contracting phase, the primary client and the facilitator are jointly responsible for identifying a presenting problem, a way to get started, and mutual responsibilities. There is never a guarantee that consulting or facilitation services will successfully lead to school improvement. However, the odds for success are enhanced when the principal and the teach-er-leader form a trusting, candid, and shared-responsibility partnership. In effective projects, the individuals in these two roles develop clarity about the following.

Relationship

- Determine mutual expectations
- Develop and maintain trust
- Establish mutual learning goals
- Identify the primary and ultimate clients

Goals

- Distinguish the presenting from the underlying problem
- Determine the desired state
- Determine specific facilitation goals, plans, working procedures, and assessment designs
- Incorporate tests for environmental impact
- Understand the system in which the facilitation is to occur
- Who will be involved in defining the problem and the desired state?
- How will you know when the project is successful?

Data

- What data is relevant?
- What data gathering and reporting mechanisms will be used?
- What perceptual filters do the stakeholders have?
- What values and principles will guide the decision making?
- What feedback loops will be established?
- Who will take responsibility for specific portions of this endeavor?

Plan

- What projects will have to be set aside to accomplish this?
- Identify interventions
- Develop a timeline
- How will you know if revising goals or strategies is called for?
- How will you know if the improvement efforts should be extended, recycled, or ended?
- How will relationships and positive energy be monitored and maintained?
- Who will take responsibility for specific portions of this endeavor?

Appendix H The Facilitator's Contracting Conversation

Purpose	Possible Process
Make a person-to-person connection to increase the comfort level of the client.	• Rapport skills • Personal disclosure
Communicate an understanding of the problem, issue, or task.	• Gather information about the client's perception of the problem. • State your understanding of the client's perception, acknowledge any uniqueness the client feels about the problem, and express positive presuppositions about the client's resources and intentions. • Inquire about aspects of the problem not yet stated. • Summarize an expanded description of the problem and watch for confirming nonverbal responses.
Clarify the desired state for the intermediate client, the primary client, and the ultimate clients.	• Inquire about the client's ultimate goals. • Ask how the client will know that the goals have been achieved. • Present the data that you as a facilitator have gathered from other sources that might influence the client's framing of outcomes. • Assist in suggesting additional behavioral descriptors of the desired state.
Test the opportunity costs.	• What's the worst possible outcome of expending energies on this issue? • What's the worst possible outcome of not dealing with this issue? • By addressing this issue, what else might have to be set aside or delayed?
Clarify what the client wants from you.	• Test a well-formed goal statement by observing affirming nonverbal responses. • Ask directly, "What do you want of me?"
State what you want in the relationship.	• Inquire about the constraints the client wants in the working arrangement with you. • Be clear with yourself about which wants are essential agreements that you must have in order to make this facilitation relationship work and which wants are merely desirable. • Describe what you want.

Describe what you can and cannot offer.	• Describe the services that you feel qualified to provide that are appropriate to your understanding of the client's wants and to achieving the desired state. • Describe the support services required for project success. • Clarify any constraints you believe you will have in this relationship. • Forecast the results you believe the two of you will be able to produce.
Define the principles and values that will guide the facilitation work.	• Who will decide what? • Who will recommend what? • What is within and beyond the scope of the group's authority?
Get an agreement and test its strength.	• Many facilitation contracts are faulty for one of three reasons: 1. The client felt some kind of coercion, however subtle or indirect. 2. The client agreed to the arrangements but increasingly felt inadequate control over what was happening. 3. The client talks a more participative game about decision making than he or she is really comfortable with. • Ask "Is this project something you really want to see happening? Are you fully satisfied with the way we have set things up? Do you feel you have enough control over how this project is going to proceed?"
Provide support.	• Make genuine supportive statements about the client's willingness to proceed.
Summarize the next steps.	• Clarify who will do what by when.

Adapted from Block (1981)

Appendix I   Structuring Conversations About Data

1. What types of data will best inform improvement efforts?

Outcome Data	Demographic Data	Process Data
Norm-referenced test results	Ethnicity, primary languages, language proficiency levels, redesignation, sex, and age	Curriculum, Instruction, Assessment: alignment; variety of curricular materials, instructional strategies; instructional delivery system; consistency across programs, grade levels, subjects, courses; quantity, quality, appropriateness of books and instructional materials
Performance assessments (portfolios, exhibitions, performance tasks)	Attendance patterns—including all students and special populations, dropout, mobility and stability, suspension and expulsion data	Resources: distribution of resources across programs, grade levels, disciplines, courses, special populations; decision-making processes relative to allocation of resources
Report card grades	Socioeconomic status, participation in free or reduced lunch program, family situations, health issues, child abuse	Staff: composition, training, credentials, certification for assignment, experience, expertise
Course enrollments, graduation and dropout rates, promotion and retention rates	Categorical programs, special needs populations, support services	Professional Development: needs assessment; nature, quality, frequency of training opportunities; participation; level of implementation; follow-up
Aggregated and disaggregated data, matched and unmatched data, longitudinal data	Parent involvement, community and business supports, volunteers	School Organization: staff-pupil ratios by grade level, program, discipline; structure of school day and year; use of facilities, support services; governance structures and decision-making processes, communication processes (among staff, with parents)

	Schoolwide trends of student intentions after graduation, by subpopulation (high school only)	School and District Growth Needs: external factors, including state and federal program mandates, community and foundation programs, school and business relationships, parent and community organizations, national and international community projections and trends (high schools)
	Staff mobility, attendance, ethnicity	

2. What organization of data will best inform improvement efforts?

Quantitative: Using Numbers	Qualitative: Using Description
Count events, products, instances	Review holistically
Display in tables, charts, graphs	Examine documents, anecdotals, artifacts
Organize by frequency, central tendencies, dispersion	Create categories Search for patterns

3. What types of analysis will best inform improvement efforts?

Asking Inquiry Questions	Generating Theory
What are the data?	What inferences might we make from the data?
What important ideas seem to "pop out"?	How might we explain the data?

What patterns or trends appear?	What might the data be telling us about the following: • Learning environment • Student attitude • Student performance • Student knowledge or skill • Teachers' work culture • Teacher attitude • Curriculum • Instruction • Assessment How do the data compare with what we would hope to see in these areas?
What are the similarities with data from other sources? What are differences with data from other sources?	How do the data compare with the literature?
What are we seeing at the class, department, grade, and school levels?	
What seems to go together?	
What seems unexpected?	
In what other ways can data be viewed?	

Appendix J   Engaging Others in Collecting and Reporting Data

Some or all of these items might have to be addressed in a school improvement plan. Decide who should be involved and at what levels of authority.

Which Person or Group Should Address These Items?	What Should Be the Level of Authority?
___ Question(s) the data should answer	___ React to ideas
___ How the data will be used	___ Adapt from a model
___ Types of data to collect	___ Provide ideas
___ Data-gathering plan	___ Select from options
___ Data-dissemination plan	___ Develop criteria
___ Instrument development	___ Develop recommendations
___ Protocol development	___ Design
___ Data-analysis plan	___ Decide
___ Feedback-to-faculty plan	___ Act
___ Action-planning design	___ Evaluate

Appendix K   The Five Stages of Change

1. Accepting the Existing Conditions
   - Seeking information on the perceptions, processes, and results of schooling
   - Examining, understanding, and owning the information
   - Recognizing the strengths and weaknesses in system performance
   - Determining how the perceptions, processes, and results might be related

2. Owning the Problem
   - Focusing dissatisfaction on the existing condition
   - Defining the dissatisfaction as a problem inherent in the system, not in the individuals
   - Understanding that the individuals are part of the system that has a problem
   - Understanding that individuals working systematically together can resolve the problem
   - Committing to active solution seeking

3. Owning the Solution
   - Developing a shared understanding of the probable causes for the existing condition; a vision of a desired condition; the skills, knowledge, and attitudes necessary to achieve it; related assumptions; and available knowledge and resources
   - Generating a range of possible solutions that are appropriate to the problem and situation
   - Analyzing the feasibility of suggested solutions, given the nature of each particular situation
   - Adapting a solution to fit the situation
   - Committing to actively participate in implementation

4. Implementing the Plan
   - Being involved in the activities that are designed to change the system's processes and results

5. Monitoring and Evaluating the Processes and Progress
   - Monitoring for implementation mutations
   - Adopting healthy mutations and excising others
   - Identifying and solving implementation problems as they arise
   - Celebrating progress
   - Accepting and owning the new reality

The Five Stages of Change

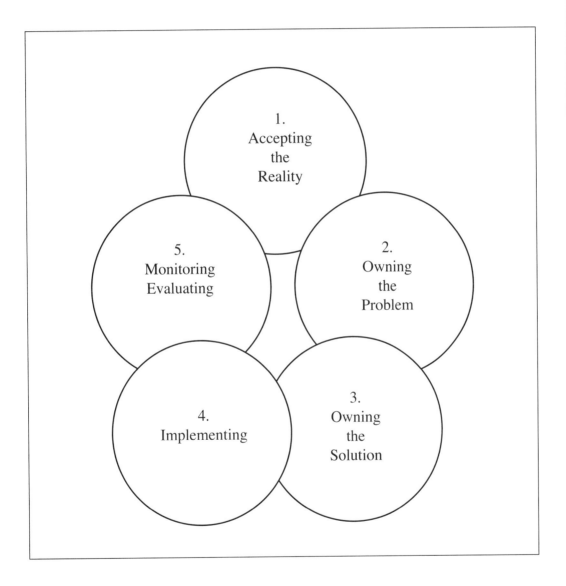

Appendix L   Meeting Inventory

Rate from 1 for don't agree to 5 for agree.

Decide Who Decides

- We were clear about who we are in the decision making process.   1 2 3 4 5
- We were clear about the decision making processes being used.   1 2 3 4 5

Define the Sandbox

- We were clear about which parts of the issue(s) we explored live in our sandbox.   1 2 3 4 5

Develop Standard

- We adhered to one process at a time.   1 2 3 4 5

- We adhered to one topic at a time.   1 2 3 4 5

- We balanced participation.   1 2 3 4 5

- The degree to which I felt listened to.   1 2 3 4 5

- The degree to which I listened to others.   1 2 3 4 5

- We engaged in productive cognitive conflict.   1 2 3 4 5

- We were clear about meeting roles.   1 2 3 4 5

Design the Surround

- We managed the environment to support our work.   1 2 3 4 5

_____   _____   _____
    Topic(s)   Date   Group

Appendix M Polarity Management: Using Conflict as a Resource

Carolyn McKanders

Polarities are chronic, ongoing tensions that are inherent in individual and organizational systems. They are unavoidable and unsolvable, they have two or more right answers that are interdependent, and they must be managed with both-and thinking.

Examples of polarities are the following:

- Individual rubrics and schoolwide rubrics
- Tight and loose structures
- Autonomy and collaboration
- Team and individual
- Home and work

Polarity Management™ is a model that involves a set of principles and tools for dealing with all polarities in life.

Betty Achinstein (2002), writing about conflict among school teachers, notes that collaboration and consensus—critical elements in building community—actually generate conflict. She found that by airing diverse perspectives in a collective setting and encouraging teachers to debate what and how to do schooling, schools generate new conflicts *because* of their commitment to creating collaborative communities.

In what ways might conflict represent a polarity?

Conflict is a manifestation of interdependence, and tensions between independence and interdependence are ever present. This inherent tension can be a source of productive energy for groups, or it can lead to unproductive interactions and create an energy drain. Groups that use tension productively distinguish between affective and cognitive conflict. Affective conflict is personalized conflict and is detrimental to group energy and productivity. Cognitive conflict is conflict over ideas and approaches, and it is a hallmark of high-performing groups. Groups that engage in cognitive conflict critically examine ideas to sort out the best practices for student learning. Thus conflict becomes a resource (Amason, Thompson, Hochwarter, & Harrison, 1995).

Achinstein (2002) quotes John Gardner's explanation of conflict, diversity, and community. Gardner states that diversity is not good simply because it implies breadth of tolerance and sympathy. A community of diverse elements has a greater capacity to adapt and renew itself in a swiftly changing world. To keep a balance between diversity and wholeness, communities must apply structures to reduce polarization, to foster communication among diverse groups, and to create mechanisms for conflict mediation.

Barry Johnson (1996) offers a set of principles, tools, and structures for identifying and utilizing the natural tensions that are created as individuals and organizations attempt to engage in cognitive conflict. These tensions often manifest as polarities: ongoing, chronic issues that are unavoidable and unsolvable. Johnson asserts that when groups can distinguish between a problem to solve and a polarity to manage and can effectively deal with both, they are able to celebrate and capitalize on diversity and convert resistance to change to a resource for sustainable strength and adaptivity.

Leaders, teams, and organizations must ask this fundamental question when they are faced with a challenge: Is this a problem to solve, or is it an ongoing polarity that we must manage well? Problems to solve are those that have one right answer or two or more right answers that are independent. For example: "How do you spell ___?" or "What should we include in our parent survey?"

In contrast, polarities to be managed are sets of opposites that can't function well independently; they require both-and thinking. Because the two sides of a polarity are interdependent, you cannot choose one as a solution and neglect the other. The objective of managing polarities is to get the best of both opposites while avoiding the limits or downside of each. Johnson (1996) uses breathing as a metaphor for all polarities. You cannot solve the inhale-exhale polarity by choosing to either inhale or exhale. You manage it by getting the benefits of each while appreciating the limits of each. It's not a static situation. It's a process, an ongoing flow of shifting emphasis from one to the other and back again. Managing this polarity requires choosing both inhaling *and* exhaling.

Some examples of polarities to manage are work and home, individual and team, stability and change, independence and interdependence, and planning and action.

A central premise of the adaptive school work is that leaders must recognize that schools are living paradoxes (i.e., polarities), operating simultaneously as "thing" and "en-

ergy" models—dynamic systems of energy and information.

The principles and tools of Polarity Management ™ support collaborative communities in accessing the richness of capitalizing on diversity and engaging cognitive conflict to liberate group energy and productivity.

The Polarity Map

The polarity map is a tool for mapping paradoxes or dilemmas, which we refer to as *polarities*. The map provides a structure for making invisible tensions visible and for addressing the whole polarity picture. Once the map is completed through collaborative conversation, it provides a focus for dialogue from diverse perspectives.

The polarity map is a square divided into four quadrants. The right and left halves are called poles. The upper part of each pole contains the positive results of focusing on that pole, referred to as its upside. The lower part of each pole contains the negative results of focusing on that pole to the neglect of the other pole and is called the downside. Creating and discovering the content of all four quadrants is essential for maximum effectiveness in managing a polarity.

Guidelines for Creating a Polarity Map

Define the challenge. Identify an ongoing, chronic issue (a) within your sphere of influence (b) that has eluded problem-solving and (c) that has to be addressed in the next 2 months.

Identify a key polarity. A polarity differs from a problem in the following ways: (a) The issue continues over time, (b) there are two interdependent alternatives, (c) you need to have the positive aspects of each of the alternatives, and (d) developing one alternative to the ne-

A Polarity Map

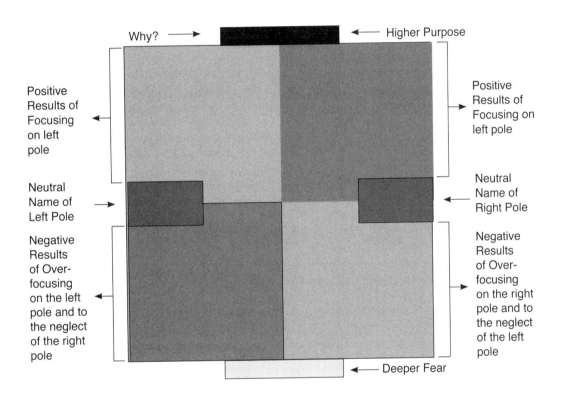

Why? →   ← Higher Purpose

Positive Results of Focusing on left pole ←   → Positive Results of Focusing on left pole

Neutral Name of Left Pole →   ← Neutral Name of Right Pole

Negative Results of Over-focusing on the left pole and to the neglect of the right pole ←   → Negative Results of Over-focusing on the right pole and to the neglect of the left pole

← Deeper Fear

glect of the other will eventually undermine your productivity. Ask the following probing questions:

1. In what ways do you continue to experience this issue over time?

2. In what ways are there two alternatives that are interdependent? This means that you can focus on only one pole for so long before you are required to focus on the other pole.

3. What is the necessity of having the upsides of both poles over time?

4. To what extent will focusing on one upside to the neglect of the other eventually undermine your productivity?

Explore the issues, opportunities, and polarities. Facilitate a conversation that is designed to create an objective description of the issues, opportunities, and polarities that are present. The skills of dialogue (chapter 4) and the norms of collaboration (chapter 3) are essential to this goal. Presume that all ideas are respected and important. Paraphrasing (chapter 4) is a primary tool in these conversations. Well-crafted paraphrases communicate "I am trying to understand you, and therefore I value what you have to say" and establish a relationship between people and ideas.

Here is an example. A high school leadership team that was conversing about staff resistance to interdepartmental collaboration concluded that there were merits to some staff members' advocacy of autonomy. During this conversation the facilitator offered the following paraphrases:

- "Sam, you believe the complaints we're getting are data worth examining."

- "A value that we all hold is that all departments working together will produce better results for all students."

- "On the one hand, we want teaming, and on the other hand, we see the necessity for individual action."

- "It sounds as if we want to honor autonomy in two ways, individuals and departments."

The facilitator provided a "shift conceptual level paraphrase" (chapter 3) to paraphrase the polarity: "Let me see if I can sum this up. We're wondering how we might collaborate while also honoring individual autonomy."

In this example the high school leadership team decided to create a collaboration-autonomy polarity map. Later they repeated this mapping process with the staff.

Agree on names for the poles. The names should be value-neutral and be agreed on by the group.

Write the pole names on the map. The polarity map is created on chart paper so that group members can see the map as it unfolds.

Brainstorm the content for each quadrant. Aim to write four to eight entries in each quadrant. Collect all ideas from the participants without judgment, criticism, or questions. Identify both upsides, asking, "What are some positives results or upsides of focusing on ____?" Then

identify both downsides, asking, "What are the negatives of focusing on ____ to the neglect of the other pole?" This order can be modified to meet individual and group needs. For example, a group that values stability over change might need to brainstorm the upside of stability and the downside of change before being ready to move to mapping the upside of change. Oppositional values and fears should be identified and respected as important.

Agree on a higher purpose and a deeper fear. Agreeing on a higher purpose and a deeper fear integrates oppositional views and provides a reason to manage the tension between them. The higher purpose is the major benefit of managing the polarity well, and the deeper fear is the major negative result of not managing the polarity well. Again, use dialogue and the norms of collaboration.

The "shift conceptual focus paraphrase" is invaluable for integrating seemingly competing values and views, elevating conversations to a common higher purpose. For example, a middle school staff dialogue about student discipline became quite emotional, with members giving example after example of student misbehavior. Some staff members insisted that more suspensions and rules were necessary; others challenged this idea, stating that the students would just become resentful, passive-aggressive, and less willing to behave. They argued that their role was to support students in learning life skills for controlling themselves.

The chairman of the committee, who was acting as the facilitator, offered a "shift conceptual level paraphrase": "Some of us feel strongly about tightening the rules to get order, whereas some believe that students might need to be taught how to use their freedom to self-regulate. It is apparent that a goal we all hold is how to support the students in exhibiting more productive behavior."

After additional conversation, the group

agreed to map the structure-freedom polarity, coming to the conclusion that both were necessary to encourage students' productive behavior.

Dialogue about the completed polarity map and explore ways to maximize the upside of each pole and minimize the downside of each pole.

Understanding How Polarities Work

A polarity map appears as a static set of ideas in four labeled quadrants: positives and values in the upside of each pole, and negatives and concerns in the downside of each pole. In fact, there is a predictable movement through a polarity situation, and we can envision it with the polarity map. As polarities work, we can predict people's movement from one pole to the other as they (a) anticipate or experience the downside of one pole, from which they want to move away, and (b) are attracted to the upsides of the opposite pole, which they want to move toward. The downside of the pole they want to leave often becomes identified as the problem. The upside of the opposite pole becomes identified as the solution. However, for a polarity to be well managed, one must remain in the upside of both poles while avoiding the limitations of the downsides of both poles. The natural energy flow of a well-managed polarity is an infinity loop, with only a slight dip into the lower quadrants.

Facilitating Polarity Mapping

Facilitation provides the focusing, directing, and organizing features that are necessary for adult conversations to produce results for students. Facilitators manage group energy through attention to three areas: (a) helping individuals work as a group, (b) engaging all members in active participation, and (c) focusing group attention.

Well-facilitated conversations around polarities and other diverse viewpoints produce the cognitive conflict and psychological safety that is necessary for highly productive dialogues that foster shared meanings, values and goals, and collective agreements.

The following are some principles and strategies that facilitators may use to support these conversations:

- *Grounding.* This is an opening inclusion activity that is used when groups come together for important or difficult work. Grounding (a) sets a norm for respectful listening, (b) brings people to the present, (c) brings everyone's voice into the room in a nonconfrontational way, (d) encourages people to connect with one another, (e) allows for expression of hopes and apprehensions, (f) values thinking and feeling, and (g) brings hidden agendas to the surface.

- *Greeting Circle.* This is another grounding activity in which each person greets and is greeted by another. In this process, everyone confronts the natural tension about greeting others. When participants are asked how they felt and what they learned, productive energy is released into the room.

- *Address One Topic at a Time.* There is a limit to what individuals and groups can attend to in the moment. When more than one topic is being discussed, the group lacks focus, and confusion reigns. Natural tensions are present when discussing polarities. Keeping the group focused on one topic and/or polarity at a time honors both the ideas and those who are generating them.

- *Address One Process at a Time.* Group processes are vehicles for collective thinking. To brainstorm, to clarify, to analyze, and to evaluate require different mental operations. In order to use one process at a time, the facilitator must make sure that all group members know what the process is, how it works, and why it is being used.

Facilitating Conversation About a Completed Polarity Map

Once a group has completed mapping a polarity on chart paper, a facilitated conversation offers group members the opportunity to view and explore the dilemma as a whole and from multiple perspectives. Furthermore, the group can now generate strategies for staying in the upsides of both poles while avoiding the downsides. The norm of putting inquiry first supports the facilitator and the group members' resourcefulness and success in these conversations.

Here are some sample questions:

- As you reflect on our collective wisdom, what new learning and insights are emerging for you?

- Given our expanded perspective, what might be some benefits for managing this polarity well?

- What might be some higher purposes that will benefit all of our students?

- What might be some of our deepest fears if we fail to manage this polarity well?

- As we reflect on phrases in each quadrant, what might be some assumptions, values, or beliefs that are present?

- Given our desire to stay in the upsides of both poles, what are some strategies?

- What are some indicators that will tell us we are moving to the downside of a pole? Who will remind us, and how?

- What seems most important to all of us here?

- What might be some impacts of collaboratively mapping a polarity?

- What are your hunches about other polarities that might exist in this situation?

- How might we apply this to other areas of our work?

Tips for Using Polarity Maps

- Remember that to pursue the benefits of one pole, you must also pursue the benefits of the other pole. The solution is not static.

- One possibility is to identify the indicators for each pole, which will let you know when you are experiencing its downside. Putting feedback mechanisms in place aids in managing the polarity. (Example: Using conversation maps and tools)

- Listen deeply and facilitate dialogue, especially with naysayers.

- Brainstorm strategies for staying in the upsides of both poles.

References

Achinstein, B. (2002). *Community diversity and conflict and diversity among schoolteachers: The ties that bind.* New York: Teachers College Press.

Albert, S., & Whetten, D. A. (1985). Organizational identity. In L. L. Cummings & B. M. Staw (Eds.), *Research in organizational behavior* (Vol. 7, pp. 263–295). Greenwich, CT: JAI.

Amason, A. C., Thompson, K. R., Hochwarter, W. A., & Harrison, A. W. (1995, Autumn). Conflict: An important dimension in successful management teams. *Organizational Dynamics, 24* (2), 20–35.

Avery, M., Aurine, B., Streibel, B., & Weiss, L. (1981). *Building United judgment: A handbook for consensus decision making.* Madison, WI: The Center for Conflict Resolution.

Bailey, S. (1996, August 8). *Sensing and managing the surround: Physical dimensions, social dimensions, symbolic, and emotional dimensions.* Paper presented at the Adaptive Schools Leadership Institute, Tahoe City, CA.

Baker, W., Costa, A., & Shalit, S. (1997). The norms of collaboration: Attaining communicative competence. In A. L. Costa & R. M. Liebmann (Eds.), *The process-centered school: Sustaining a renaissance community* (pp. 119–142). Thousand Oaks, CA: Corwin Press.

Bandler, R., & Grinder, J. (1971). *The structure of magic.* Palo Alto, CA: Science and Behavior Books.

Bandura, A. (1977). *Self-efficacy: The exercise of control.* New York: Freeman.

Beckard, R., & Harris, R. (1997). *Organization transitions: Managing complex change* (2nd ed.). Reading, MA: Addison-Wesley.

Block, P. (1981). *Flawless consulting: A guide to getting your expertise used.* San Diego: University Associates.

Bolam, R., McMahon, A., Stoll, L., Thomas, S., & Wallace, M. (2005). *Creating and sustaining effective learning communitites* (Research Brief RB637). London: Department for Education and Skills Publications. Available online at www.dfes.gov.uk/research/.

Boleman, L., & Deal, T. (2003). *Reframing organizations: Artistry, choice, and leadership* (3rd ed.). New York: Wiley.

Borko, H., Livingston, C., & Shavelson, R. (1990). Teachers' thinking about instruction. *Remedial and Special Education*, Vol.11, No. 8, pp. 40–49.

Bransford, J., Brown, A., & Cocking, R. (1999). *How people learn: Brain, mind, experience, and schools.* Washington, DC: National Academies Press.

Bridges, W. (1980). *Making sense of life's changes: Transitions.* New York: Addison-Wesley.

Bridges, W. (1991). *Managing transitions: Making the most of changes.* Reading, MA: Addison-Wesley.

Briggs, J. (1992). *Fractals: The patterns of chaos. Discovering a new aesthetic of art, science and nature.* New York: Touchstone.

Brown, A. (1994). The advancement of learning. *Educational Researcher, 23* (8), 4–12.

Bryk, A., & Schneider, B. (2002). *Trust in schools: A core resource for improvement.* New York: Sage Foundation.

Buckley, M. (2002). *ChartArt: Traceable chart art for flip charts and overheads.* Sherman, CT: MiraVia.

Buckley, M. (2005). To see is to retain. In R.

Garmston (Ed.), *The presenter's fieldbook: A practical guide* (2nd ed., pp. 181–204). Norwood, MA: Christopher-Gordon.

Calderhead, J. (1996). Teachers: Beliefs and knowledge. In D. Berliner & R. C. Calfee (Eds.), *Handbook of educational psychology* (pp. 708–725). New York: Simon & Schuster Macmillan.

Capra, F. (1982). *The turning point: Science, society, and the rising culture.* New York: Bantam.

Capra, F. (1991). *The tao of physics.* Boston: Shambhala.

Capra, F. (1996). *The web of life: A new scientific understanding of living systems.* New York: Anchor Books.

Chatwin, B. (1987). *The songlines.* New York: Penguin Books.

Chernoff, J. M. (1981). *African rhythm and African sensibility: Aesthetics and social action in African musical idioms.* Chicago: University of Chicago Press.

Chopra, D. (1993). *Ageless body, timeless mind: The quantum alternative to growing old.* New York: Crown.

Coleman, J. S., Campbell, E. Q., Hobson, C. J., McPartland, J., Mood, A. M., & Weinfeld, F. D. (1966). *Equality of educational opportunity.* Washington, DC: U.S. Government Printing Office.

Collins, J. C., & Porras, J. I. (1997). *Built to last: Successful habits of visionary companies.* New York: HarperBusiness.

Cooper, B., Sarrel, R., & Tetenbaum, T. (1990, April). *Choice, funding, and pupil achievement: How urban school finance affects students.* Paper presented at the meeting of the American Educational Research Association, Boston.

Costa, A., & Garmston, R. (2002). *Cognitive coaching: A foundation for renaissance schools.* Norwood, MA: Christopher-Gordon.

Covey, S. R. (1989). *The seven habits of highly effective people.* New York: Fireside Books.

Crum, T. (1998). *The magic of conflict.* New York: Touchstone Books.

Csikszentmihayli, M. (1993). *Flow: The psychology of optimal experience.* New York: Harper & Row.

Damasio, A. (1994). *Descartes' error: Emotions, reason, and the human brain.* New York: Avon Books.

Damasio, A. (1999*). The feeling of what happens: Body and emotion in the making of consciousness.* New York: Harcourt Brace.

Danner, D. D., Snowdon, D. A., & Friesen, W. V. (2001). Positive emotions in early life and longevity: Findings from the nun study. *Journal of Personality and Social Psychology, 80,* 804–813.

Darling-Hammond, L. (1997). *The right to learn: A blueprint for creating schools that work.* San Francisco: Jossey-Bass.

DeBoer, G. (1991). *A history of ideas in science education.* New York: Teachers College Press.

Dilts, R. (1990). *Changing beliefs with nlp.* Capitola, CA: Meta.

Dilts, R. (1994). *Effective presentation skills.* Capitola, CA: Meta.

Dilts, R. (1996). *Visionary leadership skills: Creating a world to which people want to belong.* Capitola, CA: Meta.

Doyle, M., & Straus, D. (1993). *How to make meetings work!* New York: Berkley.

Dufour, R., Eaker, R., & Baker, R. (1998). *Professional learning communities at work: Best practices for enhancing student achievement.* Bloomington, IN: National Educational Services.

Edwards, J., Rogers, S., & Sword, M. (1998). *The pleasant view experience.* Golden, CO: Jefferson County Public Schools.

Elmore, R. (1995). Structural reform and educational practice. *Educational Researcher, 24* (9), 23–26.

Elmore, R. (2000, Winter). *Building a new structure for school leadership.* Washington, DC: Shanker Institute.

Elmore, R. (2002, January/February). The limits of change. *Harvard Education Letter, 18* (1), 8.

Fredrickson, B. L., & Losada, M.F. (2005). Positive affect and the complex dynamics of human flourishing. *American Psychologist, 60* (7), 678–686.

Fullan, M. (2001). *The new meaning of educational change* (3rd ed.). New York: Teachers College Press.

Garfield, C. (1986). *Peak performers: The new heroes of American business.* New York: Morrow.

Garmston, R. (2005). *The presenter's fieldbook: A practical guide.* Norwood, MA: Christopher-Gordon.

Garmston, R., & Hyerle, D. (1988, August). *Professors' peer coaching program.* Sacramento, CA: California State University.

Garmston, R., Lipton, L., & Kaiser, K. (1998). The psychology of supervision. In G. Firth & E. Pajak (Eds.), *The handbook of research on school supervision* (pp. 242–286). New York: Macmillan.

Garmston, R., & Wellman, B. (1992). *How to make presentations that teach and transform.* Alexandria VA: Association for Supervision and Curriculum Development.

Garmston, R., & Wellman, B. (1998). Teacher talk that makes a difference. *Educational Leadership,* 55 (7), 30–34.

Gharajedaghi, J. (2006). *Systems thinking: Managing chaos and complexity* (2nd ed.). Burlington, MA: Elsevier.

Gleick, J. (1987). *Chaos: Making a new science.* New York: Viking Penguin.

Glickman, C. D. (1991). Pretending not to know what we know. *Educational Leadership, 48* (8), 4–10.

Glickman, C. (1998). *Human will, school charters and choice: A new centralized policy for public education.* Unpublished paper, University of Georgia, Athens. GA.

Goddard, R. (2001). Collective efficacy: A neglected construct in the study of schools and student achievement. *Journal of Educational Psychology, 93* (3), 467–476.

Goddard, R., Hoy, W., & Woolfolk-Hoy, A. (2004). Collective efficacy beliefs: Theoretical developments, empirical evidence, and future directions. *Educational Researcher, 33* (3), 3–13.

Goldberg, M. C. (1998). *The art of the question.* New York: Wiley.

Goleman, D. (1995). *Emotional intelligence: Why it can matter more than IQ.* New York: Bantam Books.

Goleman, D. (2006). *Social intelligence: The revolutionary new science of human relations.* New York: Bantam Dell.

Grinder, M. (1997). *The science of nonverbal communications.* Battleground, WA: Grinder.

Grinder, M. (2007). *The elusive obvious: The science of non-verbal communication.* Battle Ground, WA: Grinder.

Hall, G., & Hord, S. (1987). *Change in schools: Facilitating the process.* Albany, NY: State University of New York Press.

Hargreaves, A., & Dawe, R. (1990). Paths of professional development: Contrived collegiality, collaborative culture, and the case of peer coaching. *Teaching and Teacher Education, 6,* 277–241.

Hennessy, G. (1998). Modeling "soft" variables. *The Systems Thinker, 8* (7), 6–7.

Ho, M. (1998). *The rainbow and the worm: The physics of organisms.* Singapore: World Scientific.

Hoy, W., Tarter, J., & Woolfolk-Hoy, A. (2006). Academic optimism of schools: A force for student achievement. *American Educational Research Journal, 43* (3), 425–446.

Iwanicki, E. (1998). Evaluation in supervision. In G. Firth & E. Pajak (Eds.), *Handbook of research on school supervision* (pp. 138–175). New York: Macmillan.

Jaques, J., & Cason, K. (1994). Human capability: A study of individual potential and its applications. Falls Church, VA: Cason & Hall.

Johnson, B. (1996). *Polarity management: Identifying and managing unsolvable problems*. Amherst, MA: HRD Press.

Kegan, R., & Lahey, L. (1984). Adult leadership and adult development: A constructivist view. In B. Kellerman (Ed.), *Handbook on socialization theory and research* (pp. 199–229). Chicago: Rand McNally.

Kegan, R., & Lahey, L. (2001). How the way we talk can change the way we work: Seven languages of transformation. San Francisco: Jossey-Bass.

Kelly, E. (2006). *Powerful times: Rising to the challenge of our uncertain world*. Upper Saddle River, NJ: Wharton.

Koestler, A. (1972). *The roots of coincidence*. New York: Vintage Books.

Kolb, D., & Associates. (1994). *When talk works: Profiles of mediators*. San Francisco: Jossey-Bass.

Kreutzer, D. (1995). FASTBreak: A facilitation approach to systems thinking breakthroughs. In S. Chawla & J. Renesch (Eds.), *Developing cultures for tomorrow's workplace* (pp. 228–241). Portland, OR: Productivity Press.

LaBorde, G. Z. (1984). *Influencing with integrity: Management skills for communication and negotiation*. Palo Alto, CA: Syntony.

Lakoff, G. (2004). *Don't think like an elephant*. White River Junction, VT: Chelsea Green.

Lankton, S. (1980). *Practical magic: A translation of basic neurolinguistic progamming into clinical psychotherapy*. Capitola, CA: Meta.

Ledoux, J. (1996). *The emotional brain: The mysterious underpinnings of emotional life*. New York: Simon and Schuster.

Lee, O., & Fradd, S. (1998). Science for all, including students from non-English-language backgrounds. *Educational Researcher, 27* (4), 12–21.

Lee, V., & Smith, J. (1996). Collective responsibility for learning and its effects on gains in achievement and engagement for early secondary students. *American Journal of Education, 104,* 103–147.

Lemke, J. (1990). *Talking science: Language, learning, and values*. Norwood, NJ: Ablex.

Levinson, M. (2006). *The box: How the shipping container made the world smaller and world economy bigger*. Princeton, NJ: Princeton University Press.

Lipton. L., & Wellman, B. (1998). *Pathways to understanding: Patterns and practices in the learning-focused classroom*. Sherman, CT: MiraVia.

Little, J. W. (1982). Norms of collegiality and experimentation: Workplace conditions of school success. *American Educational Research Journal, 19,* 225–340.

Little, J. W. (1990). *The persistence of privacy: Autonomy and initiative in teachers' professional relations*. Teachers College Record, *91,* 509–536.

Little, J., & McLaughlin, M. (Eds.). (1993). *Teachers' work: Individuals, colleagues, and contexts*. New York: Teachers College Press.

Lorenz, E. N. (1993). *The essence of chaos*. Seattle: University of Washington Press.

Lortie, D. (1975). *Schoolteacher: A sociological study*. Chicago: University of Chicago Press.

Losada, M., & Heaph, E. (2004). The role of positivity and connectivity in the performance of business teams: A nonlinear dynamics. *American Behavioral Scientist, 47,* 740.

Louis, K., & Kruse, S. (1995). *Professionalism and community: Perspectives on reforming urban schools.* Thousand Oaks, CA: Corwin Press.

Louis, K. S., Marks, H. M., & Kruse, S. (1996). Teachers' professional community in restructuring schools. *American Educational Research Journal, 33* (4), 757–798.

Louis, K. S., Toole, J., & Hargreaves, A. (1999). Rethinking school improvement. In J. Murphy & K. S. Louis (Eds.), *Handbook of research on educational administration* (pp. 251–275). San Francisco: Jossey-Bass.

McLaughlin, M. (1990, December). The RAND change agent study revisited: Macro perspectives and micro realities. *Educational Researcher*, Vol. 19, No. 9, 11–16.

McLaughlin, M., & Talbert, J. (1993). *Contexts that matter for teaching and learning: Strategic opportunities for meeting the nation's education goals.* Stanford, CA: Stanford University Center for Research on the Context of Secondary School Teaching.

McLaughlin, M., & Talbert, J. (2001*). Professional communities and the work of high school teaching.* Chicago: University of Chicago Press.

McLaughlin, M., & Talbert, J. (2006). *Building school-based teacher learning communities: Professional strategies to improve student achievement.* New York: Teachers College Press.

Miller, G. (1963). The magical number seven, plus or minus two: Some limits in capacity for processing information. *Psychological Review, 63*, 81–97.

Newman, F., & Associates. (1997). *Authentic achievement.* San Francisco: Jossey-Bass.

Newman, F., King, B., & Rigdon, M. (1997, Spring). Accountability and school performance: Implications for restructuring schools. *Harvard Educational Review, 67* (1), 41–74.

Newman, F., & Wehlage, G. (1995). *Successful school restructuring.* Madison, WI: Center on Organization and Restructuring of Schools.

Palmer, L. J. (1998). *The courage to teach: Exploring the inner landscapes of a teacher's life.* San Francisco: Jossey-Bass.

Peck, S. (1987). *The different drum: Community making and peace.* New York: Touchstone.

Perkins, D. (1992). *Smart schools.* New York: Free Press.

Poole, M. G., & Okeafor, K. R. (1989, Winter). The effects of teacher efficacy and interactions among educators on curriculum implementation. *Journal of Curriculum and Supervision, 4* (2), 146–161.

Pruitt, D., & Carnevale, P. (1993). *Negotiation in social conflict.* Pacific Grove, CA: Brooks/Cole.

Rosenholtz, S. (1991). *Teachers' workplace: The social organization of schools.* New York: Teachers College Press.

Rowe, M. B. (1986, January-February). Wait time: Slowing down may be a way of speeding up! *Journal of Teacher Education*, 43–49.

Saban, J., Wensch, L., Costa, A., Garmston, R., Battaglia, A., & Brubaker, W. (1998, Spring). Designing the holonomous school building. *Journal of School Business Management, 10* (1), 35–39.

Sanders, W., & Rivers, J. (1996). *Cumulative and residual effects of teachers on future student academic achievement.* Knoxville, TN: University of Tennessee Value-Added Research and Assessment Center.

Sanford, C. (1995). Myths of organizational effectiveness. In *At work* (pp. 10–12). Battle Ground, WA: Springhill.

Saphier, J., Bigda-Peyton, T., & Pierson, G. (1989). *How to make decisions that stay made.* Alexandria, VA: Association for Supervision and Curriculum Development.

Saphier, J., Haley-Speca, M., & Gower, R. (2008). *The skillful teacher: Building your teaching skills.* Acton, MA: Research for Better Teaching.

Sarason, S. (1990). *The predictable failure of educational reform.* San Francisco: Jossey-Bass.

Schein, E. (2004). *Organizational culture and leadership* (3rd ed.). San Francisco: Jossey-Bass.

Schwarz, R. (2002). *The skilled facilitator: Practical wisdom for developing effective groups.* San Francisco: Jossey-Bass.

Senge, P. M. (1990). *The fifth discipline: The art and practice of the learning organization.* New York: Doubleday/Currency.

Sergiovanni, T. (1994). *Building community in schools.* San Francisco: Jossey-Bass.

Shulman, L. (1987). Knowledge and teaching: Foundations of the new reform. *Harvard Educational Review, 57* (1), 1–22.

Sibbit, D. (2002). *Principles of facilitation: The purpose and potential of leading group process.* San Francisco: Grove Consultants.

Stacey, R. (1992). *Managing the unknowable: Strategic boundaries between order and chaos in organizations.* San Francisco: Jossey-Bass.

Sternberg, R., & Horvath, J. (1995, August-September). A prototype view of expert teaching. *Educational Researcher,* 9–17.

Stiggins, R. (2007, May). Assessment through student's eyes. *Education Leadership, 64* (8), 22–26.

Thibaut, J., & Kelley, H. (1959). *The social psychology of groups.* New York: Wiley.

Tschannen-Moran, M., Woolfolk-Hoy, A., & Hoy, W. (1998). Teacher efficacy: Its meaning and measure. *Review of Educational Research, 68,* 202–248.

Tyack, D. (2003). *Seeking common ground: Public schools in a diverse society.* Cambridge, MA: Harvard University Press.

Tyack, D., & Cuban, L. (1995). *Tinkering toward utopia. A century of public school reform.* Cambridge, MA: Harvard University Press.

Tyler, R. (1949). *Basic principles of curriculum and instruction.* Chicago: University of Chicago Press.

Waldrop, M. (1992). *Complexity: The emerging science at the edge of order and chaos.* New York: Simon and Schuster.

Waters, T., & Grubb, S. (2004). *Leading schools: Distinguishing the essential from the important.* Aurora, CO: Mid-Continent Research for Education and Learning.

Waters, T., Marzano, R. J., & McNulty, B. (2003). *Balanced leadership: What 30 years of research tells us about the effect of leadership on student achievement.* Aurora, CO: Mid-Continent Research for Education and Learning.

Weinraub, R. (1995). Transforming mental models through formal and informal learning. In S. Chawla & J. Renesch (Eds.), *Learning organizations: Developing cultures for tomorrow's workplace* (pp. 417–430). Portland, OR: Productivity Press.

Wellman, B., & Lipton, L. (2004). *Data-driven dialogue: A facilitator's guide to collaborative inquiry.* Sherman, CT: MiraVia.

Wheatley, M. (1992). *Leadership and the new science: Learning about organizations from an orderly universe.* San Francisco: Barrett-Koehler.

Wheatley, M., & Kellner-Rogers, M. (1996). *A simpler way.* San Francisco: Berrett-Koehler.

Wiggins, G., & McTighe, J. (2005). *Understanding by design* (2nd ed.). Alexandria, VA: Association for Supervision and Curriculum Development.

Zais, R. (1976). *Curriculum principles and foundations.* San Francisco: Harper & Row.

Zoller, K. (2005). The new science of nonverbal skills. In R. Garmston, *The presenter's fieldbook: A practical guide,* 2nd ed. Norwood, MA: Christopher-Gordon.

Zoller, K. (2007). *Nonverbal patterns of teachers from five countries: Results from the timss-r video study.* Unpublished dissertation, California State University, Fresno, CA.

Index

About the Authors

ROBERT J. GARMSTON, ED.D., presents to educators and managers throughout the United States as well as in Canada, Africa, Asia, Australia, Europe, the Middle East and South America. Emeritus Professor of Educational Administration at California State University, Sacramento, Bob has previously been a classroom teacher, principal, director of instruction and acting superintendent. Co-developer of Cognitive Coaching with Dr. Arthur Costa and co-founder of the Center for Adaptive Schools with Bruce Wellman, www.thinkingcollaborative.com, his work has been translated into Arabic, Hebrew, Italian and Spanish. He is director of Facilitation Associates, a consulting firm specializing in leadership, learning, personal and organizational development. Bob lives near Sacramento, California, with his wife Sue and close to his five adult children and grandchildren, who are, of course, cute and bright.

BRUCE M. WELLMAN is co-director of MiraVia, LLC. He consults with school systems, professional groups and organizations throughout the United States and Canada, presenting workshops and courses for teachers and administrators on the patterns and practices of learning-focused classroom, learning-focused conversations for supervisors and mentors, presentation skills and facilitating and developing collaborative groups.

Mr. Wellman is an award-winning writer whose work has been honored by the Education Writers Association and the National Staff Development Council. He is the author and co-author of numerous publications related to organization and professional development, mentoring, quality teaching and improving professional cultures.

Mr. Wellman has served as a classroom teacher, elementary science curriculum coordinator, and staff developer in the Oberlin, Ohio and Concord, Massachusetts public schools. He holds a B.A. degree from Antioch College and an M.Ed. from Lesley College. He lives in Southern Vermont with his wife Leslie Cowperthwaite, where they enjoy gardening and natural history.

Here are some other Adaptive Schools resources that you may find helpful:

The Meeting Manager

The Meeting Manager is a laminated mat to take to meetings to elicit key skills and concepts that enhance meeting success. Included on the two sides of the mat are: adaptivity, promoting a spirit of inquiry, norms of collaboration, paraphrasing, meeting success structures, two ways of talking, stems of connection, meeting purposes, energy sources, and selected strategies.

Adaptive Schools Banners

In *Smart Schools* David Perkins asserts that elements in the emotional and physical environment interact with thinking and become points of mediation.

1. Two Ways of Talking
2. 7 Norms of Collaboration
3. Meeting Standards

Three 3' x 4' banners, digitally printed on white 10 oz. vinyl—ready to hang with 6 grommets.

Contact www.thinkingcollaborative.com for prices and to order items listed.